NIGERIA AT FIFTY

NIGERIA AT FIFTY

Contributions to Peace, Democracy, and Development

edited by
Attahiru M. Jega
Jacqueline W. Farris

SHEHU MUSA YAR'ADUA FOUNDATION

Published in Nigeria in 2010 by
The Shehu Musa Yar'Adua Foundation
One Memorial Drive
Abuja, Nigeria
www.yaraduacentre.org

ISBN: 978-978-907-7823

Printed and bound in the United States of America

∞ The paper used in this publication meets the requirements
of the American National Standard for Permanence of
Paper for Printed Library Materials Z39.48-1992.

5 4 3 2 1

In memory of
Shehu Musa Yar'Adua

May we one day realize his vision
for a fairer, more just, and peaceful world

Contents

Acknowledgments

Working on this project has been an intellectually enriching experience of collegial partnership and collaboration, the memories of which will linger for a long while. Of course, in a work of this nature many debts are owed and need to be appropriately acknowledged.

In particular, we thank Dr. Kole Shettima, who conceived the idea, and Dr. Jibrin Ibrahim, whose initial effort brought together a team of seasoned academics. Many thanks to the Steering Committee members: Dr. Jibrin Ibrahim, Dr. Kole Shettima, Hajia Amina az'Zubair, Dr. Hamid Bobboyi, Professor Okello Oculi, Dr. Andrew Okolie, Mr. Ken Saro Wiwa, and Dr. Adeolu Akande, whose hard work, sustained interest, and commitment have contributed significantly to the completion of this work.

Ambassador Baba Gana Kingibe, former minister of foreign affairs and former secretary to the government of the federation, availed us of his wealth of experience and insight in a series of meetings that clarified issues and shed light on the dynamics of Nigeria's foreign policy, for which we are extremely grateful. We have also benefitted from diplomats whose contributions have greatly enriched the book. In particular, we thank Professor Osita Eze, director-general of the Nigerian Institute of International Affairs, and Ambassador Daniel Hart, senior special assistant to the president on foreign relations, who participated in a workshop organized by the Yar'Adua Centre.

Professional colleagues read, reviewed, and commented on the manuscript and offered useful suggestions: Warisu Alli of the Department of Political Science, University of Jos; Alade Fawole of the Department of International Relations, Obafemi Awolowo University, Ife; Habu Mohammed of the Department of Political Science, Bayero University, and the Aminu Kano Centre for Democratic Research and Training, Kano

(AKCDRT); and Moses Aluaigba, also of AKCDRT. We appreciate their contributions to improving the quality of the book and thank them immensely. They share no blame for any errors that may remain.

The John D. and Catherine T. MacArthur Foundation provided initial funding for the project. Dr. Jonathan Fanton, the immediate past president of the foundation, showed remarkable interest and commitment far beyond the call of duty. He spared time during one of his visits to Abuja to participate in a workshop during which he shared with contributors his rich insights and perspectives on political developments in Nigeria and the global expectations that accompany them. The Ministry of Foreign Affairs, too, has contributed funds towards publication of the book, which we gratefully acknowledge. In particular, we are indebted to Ojo Maduekwe, the immediate past minister of foreign affairs, who, once briefed, took interest in the project and encouraged his ministry to endorse and support the work. We also acknowledge the support of Professor Mahmoud Yakubu, executive secretary of the Education Trust Fund (ETF), and the financial assistance provided by the ETF towards publication of the book. Amina az-Zubair, senior special assistant for the Millennium Development Goals, was also instrumental in providing funding and support.

We give special thanks to the Yar'Adua Centre for coordinating, facilitating, managing, and generally superintending the research, production, and publishing of this book. We are grateful to the Centre's indefatigable support staff, especially Mrs. Rose Ugorji for her administrative and secretarial services.

In any event, the chapter contributors and editors collectively share responsibility for any errors of omission or commission that may be found.

Attahiru M. Jega
Jacqueline W. Farris

NIGERIA
AT FIFTY

1

Nigeria's Foreign Policy and the Promotion of Peace, Development, and Democracy

Attahiru M. Jega

As Nigeria commemorates fifty years of independence from colonial rule in October 2010, it is important to review and assess Nigeria's foreign policy focus on peace, development, and democracy and attempt to answer the following questions: What has the purported leader of Africa done, inside and outside of Africa? How and why? How well conceptualized and executed is the focus? With what impact and consequences? Contributors to this book address these pertinent and increasingly primary themes in Nigeria's foreign policy, often subsumed under "Africa is the centrepiece of Nigeria's foreign policy" blanket, but yet not sufficiently analysed, explained, and understood.

Studies on Nigeria's foreign policy have tended to be general broad strokes, covering virtually every conceivable topic. We have chosen instead, in this volume, to focus on a thematic area of growing relevance and significance in international relations, targeting issues pertaining to the emerging discourses on global citizenship. For example, in a conflict-ridden world, with occasional violent eruptions, genocidal tendencies, and enormous humanitarian problems, contributions to solving conflicts, promoting peaceful coexistence, and facilitating good governance and democratisation have become important objectives of foreign policy. With the decline of superpower rivalry in the post–Cold War era, the threat of nuclear conflagration has reduced, such that the United Nations and its Security Council, as well as other regional and multilateral organisations, are giving greater attention to solving conventional conflicts and humanitarian crises. For many often contradictory reasons, Nigeria has long recognised this and has played increasing roles in regional, subregional, and global peacekeeping/peacebuilding operations. Nigeria has also pursued, as a foreign policy objective, issues concerning national development through bilateral and multilateral relations and democracy promotion—the latter more a child of necessity and circumstance than a well-targeted and pursued agenda.

A reassessment and reevaluation of Nigeria's foreign policy, in all its ramifications, is indeed necessary and long overdue, and the fiftieth commemoration of Nigeria's independence provides a welcome opportunity for this. The existing structure, processes, and machinery of foreign policy formulation and implementation, which have served Nigeria relatively well up to the early 1980s, now leave much to be desired. The contradictions, constraints, and inherent weaknesses are glaringly manifest; hence the urgent need to strengthen and reevaluate policy in line with the requirements of a fast-changing and rapidly globalising world. Present-day foreign policy decisions and actions need to focus on addressing the challenges of national survival, human security, progress, and development in the new millennium. Indeed, the defined foreign policy objectives in the 1999 Constitution of the Federal Republic of Nigeria require reexamination, if not redefinition, to accommodate a focus on new issues and challenges confronting Nigeria. While the old issues of sovereignty protection, territorial integrity, and national security are still relevant, new emerging issues—for example, national competitiveness in the globalised economy, promotion and defence of universal rights, environmental protection and sustainable development, and the promotion of peaceful coexistence and democratisation—have assumed primacy.

As Nigeria increasingly comes to terms with these additional concerns in its foreign policy pursuits, a carefully defined framework is needed to guide decisions and actions. Studies on Nigeria's foreign policy have pointed to the structures' and processes' incapacity for conceptualising and implementing foreign policy decisions to meet the challenges of the rapidly changing reality of the contemporary international system (Akindele 1990; Adebajo and Mustapha 2008). This inadequacy will only worsen unless reforms are introduced and institutionalised to address it. There is perhaps no better time for a reflection and reform initiative than the occasion of the commemoration of the fiftieth anniversary of Nigeria's independence from colonial rule.

At the conceptual and theoretical levels, as Asobie has observed, "The study of Nigeria's foreign policy is grossly underdeveloped" (1991, p. 3). Despite its being a copious and voluminous industry, the study of Nigeria's foreign policy has been unsystematic, basically idiosyncratic, and lacking in theoretical and empirical rigour. As Ambassador Hart (2009) aptly noted, foreign policy studies in Nigeria have generally been narrative inclined; they are not analytical and offer little if any basis for a choice of scientific framework to guide conceptualisation, implementation, or study and understanding of Nigeria's foreign policy.

This book is also a modest attempt to contribute to the need for a more scientific and systematic study, especially in the key thematic areas of peace, development, and democracy. Equally significant, it hopes to facilitate restrategising, streamlining, and refocusing Nigeria's foreign policy towards better attainment and satisfaction of the needs and aspirations of citizens, domestically and internationally. A strategy to pursue the national interest and foreign policy objectives is needed. In the context of a rapidly globalising world, Nigeria's foreign policy should be driven by forward-looking initiatives and exemplary leadership in policy conceptualisation and execution. Additionally, it should be backed by strong and stable institutions, agencies, and processes. It is inconceivable that a country that muddles through its domestic and foreign policies would prosper in the contemporary world.

History and Context

Nigeria has come a long way in international relations, from the immediate postindependence era of the early 1960s when US President Lyndon B. Johnson kept confusing Nigeria with Algeria (Alkali 2003, p. 190, quoting Wayas) to this first decade of the new millennium when virtually every US household knows Nigeria, though unfortunately due more to the dubious distinction of its citizens' involvement in global crimes, ranging from drug-trafficking to fraud ("419") and now terrorism following a botched attempted bombing of an aircraft in a US city on December 25, 2009, by a young Nigerian citizen. From the early 1960s when Britain was virtually Nigeria's only trading partner, to which it exported primarily agricultural commodities, to the new millennium when Nigeria is one of the world's major oil-exporting countries and a major exporter of that commodity to the United States (indeed, its largest trading partner in sub-Saharan Africa), Nigeria has become an important player in international relations, an assumed potential leader of Africa, and a major contributor to international peacekeeping and peacebuilding operations, both regionally and globally.

Given its size, population, and vast natural resource endowment, Nigeria was perceived at independence from colonial rule as a country destined to play crucial roles for progress and development throughout the world and a natural leader on the African continent (Phillips 1964;

Thiam 1965). Although the immediate postindependence Balewa government defined broad foreign policy objectives, which it pursued rather cautiously, it set the stage for such a claim to leadership. For example, Nigeria opposed France's testing of atomic weapons in the Sahara desert and severed diplomatic ties with France in 1961 as a result, became involved in peacekeeping operations in the Congo and in Lebanon, helped thwart a coup attempt in Tanzania, covertly funded and provided military assistance to the African National Congress (ANC) in South Africa, and played a decisive role in the formation of the Organisation of African Unity. Although Prime Minister Tafawa Balewa abhorred radical ideologies and regimes, "[H]e was passionate about Africa and African issues to which he gave significant attention" (Fawole 2003, p. 40). However, critiques have characterized Balewa's foreign policy as not only conservative but also hesitant and moralistic, and lacking in content and consistency (Idang 1973; Alkali 2003). Some have argued that the first phase of Nigeria's foreign policy under the Balewa government was driven by altruistic motives (Hart 2009). It was also said to be broadly pro-Western to excessively accommodate British colonial interests.

In any case, successive Nigerian governments, especially under military rule, have striven to assume or claim a leadership position through foreign policy declarations and actions and other modes of international engagements. This commenced with General Yakubu Gowon's drive for regional integration and key role in the formation of the Economic Community of West African States (ECOWAS). Increased oil revenues enabled Nigeria's more generous foreign policy undertakings, proactive engagements, and the emergence of hegemonic ambitions.

From the mid-1970s, Nigeria's military leaders began to define the country's foreign policy objectives in the context of its perceived power and continental aspiration for leadership. Under Generals Murtala Mohammed and Olusegun Obasanjo (1975–1979), Nigeria was a leader on African issues with an enthusiastic, some say radical, thrust. Nigeria's foreign policy objectives were more coherently defined than was hitherto the case. Africa was made the centrepiece or cornerstone of Nigeria's foreign policy. Although protection and defense of the country's territorial integrity, as well as pursuit of economic development have remained core objectives, they were in practice subsumed under the Afro-centric thrust of the defined national interests. Nigeria's foreign policy profile rose significantly due to its commitment and assistance to liberation struggles in southern Africa during this period—in recognition of which it earned membership in the Frontline States as well as chairmanship of the UN Anti-Apartheid Committee. Its influence over African matters was such that "if Nigeria wasn't at a table where African issues were discussed, [the discussion] is incomplete" (Eze 2009).

From the 1980s to the 1990s, however, Nigeria's foreign policy concerns shifted to a preoccupation with peacekeeping at the subregional level and economic diplomacy at the international level. Increased civil strife and military conflicts in the West African subregion, especially in Liberia, Sierra Leone, and Cote d'Ivoire, gave rise to concerns with national sovereignty, territorial integrity, and a possible spillover effect to the rest of the countries in the subregion. Good neighbourliness was threatened, and there were fears of the destabilising implications of massive inflows of refugees from war-torn areas in the subregion. In spite of declining revenues and the onset of an economic crisis, Nigeria maintained peacekeeping operations at high costs.

The pursuit of economic diplomacy as an additional plank of Nigeria's foreign policy was aimed at cushioning the damaging impact of the economic crisis that engulfed Nigeria in the 1980s and at assuaging the consequences of the structural adjustment measures introduced to contain the crisis. Foreign policy was redirected from a predominantly political focus to an economic one in which foreign policy instruments were used to advance domestic economic development objectives (Ogwu and Olukoshi 1991). Through economic diplomacy, launched by the Babangida government in 1988, Nigeria hoped to improve relations with its development partners, attract foreign investment, mitigate the burden of indebtedness, and garner international assistance from bilateral and multilateral sources for the country's socioeconomic development. As Okechukwu Ibeanu points out in Chapter 2, this thrust of economic development was an important feature of what he terms the "realist" phase of Nigeria's foreign policy in the 1980s and the 1990s.

To what extent the objectives of economic diplomacy, in particular the quest to attract foreign investment and garner new export markets and at the same time be an acknowledged subregional and regional African leader, have succeeded is a subject of intense debate and contestation. What can be said without doubt is that it is one thing to perceive oneself a leader but quite another thing to be recognized as such by others. Thus, converting the perception of Nigeria's leadership role in Africa into reality has remained a formidable challenge fifty years later. Substantial commitments of human and material resources to back up foreign policy decisions and actions, especially in conflict resolution and peacekeeping, have not yielded the desired respect and influence for Nigeria in Africa or elsewhere. Neither has it yielded any significant dividend in terms of investment opportunities for Nigeria in the countries that it helped nor garnered popular acceptance and support domestically as Julie Sanda and Obadiah Mailafia have shown in Chapters 5 and 9, respectively. The pertinent question is: Why?

The long-recognized link between domestic processes and the conduct of foreign policy goes a long way to explain Nigeria's growing frustration in the actualisation of its coveted leadership role in Africa. Weak economic and political structures, ineffective institutions and processes, and bad governance, characterized by quarrelsome, inept, and corrupt public officers, have combined to undermine, except for a brief period (1975–1979), the influence and respectability that ought to have accrued to Nigeria's foreign policy undertakings in the past fifty years. Although Nigerians, especially their leaders, are still presumptive about their country's leadership role in Africa, many observers and scholars think otherwise. A range of suggestive phrases are now being used to describe Nigeria and its relationship with the rest of the world: "a crippled giant" (Osaghae 1998); "open sore of a continent" (Soyinka 1996); "a giant with clay feet," "hegemony on a shoestring," "crumbling Tower of Babel," and "Africa's Gulliver faced the threat of becoming the Lilliput of the globe" (Adebajo and Mustapha 2008); and so forth.

Domestic instability and insecurity and the majority of citizens' lack of prosperity have affected Nigerians' appreciation of and support for their country's worthy endeavours in foreign policy and global politics. With a projected population of 159.4 million in 2010, Nigeria is one of the ten most populous countries in the world. Its population represents one-quarter of sub-Saharan Africa and one-fifth of the black race. With an estimated gross domestic product (GDP) of US$183 billion (in 2008) and a growth rate of 3.8 percent, as well as abundant resources, it is potentially Africa's largest economy. Yet, Nigeria is one of Africa's most chronically unstable and conflict-ridden countries. Multicultural diversity has been complicated by negative elite mobilisation of ethnicity and religion, and compounded by one of the highest incidences of poverty on the African continent. In spite of attempts by the Obasanjo (1999–2007) and Yar'Adua (2007–2010) governments to "eradicate" poverty, statistics still point to a bleak picture, standing at about 70 percent (Usman 2007, p. 4). Industrial growth production rate is estimated at –1.8 percent, levels of unemployment are high, life expectancy is 55 years, and the overall literacy rate is 64 percent. Nigeria continues to be overdependent on the oil sector, which still accounts for 95 percent of foreign exchange earnings and 80 percent of budgetary revenues. However, oil revenues have not been properly harnessed for socioeconomic development, as evidenced by dilapidated infrastructure, chronic power outages, and institutional decay.

The contradiction of being a rich country with very poor people is explained or accounted for by the recklessness of a greedy and self-serving Nigerian elite who have mismanaged the economy, undermined infrastructure and socioeconomic development, and basically squirreled away the country's resources into their private coffers. There is no doubt, therefore, that the domestic environment, characterised by insecurity, poverty, ethno-religious mobilisation, and youth unemployment, has negatively constrained and influenced or otherwise conditioned the making and execution of foreign policy.

Nonetheless, in the fifty years of Nigeria's foreign policy, despite significant external and domestic constraints, there are notable and noteworthy accomplishments. which are suggestive of a broader scope of achievements, if only lessons could be learnt and reform initiatives launched appropriately. No doubt there are discernable discontinuities as much as there are continuities, as Ibeanu has highlighted in Chapter 2, but, as a whole, and as most chapter contributors have shown, Nigeria has actively participated as a global player for the resolution of conflicts, promotion of peace, and advancement of democratisation, even if the latter was an unplanned but concomitant outcome of the former. The chapters in the book have together brought out the array of not only notable accomplishments but also the formidable challenges that Nigeria has had to contend with in its fifty years of foreign policy, as the following brief summary of the chapter contributions highlights.

Summary of Chapters

In Chapter 2, Ibeanu contends that Nigeria's role in global politics can best be understood by classifying the thrust of its foreign policy into three phases: (1) conservative, (2) radical, and (3) realist. Each corresponds with a particular period with unique factors that shaped developments in and outside Nigeria. For instance, the conservative phase covers 1960 to 1970 when Nigeria was concerned with issues such as attainment of political freedom from colonialism, protection and defence of national sovereignty, and noninterference in the internal affairs of other African states. Nigeria's approach to global and African issues in this period was conservative and pragmatic. While trying to ensure global stability, Nigeria was deeply concerned with the requirements of managing the country's fragile nature.

In the radical phase (1970–1980), Nigeria was more assertive because of factors that spurred its self-confidence, such as the successful execution of the civil war, an increase in oil wealth, and the dominance of domestic politics by relatively radical military regimes. In the realist phase—from the 1980s onwards—as a result of the problems created by the economic crisis of that decade, Nigeria preoccupied itself with improving relations with creditors such as Bretton Woods institutions and forging other bilateral and multilateral economic relations, essentially for redressing the damaging impact of the crisis and for sustained economic development. Thus, during this period Nigeria essentially relegated to the background its hitherto keen concern about African liberation from colonialism and imperialism and instead focused more on economic competitiveness in the era of globalisation and forging relationships compatible with economic growth and development.

Okello Oculi discusses, in Chapter 3, the continuities inherent in Nigeria's foreign policy and how these have been manifested through the country's membership in key international organizations such as the United Nations, the Commonwealth of Nations, and the Non-Aligned Movement. For instance, Nigeria's stance as a UN member was made clear when Balewa's speech to the United Nations in October 1960 emphasised that the country's foreign policy principle included sustained relations with Britain and regional groupings, rejection of regime change in Africa through military coup, preference for aid to Africa from multilateral UN agencies, more African voices in global affairs, and the notion of placing African affairs first in Nigeria's foreign policy. Oculi also discusses how Nigeria has used its membership in the Commonwealth to demonstrate its influence and foster African interests such as the fight against apartheid, hosting of the Commonwealth Heads of Government Meeting in 2003, and the use of Nigerian diplomats to resolve African crises (as in Kenya). These issues have consistently shown the nature of Nigeria's foreign policy focus in the past fifty years, which is centred on Africa.

In Chapter 4, Eghosa Osaghae analyses the role Nigeria has played as a subregional power in the democratisation processes in Liberia, Sierra Leone, Togo, and Equatorial Guinea. He shows how Nigeria demonstrated its influence as a leader in the West African subregion by either unilaterally or multilaterally intervening in these countries' crises, using the Economic Community of West African States (ECOWAS) as a platform and springboard. These case studies aptly illustrate

Nigeria's role as an active promoter of conflict resolution, peacebuilding, collective security, and democratisation. This role, of course, has been replete with contradictory dynamics. For one, the reluctance of global powers to be actively engaged in African conflicts, especially after the United States' bitter experience in Somalia, created an opportunity for Nigeria to play a leadership role. For another, arising from its role in peacekeeping and conflict resolution, Nigeria soon recognised the imperative of democratisation for sustainable peacebuilding and became preoccupied with transition to democracy projects in other West African countries as an integral part of its peacebuilding mission, even while under the tutelage of authoritarian military regimes. The need to resolve this contradiction may have had significant bearing in subsequent politics of transition in Nigeria itself in the 1990s. For example, pro-democracy civil society organisations gained much mileage by hammering on the contradiction in which military authoritarian rulers in Nigeria, without democratic credentials, were exporting democracy to West African neighbours. In any case, Nigeria's role in promoting and bringing about peace and democratic development in these countries has enhanced its status as a regional and subregional leader and as a major player in the United Nations' preoccupation with global and human security, as well as democratisation.

In Chapter 5, Julie Sanda focuses on Nigeria's role in enhancing global stability through peacekeeping and peacemaking. Using Nigeria's contributions in Congo, Lebanon, and Bosnia-Herzegovina, Sanda describes how Nigeria has made globally acknowledged contributions, albeit at tremendous costs. She underscores the fact that, despite a commitment of enormous human and material resources to peacekeeping and peacemaking in other countries, Nigeria has been unable to benefit substantially because of the absence of clearly defined objectives and goals underlying the interventions, targeted at maximising the actualisation of Nigeria's national interest. Similarly, she points to poor coordination and cooperation among institutions and individuals involved in the policymaking and execution processes, which are largely responsible for the inability of the country to develop well-defined goals and a strategic framework for international peacekeeping adventures.

In Chapter 6, Andrew Okolie undertakes a discussion on Nigeria's role in African regional and continental peacekeeping, peacemaking, and peace enforcement with particular reference to Sierra Leone, Liberia, Darfur, and Somalia. Okolie notes that peacekeeping in Liberia, Sierra Leone, Chad, and even Guinea-Bissau were carried out under the auspices of the Economic Community of West African States

Monitoring Group (ECOMOG). In all these operations, Nigeria's peace-keeping efforts were initially unilateral (as in the case of Chad) but later became multilateral (as in the cases of Liberia, Sierra Leone, and Guinea-Bissau) when Nigeria collaborated with other member states of ECOW-AS. To Okolie, ECOMOG succeeded mainly because of the political will and doggedness of ECOWAS members, especially Nigeria, and because of the authoritarian nature of the governments of the major powers (Nigeria and Ghana) that formed ECOMOG, as well as the enormous resources at the disposal of Nigeria. However, the main challenges ECO-MOG faced in peacekeeping in these countries included the brutal and protracted nature of the conflicts, ECOMOG's legitimacy problem, linguistic and geopolitical divisions/rivalries, obsolete military equipment, and poor logistics and training. The success of ECOMOG further confirmed Nigeria as a hegemonic power in West Africa, in particular, despite the shortcomings and limitations of ECOMOG.

In Chapter 7, Hamid Bobboyi analyses what, arguably, is Nigeria's major foreign policy triumph: The creation and nurturing of ECOWAS. He discusses the crucial role Nigeria played in its formation and assesses its main achievements, as well as the challenges it faces. The creation of ECOWAS was a realisation of earlier efforts aimed at economic integration and collective self-reliance in an increasingly asymmetrical world in which primary commodity producers are at the mercy of industrialised countries. The main achievements include implementation of the peace and security protocol that saw the establishment of ECOMOG and its crucial roles in ensuring peacekeeping and conflict resolution at the subregional and even regional/continental levels; implementation of the free movement of persons and goods protocol, which abolished visas and catalyzed closer socioeconomic relations among member states; and the implementation of the democracy and good governance protocol, which facilitates election monitoring and collective sanctioning of military coups among member states. However, persistent challenges include substantial nontariff barriers and other protectionist measures that have prevented the successful implementation of the ECOWAS Trade Liberalization Scheme (ETLS) and that have obstructed the fundamental objective of closer subregional economic integration; relatively low manufacturing capacity in member states, which has minimised the tapping of benefits of the raw materials being promoted by the ETLS; the inability to harmonise monetary policy and introduce a single currency; and the inability to tackle poverty and its impact on the socioeconomic development of the subregion. Significant recommendations are made on how best to consolidate and sustain the ECOWAS initiative by addressing key challenges. In so doing, leadership, political will, and vision are considered essential.

In Chapter 8, Abubakar Siddique Mohammed discusses how the oil resource–based economic character of Nigeria has defined its position in OPEC and its relations with the Arab world and the West. Mohammed shows how the discovery of oil, its exploration, and exploitation were not controlled by Nigeria until long after independence. Thereafter, with oil becoming the major revenue source and foreign exchange earner for Nigeria, the country became a major player in the global oil market as an exporter of high-quality crude oil. The emergence of OPEC and its dominance by oil-producing countries of the Middle East subsequently impacted the way Nigeria related with its oil companies at home, the Middle East, and Western oil-consuming countries such as the United States and Britain, especially when Nigeria joined OPEC in 1971. Mohammed further shows how the politics of regulating oil production quotas in OPEC and the conflicts in the Middle East (Arab–Israeli conflict and Iran–Iraq War) drew the United States and its Western allies closer to Nigeria when the West refocused its attention to the Gulf of Guinea (dominated by Nigeria) as a strategic alternative source of energy.

Mailafia, in Chapter 9, analyses Nigeria's bilateral and multilateral economic assistance to African countries and assesses its impact on Nigeria's domestic economy and on the relationship between it and other countries in the continent as well as how this assistance has influenced Nigeria's foreign policy direction. Mailafia asserts that Nigeria has used the ECOWAS platform to dramatise its economic and political dominance in West Africa through direct assistance to its members and other needy African states. Examples include the over US$60 billion financial assistance to Benin Republic, Zimbabwe, Cape Verde, Guinea, Senegal, Niger, Togo, Liberia, and Mali. Additional avenues Nigeria has used to assist others include the Technical Aids Corps Scheme, Nigeria Trust Fund, and Nigeria Technical Cooperation Fund.

Mailafia notes, however, that dwindling oil revenues and domestic economic constraints have subjected Nigeria's charity to intense questioning within Nigeria, especially given the battered international image of the country despite this assistance, and the worsening condition of infrastructure at home with poor socioeconomic indices. Mailafia proposes redirecting Nigeria's national interest to focus on solving Nigerian socioeconomic problems while being more selective in providing development assistance.

In Chapter 10, Tijjani Bande assesses the significance of transnational waters and how Nigeria has utilised these to foster good neighbourliness as well as its own national interest. He uses the Lake Chad Basin Commission and the Niger Basin Authority to illustrate how these institutions can facilitate integration in the West African subregion as well as serve as sources of livelihood for Nigerians and other nationals living along and around the River Niger and Lake Chad basins. He also points to the danger posed by the bureaucracy in these organisations, including internal politics and the lackluster attitude of member states, which could jeopardise Nigeria's national interests and the prospects of subregional integration.

Chapter 11, the concluding chapter, summarises and reviews the major postulations of contributors and articulates a framework for repositioning, if not redefining, Nigeria's foreign policy in order to more effectively meet the challenges of twenty-first-century preoccupations with human security, development, and democratisation.

It is evident from the chapter contributions that fifty years of Nigeria's foreign policy are replete with an array of accomplishments, trials, and challenges pertaining to Nigeria's role in peacemaking, development, and democratisation at the global, regional, and subregional levels. Similarly, it is clear that regardless of the phase or time periods in which Nigeria's foreign policy could be classified, there are discernable continuities, especially with regard to a focus on African issues, particularly relating to conflict resolution, peacebuilding, economic integration, and, more recently, democratisation. The extent to which these core continuities have been pursued, however, has been essentially conditioned or affected by the dynamic domestic and external environments. Significantly, as Osaghae asserts in Chapter 4:

> In an increasingly relegated Africa, whose conflicts the international community failed to respond promptly to, it was clear that, benign colonialism or not, African regional powers were going to play more active roles in the affairs of their subregions in the post–Cold War period. They have indeed done so mostly in the name of defending democracy and constitutional rule or preventing escalation of conflicts, which seems to be the most politically correct and acceptable justification to the global superpowers and international community at large for intervening in the internal affairs of other countries.

As a regional power, Nigeria has played crucial and influential, though some say hegemonic, roles with varied impacts and consequences. These roles, however, have lacked well-defined objectives, as well as conceptual and operational frameworks—deficiencies that have imposed constraints on the extent to which the roles have aided the pursuit of

Nigeria's national interest. As Nigeria looks forward to the next fifty years of the new millennium, a redefinition and reconceptualisation of Nigeria's foreign policy objectives are required. Equally significant, a reprioritisation of issues and concerns in Nigeria's foreign policy development is also needed. These are attempted in the concluding chapter.

Bibliography

Adedeji, A., 2004, "ECOWAS: A Retrospective Journey," in A. Adebajo and I. Rashid, eds., *West Africa's Security Challenges: Building Peace in a Troubled Region*, Lynne Rienner, Colorado and London, p. 46.

Adebajo, A., and Mustapha, A.R., eds., 2008, *Gulliver's Troubles: Nigeria's Foreign Policy after the Cold War*, University of Kwazulu Natal Press, Scottsville, South Africa.

Akindele, R.A., 1990, "Constitutional Structure of Nigeria's Foreign Policy," in G. Olusanya and R.A. Akindele, eds., *The Structure and Processes of Foreign Policy Making and Implementation in Nigeria, 1960–1990*, Vantage Publishers International, Ibadan, Nigeria, pp. 55–71.

Alkali, R.A., 2003, *International Relations and Nigeria's Foreign Policy*, Northpoint Publishers, Kaduna, Nigeria.

Asobie, H., 1991, "Nigeria: Economic Diplomacy and National Interest," *Nigerian Journal of International Affairs*, vol. 17, no. 2.

Berger, S., 2000, "A Foreign Policy for the Global Age," *Foreign Affairs*, vol. 79, no. 6, pp. 22–39.

Dewar, B., 2010, "Challenges for Nigerian Political Leadership," *The Guardian*, February 3, p. 51.

Eze, O., 2009. Contribution to Methodology workshop organised by the Yar'Adua Centre, Abuja, Nigeria, October 15.

Fawole, W.A., 2003, *Nigeria's External Relations and Foreign Policy Under Military Rule, 1966–1999*, Obafemi Awolowo University Press, Ile-Ife, Nigeria.

Gambari, I.A., 1991, "Federalism and Management of External Relations in Nigeria: Lessons from the Past and Challenges for the Future," *Publius*, vol. 21, no. 4.

Hart, T. 2009. Contribution to Methodology workshop organised by the Yar'Adua Centre, Abuja, Nigeria, October 15.

Hoffman, A., 1995–1996, "Nigeria: The Policy Conundrum," *Foreign Policy*, no. 101.

Idang, G.J., 1973, *International Politics and Foreign Policy*, Oxford University Press, Ibadan, Nigeria.

Ogwu, U.J., ed., 2005, *New Horizons for Nigeria in World Affairs*, Nigerian Institute of International Affairs, Lagos, Nigeria.

Ogwu, U.J., and Olukoshi, A., eds., 1991, *Economic Diplomacy in the Contemporary World and the Nigerian Experience*, special issue of *Nigerian Journal of International Studies*, vol. 15, no. 1 and 2.

Okpokpo, E., 1999, "The Challenges Facing Nigeria's Foreign Policy in the Next Millennium," *African Studies Quarterly*, vol. 3, no. 2.

Osaghae, E.E., 1998, *Nigeria Since Independence: Crippled Giant*, Indiana University Press, Bloomington, IN, US.

Phillips Jr., C.S., 1964, *The Development of Nigerian Foreign Policy*, Northwestern University Press, Evanston, IL, US.

Soyinka, W., 1996, *The Open Sore of a Continent: A Personal Narrative of the Nigerian Crisis*, Oxford University Press, Oxford, UK.

Thiam, D., 1965, *The Foreign Policy of African States*, Praeger, New York, US.

Usman, Shamsuddeen, 2007, "Nigeria: Scorching the Resource Curse," Presentation by the minister of finance, Federal Republic of Nigeria, at the London School of Economics and Political Science, October 11.

PART 1

PROMOTING FREEDOM AND DEMOCRACY

2

Nigeria's Role in the Promotion of the OAU/AU and Membership of the Frontline States

Okechukwu Ibeanu

In fifty years of independence, Nigeria's foreign policy has focused principally on Africa. Successive Nigerian leaders professed Africa as the centrepiece of Nigeria's foreign policy. Indeed, Nigeria sees itself and is widely seen as a leader of Africa, and this has profoundly influenced the perception of its role, both on the continent and globally. However, Nigeria's foreign policy in Africa, though generally consistent, has been nuanced by a number of domestic and external factors. The impact of these factors has been to give Nigeria's approach to African affairs certain specificities over time. This chapter contends that these specificities create three principal phases in Nigeria's foreign policy in Africa, which for lack of better characterisation may be termed the conservative, the radical, and the realist phases. We also propose that Nigeria's role in the formation of the Organization of African Unity (OAU) and its participation in the activities of the Frontline States, as well the pivotal role it played in the transformation of the OAU into the African Union (AU) respectively correspond to these three phases of its African foreign policy (see Table 2.1 and Figure 2.1).

First, the conservative phase corresponds roughly to the period between independence in 1960 and the end of the civil war in 1970. Its characteristics matured between 1960 and 1963, a period during which Nigeria's perspective on Africa was principally state-centric and political. Questions of political freedom from colonialism and protection of national sovereignty within a system of sovereign equality of states, as well as the principle of noninterference in the internal affairs of African states, were primary interests. Nigeria's approach to African issues during this period was essentially conservative and pragmatic, while advocating global stability, which largely implied maintaining existing global

17

Table 2.1   Characteristics of the Three Phases of Nigeria's Foreign Policy in Africa

Aspects of Foreign Policy	Conservative Phase (1960–1970)	Radical Phase (1970–1980)	Realist Phase (1980–date)
Perspective on Africa	Principally state-centric and political. Major issues: independence, sovereign equality of states, and noninterference in internal affairs of states.	Principally people-centred and populist. Major issues: economic emancipation, protection of citizens, and new world economic order.	Principally econo-centric. Major issues: economic diplomacy, overcoming the economic crisis triggered by collapse in oil revenues, and relations with creditors and Bretton Woods.
Major domestic impetus	Fragility of nation-building and national integration coupled with fears of external radicalisation and domestic secession; plus a conservative political leadership.	Successful prosecution of a civil war, widely considered a war of national unity, plus geometric rise in oil wealth and a radical/ populist military regime between 1975 and 1979.	Collapse of oil revenues and deepening economic crisis, plus a series of unpopular civilian and military governments.
Approach to African issues	Conservative and pragmatic.	Radical and assertive.	Realist and pragmatic.
Orientation to global power structures	Pro-global stability implying the maintenance of existing global power structures.	Pro-reconstitution of existing global power structures.	Adaptation and adjustment to existing global power structures.
Ideological orientation	Pro-West and largely antisocialist.	Radical-nationalist.	Realist and largely pro-West.
Definition of diplomacy in Africa	Principally anticolonial (diplomacy of decolonisation).	Principally anti-imperialism (diplomacy of popular liberation).	Principally functionalist (economic diplomacy).
Understanding of African liberation	Essentially political, consisting of liberating the African state from colonial rule.	Essentially socio-economic, consisting of liberating people from imperialism.	Essentially economic, consisting of overcoming the economic crisis.
Future survival of Africa	Depends on *unity* of African states.	Unity of Africa's peoples and *union* of African states.	Integration of African economies and adjustment to the capitalist world economy.
Defining markers	• Balewa government • Independence from Britain • Participation in the Monrovia Group • Entering into the botched Anglo-Nigeria defence pact • Joining the Commission for Technical Cooperation in Africa whose headquarters was later relocated to Lagos • Formation of the OAU in 1963	• Post-civil war Gowon administration • Murtala-Obasanjo-Yar'Adua government • Nigeria's participation in the Frontline States • Nationalisation of British Petroleum over Zimbabwe • Massive support for liberation movements in Zimbabwe, Angola, Mozambique, Namibia, and South Africa	• Lagos Plan of Action • Abuja Treaty of African Economic Community • Babangida government • Babangida's economic diplomacy • Nigeria's ratification of the Constitutive Act of the African Union, bringing it into force in 2001 • Establishment of New Partnership for Africa's Development (NEPAD)

Figure 2.1   Characteristics of the Three Phases of Nigeria's African Policy

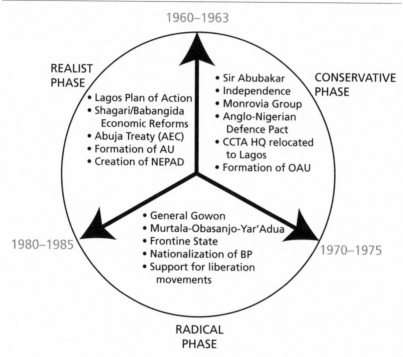

power relations. Domestically, the principal factor that shaped this early conservative phase was the fragility of the nation-building project in Nigeria and the lingering threat that the country would be torn apart by ethnic conflicts. This anxiety was further deepened by fears of external-ly motivated radicalisation capable of speeding up centrifugal forces. The main suspect at the time seemed to be Ghana under Prime Minister Kwame Nkrumah.

Second, the radical phase, which may be dated between 1970 and 1980, was marked by a more assertive Nigerian global citizenship, with Africa the focus of that citizenship. The major domestic stimuli were the successful prosecution of the civil war, by which Nigeria avoided breakup; an unprecedented increase in oil wealth; and a period of radical military rule (1975–1980). During this period, Nigeria's perspective on Africa was principally people-centred and populist. Issues such as eco-nomic emancipation, protection of citizens, and a new world economic order were central concerns. Ideologically, Nigeria tended to be radical and assertive, its main African objective being the end of colonial rule on the continent and apartheid in South Africa.

Finally, the realist phase is rooted in Nigeria's economic problems of the 1980s, particularly under the administrations of Alhaji Shehu Shagari and General Ibrahim Babangida. The principal concern during the period was economic diplomacy aimed at overcoming the economic crisis that was triggered by a collapse in oil revenues, as well as improving relations with external creditors, especially the Bretton Woods institutions (International Monetary Fund [IMF] and World Bank). Consequently, Nigeria neglected a number of its traditional concerns in Africa and increasingly sought to accommodate some of the erstwhile adversaries of Nigeria's global citizenship—all justified in populist, pragmatist, and realist terms.

Some clarifications are necessary in order to properly understand this three-phase taxonomy representing continuities and discontinuities in Nigeria's foreign policy. Discontinuities exist because each phase is broadly different from others, yet there are strong continuities between the phases. An overlap is to be expected because sometimes the same officials were prominent between phases, the foreign policy bureaucracy persisted over time, and a measure of long-term elite (interests) consensus was at play. These served to create a dialectic of *continuity in discontinuity*. Thus, Figure 2.2 shows that the pan-African fervour of the conservative phase, albeit antipolitical union, persisted during the radical phase, and pragmatism was also exhibited during the conservative phase and expressed strongly during the realist phase. At the same time, the populism of the realist phase, particularly as expressed ostensibly in commitment to the economic well-being of the Nigerian citizen, seems to be a continuation of the popular nationalism of the radical phase. The point then is that each phase was not exclusively conservative, radical, or realist. In fact, these categories are broad and may not effectively capture the varied nature of foreign policy decisionmaking and implementation during each period. However, they provide an heuristic tool for understanding the broad perspectives that dominated each phase.

Secondly, each phase took some time to mature (approximately three to five years), often starting under one government and fully crystallising in the succeeding one. For instance, the economic diplomacy of the Babangida period already found strong antecedents in the Shagari government's concerns with the deepening economic crisis and taking a lead in the Lagos Plan of Action. Again, the same concerns were clear in the economic accent of the foreign policy of the Buhari government, including the resort to countertrade (bartering Nigerian oil in exchange

Figure 2.2   Continuities and Discontinuities in the Three Phases of Nigeria's African Policy

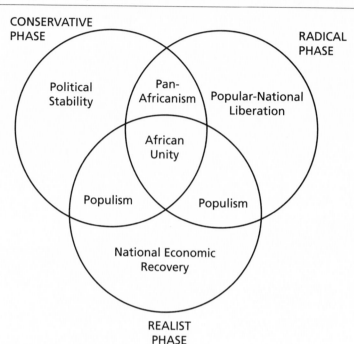

for imports). Again, it has been suggested that the radical posture of the Murtala Mohammed government towards Angola was in fact a carry-over from the Gowon government. Thus, the Gowon government may have been on the verge of recognizing the Popular Movement for the Liberation of Angola (MPLA) before it was overthrown.

Finally, it is important to note the role of interactions between both structure and agency in shaping each phase. Indeed, we can speak here of *structured agency*, referring to the complex interaction of structures and leaders in giving each phase its specific character. For example, at Nigeria's independence, the importance of structures created by colonialism and the rising influence of radical forces in neighbouring African countries combined with the character of leadership provided by Sir Abubakar Tafawa Balewa to produce a largely conservative-pragmatic foreign policy during the first phase. This is not to suggest that the Balewa government was necessarily in hock to the West, as some analysts have suggested. To illustrate, Nigeria sponsored the expulsion of apartheid South Africa from the Commonwealth in 1961 against the wishes of its Western allies, and the government abandoned the Anglo-Nigeria Defence Pact following domestic opposition (Ojo 1990).

Conservative Phase:
Nigeria and the Formation of the OAU

For over half a century before the OAU was created on May 25, 1963, different strands of the African unity movement had existed, culminating in what became the pan-African movement. These strands variously expressed a desire for the return of the African Diaspora to the continent, cultural revival, and political freedom and unity, as well as economic emancipation. However, these strands were by no means homogenous. Indeed, in many cases they were deeply contradictory. As such, the African unity project has always been built on compromise, which observers sometimes see as self-serving. Thus, Julius Nyerere described the OAU as a "trade union of African heads of state"; and Claude Ake's reflection is that OAU leaders were people of limited vision and tyrannical inclinations, hanging on desperately to power without legitimacy, and that the OAU only expressed internal contradictions that were deepening underdevelopment in Africa (Mwalilino 2000).

The formation of the OAU in 1963 was not the first attempt at inter-Africa unity. The 1961 conference held in Casablanca, Morocco, dealt with the possibilities of an African common market and an African military command. Similarly, in 1960 and 1961, twelve French-speaking African countries signed a charter establishing the Union Africaine et Malgache, which later became the Organization Commune Africaine et Mauriciene. Also in 1961, a conference was held in Monrovia, Liberia, which resulted in the formation of the Organisation of Inter-African and Malagasy States. In addition, there was the Pan-African Movement for East and Central Africa, as well as the Ghana-Guinea-Mali Union. All these show that the process of the OAU's emergence profoundly expressed longstanding divergences within the African unity movement, particularly the desirable level of unity. While some strands preferred functional unity, others strove for full political unification. In addition, the pace of unification differed. While some desired a fast tracking of African unification, others preferred a gradual process of cooperation and common institution building before ultimately reaching full political integration.

However, in the final buildup to the formation of the OAU, the different tendencies, expressed in the divergent positions of the continent's various political leaders, essentially divided into the Casablanca and Monrovia groups. The Casablanca Group was smaller in number and counted among its ranks radical governments such as Nkrumah's Ghana, Nasser's Egypt, and Sekou Toure's Guinea. By comparison, the larger Monrovia Group was more conservative and gradualist, and its important members were Nigeria, Liberia, Senegal, Ivory Coast, and later Ethiopia. These two groups came together to form the OAU.

It therefore seems that the formation of the OAU was yet another compromise with Nigeria at the forefront. To appreciate this central role of Nigeria, we need to understand the mindset in Lagos that produced it. For Nigeria's political leadership at the time, the country had just become independent, which itself was a compromise among Nigeria's ethnic nationalists and between them and the British colonialists. The country was therefore struggling with internal problems of cohesion and disarticulated state-making. At the same time, Nigerian leaders perceived the country as economically weak and requiring the support of its former colonial masters and their friends for economic development. Finally, they perceived that the country was surrounded by not-so-friendly French colonies and radical regimes, particularly Ghana. However, beyond its own specific considerations, Nigeria considered that most African countries were still grappling with the challenges of state building, arising particularly from the yet largely contested colonial boundaries. Consequently, a continental government would have been impossible at the time.

In the circumstance, it was not surprising that Nigeria became a member of the Monrovia Group, which placed emphasis on economic cooperation among sovereign African states and less on political unification of these states. This group also took a regional approach to problem solving but a hands-off approach to members' internal affairs and problems (Advameg 2010). On the other hand, the Casablanca states were more radical, particularly because of their desire for immediate unification of Africa and opposition to economic imperialism on the continent. These positions were epitomised by the policies of Nkrumah's Ghana, Nasser's Egypt, and Toure's Guinea. Despite these differences, the two groups came together in 1963 and subsequently agreed to establish the OAU. Nigeria was central to brokering the compromise that made this possible. Olukoshi (2006) rightly observes that the compromise forged by the Casablanca and Monrovia blocs spanned the objectives, mandates, procedures, and institutional structures of the OAU, and this subordinated the autonomy of the continental body to the sovereignty and sovereign equality of members within the framework of the national boundaries set in Berlin in 1884–1885 and inherited at independence. This contributed in no small measure to the perceived ineffectiveness of the organisation later in its existence.

We can surmise cardinal features of Nigeria's role in the formation of the OAU. First, Nigeria provided the rallying point for moderates across Africa on the burning issues to the continent at the time. By providing this platform, Nigeria helped to create the context for bargaining and compromise that created the OAU in 1963. Indeed, it was at the Lagos meeting of the Monrovia Group that the core members of the bloc (Nigeria, Liberia, Senegal, Cameroon, Ivory Coast, and Togo) stepped up their attack on the Casablanca Group, condemning it on various issues, including its failure to denounce the perceived interference in the internal affairs of member states by other African countries. Dr. Nnamdi Azikiwe, the Nigerian president, publicly acknowledged the obvious split between his group and the Casablanca group. Paradoxically, however, it was this public rift between the two groups that provided the window of opportunity for Ethiopian Foreign Minister Ketama Yifru, on a mission to bring the two groups together, to successfully lobby conference participants to attend the 1963 Addis Ababa Conference that gave birth to the OAU.

Second, although Nigeria provided a rallying point for moderates and although the Abubakar government took a gradualist approach to African issues, it did so without being obstructionist. By so doing, Nigeria became a respected voice on Africa, both within the continent and globally. Osuntokun rightly observes that:

> Sir Abubakar's regime was characterised by caution and conservatism but not inaction. His government was respected as a senior member of the Commonwealth and whenever Nigeria spoke it was listened to with respect. Sir Abubakar's opposition to apartheid was a contributory factor to the expulsion of South Africa from the Commonwealth in 1961. He single-handedly defended Africa against French atomic explosion in the Sahara in the 1960s. His government was also involved in founding the Organization of African Unity, which in spite of its limited and conservative agenda provided a forum for Africa to act together in the defence of the people's interests. (2005, p. 38)

Finally, it was obvious that Nigeria's domestic concerns and issues of national integration, particularly how to hold its disparate and sometimes centrifugal ethnic groups together, shaped its attitude of opposition to more radical tendencies that favoured strong continental unity and questioned the boundaries of existing African states. Thus, Nigeria, contrary to more radical leaders of the day such as Kwame Nkrumah, preferred an

OAU that would protect the territorial integrity of fragile states. Nigeria therefore opposed ethnic groups' right to self-determination within member states of the OAU (Stremlau 1981, p. 46). At the same time, Nigeria's pragmatism led to a realisation that it needed the West, including previous colonial countries, for its future economic development. This would have fallen through had Nigeria adopted a more radical, anti-imperialist approach at the formation of the OAU. With the benefit of hindsight, this position may not have served Nigeria as well as intended. However, we should not lose sight of the fact that at the time it was a rational, realistic, and informed position.

Radical Phase:
Nigeria's Membership in the Frontline States

Frontline States refer to the group of independent southern African countries bordering apartheid South Africa: Angola, Botswana, Lesotho, Mozambique, Zambia, and Zimbabwe. Formed in 1970, the group was meant to create a harmonised response to apartheid South Africa and to provide support, albeit covert, for the liberation struggle in South Africa. However, *ab initio*, this body suffered from a number of weaknesses vis-à-vis South Africa, which made it difficult for it to achieve its objective of ending apartheid. First, the countries were heavily dependent on South Africa economically, as it was the clear economic hegemonic power in the region. For instance, substantial numbers of Frontline States' citizens were migrant workers in South Africa. In addition, most of the Frontline States' members belonged to the Southern African Customs Union, which depended heavily on South Africa for port facilities and collection of customs revenue, which they shared among themselves.

Second, apart from being the regional economic hegemonic power, South Africa was militarily far superior to the combined capabilities of all Frontline States. Importantly, South Africa had on many occasions shown that it was not shy of using its military and economic superiority to whip the Frontline States in line with its wishes. All these combined with the fact that these countries were generally poor, some of them only just emerging from long periods of colonial and/or white minority rule. Consequently, the Frontline States could only provide covert support to the anti-apartheid liberation struggle in South Africa. In fact, on occasions some Frontline States dissuaded the military wing of the African National Congress (Umkhonto we sizwe) from using its territories for launching attacks against South Africa, particularly after South Africa claimed the right to hot pursuit of guerrillas into its neighbours' territories.

The invitation extended to Nigeria to join the Frontline States held the possibility of redressing some of these disadvantages. Not only had Nigeria repeatedly shown leadership on issues of liberating southern African countries from colonial and white supremacist rule, it had the financial muscle to stand up to South Africa. Nigeria's participation in the Frontline States should be properly understood in the context of its increased radicalisation of both domestic and foreign policies in the immediate aftermath of the civil war. By policy radicalisation, we mean principally the far-reaching changes in Nigerian leaders' attitude from the predominantly pro-West and stability orientations of the First Republic. The successful prosecution of the civil war had given the Gowon administration unprecedented confidence in the conduct of both domestic and foreign policy, particularly in dealing with powerful external forces, including Western powers and multinational corporations. Disagreements with some interests in the West over aspects of the prosecution of the civil war, particularly in the initial refusal of multinational oil companies to remit petroleum revenues to the federal government, encouraged the military regime to increasingly look away from its erstwhile allies in the West. Support received by the federal government from the Soviet Union during the war encouraged a more balanced conduct of policy after the war. The Second National Development Plan clearly indicates the intention of the Gowon regime in the immediate post–civil war era to be a major player in Africa and the world.

> In the context of modern power relations in the world and especially of the international threats facing the African peoples, Nigeria cannot be truly strong and united without a prosperous economic base. Material power exerts a disproportionate influence on international morality. Nigeria will, therefore, pursue relentlessly the task of development to make the national economy strong, dynamic, and responsive to the challenge of world competition. (Ekundare 1971, p. 157)

A number of events illustrate this new confidence. First, in 1971, Nigeria joined OPEC against the wishes and expectations of Western countries and oil multinationals, which until then dominated the Nigerian oil sector. Second, in 1972, the federal government promulgated the Indigenization Decree, which nationalised several foreign-owned enterprises, many of which were controlled by Western interests. Third, in the same year, the federal government of Nigeria proposed the formation of a joint African military task force to which all OAU members would contribute. The task force would be stationed in independent states bordering the Portuguese colonies to provide support to liberation movements (particularly against Portuguese colonial regimes) and to defend independent states hosting freedom fighters from colonialist attacks.

However, the radicalisation of Nigeria's diplomacy fully matured in the Murtala-Obasanjo era. From its inception on July 29, 1975, the administration took a number of domestic decisions that made it popular among Nigerians, particularly an extensive fight against corruption. Regarding southern Africa and by extension Nigeria's role in the Frontline States, two events stood out: Recognition of the MPLA in Angola and nationalisation of assets of British Petroleum (BP) in Nigeria. On Angola, the initial position of the government over the vexed issue of which was the authentic liberation movement following independence in 1975 was one of balanced interaction with the various liberation movements. By extension, Nigeria supported the OAU position of establishing a Govern-ment of National Unity in Angola consisting of elements of the major liberation movements: MPLA, Union for the Total Independence of Angola (UNITA), and the National Front for the Liberation of Angola (FNLA). However, things changed dramatically with the open support given to UNITA and FNLA by South Africa. On November 25, 1975, Nigeria announced its support for MPLA, thereby weakening South Africa's influence in Angola (Sotunmbi 1990). The decision came as a surprise to observers of Nigeria's foreign policy because Nigeria had often taken a moderate and soft, pro-OAU approach to such issues.

The nationalisation of BP assets in 1979 is another illustration of the radicalisation of foreign policy and a new level of commitment to African liberation, which justified Nigeria's membership in the Frontline States. It was a far-reaching shift from Nigeria's pattern of engagement with Britain, its former colonial master, and a radical response to Britain's decision to continue support for the puppet and racist government in Salisbury, Southern Rhodesia (later Harare, Zimbabwe), as well as the apartheid government in South Africa. Nigeria was angered by the widespread suspicion that BP intended to lift Nigerian oil for supply to South Africa, at the time regarded by Nigeria as a principal adversary (Aluko 1990). At the same time, Britain was stalling on ending the racist, unilateralist regime in Rhodesia. The nationalisation of BP by the Nigerian government contributed to the Lancaster House process, which ended in the signing of an agreement on December 21, 1979, which covered the terms of an Independence Constitution, elections, and particularly land ownership in Zimbabwe. For one, the timing coincided with the meeting of the

Commonwealth Heads of Government in Lusaka, Zambia, August 1–7, 1979. Immediately after the meeting and in the wake of the nationalisation of BP, the British government invited the Zimbabwe–Rhodesia government led by Bishop Abel Muzorewa, widely seen as a puppet of Britain and propped up by Ian Smith, and the Patriotic Front (ZANU-ZAPU), led by Robert Mugabe and Joshua Nkomo, to a Constitutional Conference at Lancaster House, London.

The radical stance of the Murtala-Obasanjo regime on southern Africa carried over into at least the early years of the new civilian regime of Shagari. In 1981, Nigeria hosted an emergency summit of the Frontline States that called on all OAU members to extend urgent assistance, especially military aid, to Angola to repel South African forces. This was a radical stance, notwithstanding that the concept of an African high command had not gained widespread support on the continent at that time. However, some African states advocated a mission limited to defense against racist and imperialist threats but not intra-African conflicts or insurgencies within independent African states. Others argued for a continental military command to deter external attacks; to intervene in domestic disorders, especially to prevent or suppress military coups; and to counter South African forces (www.country-data.com 1991).

In summary, Nigeria's membership in the Frontline States was not only a recognition of its longstanding role in African liberation but a reflection of growing confidence in its external relations, largely buoyed by growing petroleum wealth during the radical phase. Domestically, a radical military regime, which was made popular by its commitment to returning the country to democratic rule in 1979, drove this new foreign policy focus on national liberation in southern Africa. The domestic popularity of the regime, particularly during the period General Murtala Mohammed was at the helm, coupled with a high-profile involvement of radical intellectuals in crucial foreign policy decisions, contributed to the wide-ranging success achieved by Nigeria in the liberation of African countries from colonialism and racism during this period.

Realist Phase: Nigeria and the Formation of the AU

Clearly, Nigeria played a crucial and defining role in the transformation of the OAU into the AU from the very beginning. In April 2006, Nigeria ratified the Constitutive Act of the AU, which began the thirty-day waiting period that brought the treaty into force (see Article 28 of the Constitutive

Act, African Union 2003). This was followed by a one-year transitional period to enable the OAU and African Economic Community (AEC) to wind down, as provided for in Article 33 of the Constitutive Act. This process culminated finally in the launch of the AU in Durban, South Africa, on July 9, 2002.

Apart from the specific challenges that have been raised regarding the OAU Charter and its implementation, the two most important precursors to the AU are the Lagos Plan of Action (1980) and the Abuja Treaty of the African Economic Community (1991). These documents clearly emphasise one of the perceived longstanding missing gaps in the OAU, namely the effective economic integration of Africa. Between 1968 and 1980, a series of resolutions by the OAU in which Nigeria strongly participated point to the profound connections between economic integration and the attainment of the organisation's goals (Parker and Rukare 2002, p. 365). These facts signify, first, the inevitability of economic development content to the AU and, second, the central role Nigeria played in its emergence.

Although the pursuit of economic development has been at the heart of Nigeria's foreign policy and diplomacy since independence in 1960, it was in the 1980s that it became the central, if not the singular, focus of its foreign policy. Its role in the transformation of the OAU into the AU was set within this context. However, the broader context was the crippling economic crisis that the country began to experience in the late 1970s, which fully matured under the civilian government of 1979–1983. This new theme of grounding African unity on economic integration resonated with Nigerian governments as a result of the country's economic difficulties.

In 1977, following a palpable decline in government revenues, the Obasanjo military government declared a programme of "belt tightening" entailing cuts in government spending. By 1981, two years into the new civilian government of Shagari, monthly imports were running on average of over N1 billion. In that year, food imports alone stood at over N2.1 billion out of a total imports bill of more than N12.7 billion. Exports declined as the country's exports revenues fell by N3.16 billion in 1981. The trade deficit for the year stood at N1.7 billion, down from a surplus of N5.1 billion the previous year. Consistent goading by foreign creditors to curb the nation's mostly consumerist policies failed and when it finally heeded in April 1982 with the announcement of a Stabilization Act, it was deemed "half-hearted" by IMF standards. In fact, the Stabilization Act may have been a mere façade for obtaining the IMF facility of US$2.26 billion, which the government was seeking at the time. The Shagari government had hoped that a pro-Western foreign policy, as demonstrated by Nigeria's positions on the Chadian crisis, the Saharawi Arab Democratic Republic membership of the OAU, and Qaddafi's bid to head the OAU, would guarantee Western economic support. The calculation failed. When the Shagari government was ousted in December 1983, the Buhari regime that was subsequently in power for approximately one and a half years brought increased Western economic pressures on Nigeria by rightly rejecting some of the policies of the Bretton Woods institutions and particularly questioning the context in which Nigeria's huge external debt was accumulated (Ibeanu 1988; Olukoshi and Abdul-Raheem 1985).

It was in this context of rapid economic decline and political authoritarianism that Nigeria's foreign policy in the mid-1980s was shaped, particularly the new emphasis on economic diplomacy under General Babangida (Asobie and Ibeanu 2005). The single-minded objective of Babangida's economic diplomacy lay in furthering the goals of the Structural Adjustment Programme through the promotion of exports (especially nonoil exports), attraction of foreign investments and loans, and rescheduling of the country's over US$30 billion external debt. In 1986, then external affairs minister Professor Bolaji Akinyemi called for a redirection of Nigeria's foreign policy away from the core areas of decolonisation and end of apartheid to the new imperative of economic development. He reasoned that the impression of Nigerian leaders in the past tended to be that the country's vital interests were limited to the elimination of colonialism and apartheid. He argued that Nigeria had other interests, which were more closely tied to the survival of the Nigerian state, the welfare of Nigerian citizens, and Nigeria's leadership role in Africa and the black world. The most critical of these interests was Nigeria's economic development (Asobie 1991, p. 57).

The same preoccupation continued after the exit of Akinyemi as foreign minister. In June 1988, the new external affairs minister, Ike Nwachukwu, outlined the basic elements of Nigeria's diplomacy:

> We feel that it is the responsibility of our foreign policy apparatus to advance the course of national economic recovery. This entails negotiations and activities that will attract both foreign investment and other assistance required for the successful accomplishment of our national economic goals. (Asobie 1991, p. 60)

For him, this position captured the "ball-game" in international relations of the day, "self-interest and economic development" (Ogwu and Olukoshi, 1991, p. 6).

Babangida's economic diplomacy was based on a realignment of Nigeria's foreign policy such that its pro-Western, pro-imperialist, and antiradical contents loomed large. In a 1991 speech to Nigerian ambassadors, Nwachukwu summarised this strategy:

> In your utterances and in your behavioural pattern, please remember that Nigeria is a developing country. It needs support from the international community and that support can only come when you can win the confidence of those whose support you seek. . . . You begin to win that confidence through friendliness and loyalty to their cause (i.e. the cause of those whose support you seek). What matters is your ability to win for Nigeria what we cannot for ourselves, that is, the economic well-being of our people and physical well-being of Nigeria. (Ogwu and Olukoshi 1991, p. 6)

One casualty of this newfound economic diplomacy was Nigeria's role in the Frontline States. First, although Nigeria had traditionally backed the Frontline States, militarily if necessary, it refused to intervene in Mozambique in the face of the combined military pressure of RENAMO (Resistência Nacional Moçambicana) and South Africa. Second, the Babangida administration mended fences with apartheid South Africa. According to *Africa Confidential*, the two countries are "no longer poles apart." The leaders even shared the belief in what they considered the "four growth poles" of Africa: "Nigeria and South Africa are the most significant for Africa in terms of economic muscle and population" (*Africa Confidential* 1992, p. 2). South Africa President F. W. de Klerk visited Nigeria in 1991, and Nigeria relaxed its embargo on trading with South Africa. The Nigerian government planned to offer "African discounts" in order to lure South Africa into a long-term crude oil supply agreement. However, the South Africans preferred a quasi-barter deal in which Nigeria would buy South African manufactures or capital goods equivalent to the value of Nigeria's oil exports to South Africa. Finally, the Babangida government forged close relations with the leader of the UNITA rebels in Angola, Jonas Savimbi, and the discredited leader of RENAMO, Afonso Dhlakama, was granted an audience by Babangida on June 13, 1992.

We see then that the emergence of the AU and particularly its alter ego, NEPAD, consummated the transformation from the radical period of Nigeria's foreign policy in Africa, which focused on African liberation and the end of apartheid, to a more self-interested emphasis on economic development. Nigerian leaders have since continued to play central roles in the evolution of this new African unity grounded in the economic development project. Indeed, the dissolution of the OAU and the emergence of the AU cannot be dissociated from the specific roles of the principal actors associated with NEPAD's emergence. NEPAD had its genesis at the OAU Extraordinary Summit held in Sirte, Libya, in September 1999. The summit mandated Presidents Thabo Mbeki of South Africa and Abdul-Aziz Bouteflika of Algeria to engage Africa's creditors on the total cancellation of Africa's external debt (Iwuamadi 2003). Following this, the South-South Summit of the Non-Aligned Movement and the G77, held in Havana, Cuba, in April 2000, mandated Presidents Mbeki and Obasanjo to convey the concerns of the South to the G8 and the Bretton Woods institutions and also to engage them with a view to developing a constructive partnership for the regeneration of Africa.

At the G8 summit in Japan in July 2000, the three African presidents (Obasanjo, Mbeki, and Bouteflika) were invited and presented the issue of partnership with the G8 leaders. The work on developing NEPAD at that stage was known as the Millennium Partnership for the African Recovery Programme (MAP). Then began in earnest a process of engagement on a bilateral and multilateral level. During the Fifth Extraordinary Summit of the OAU held in Sirte, Libya, March 1–2, 2001, President Obasanjo made a presentation on MAP while President Abdoulaye Wade of Senegal presented the OMEGA Plan. The work done by the four presidents—Mbeki, Obasanjo, Bouteflika, and Wade—was endorsed, and it was decided that every effort should be made to integrate all initiatives being pursued for the recovery and development of Africa, including the Economic Commission for Africa.

In reaching this decision, the summit recognized the synergy that existed between the various initiatives, and, on July 11, 2001, the New African Initiative (NAI) was adopted as a working title for the purposes of the OAU summit. The NAI was finally presented to the OAU Summit of Heads of State and Governments in Lusaka, Zambia, in 2001, providing a vision for Africa, a statement of the problems facing the continent, and a programme of action to resolve these problems in order to achieve the vision. Hence, NEPAD was enthusiastically received and unanimously adopted in the form of Declaration 1 (xxxvii) as Africa's principal agenda for development, providing a holistic, comprehensive, and integrated strategic framework for the socioeconomic development of the continent within the institutional framework of the AU (Iwuamadi 2003). Under this declaration, a Head of State and Government Implementation Committee was established to ensure follow-up and implementation. The committee, composed of Algeria, Botswana, Cameroon, Egypt, Ethiopia, Gabon, Mali, Mauritius, Mozambique, Nigeria, Rwanda, Sao-Tome and Principe, Senegal, South Africa, and

Tunisia, finalised a name for the initiative: New Partnership for Africa's Development (NEPAD).

From all indications and looking at the series of OAU summits before the emergence of AU, it is clear that the final movement that led to the transformation of OAU into AU started in Nigeria, precisely with the adoption of the Lagos Plan of Action (Browne and Cummings 1984). Some of the major provisions of the Lagos Plan were later translated into a treaty in Abuja, Nigeria, in June 1991, when the OAU Heads of States and Government signed the treaty establishing the AEC. The AEC treaty provided a framework to achieve regional integration in Africa by consolidating national economies into a single continental market and, perhaps more importantly, set in motion the process of transforming the OAU into the AU (Onunaiju 2009). Indeed, the Abuja Treaty eventually led to the Fourth Extraordinary Session of the OAU Assembly of African Heads of State and Government in September 1999 in Sirte, Libya. Following the Sirte Declaration, the Constitutive Act of the African Union was adopted during the Lome Summit of the OAU on July 11, 2000, to replace the OAU Charter. Subsequently, the AU came into effect officially on May 26, 2001.

Many critics have wondered if the AU, which Nigeria played a central role in creating, is not a mere parody of the European Union (EU), thus suggesting a return to the pro-West policy of the conservative phase of the country's foreign policy. Indeed, it does seem that the AU is largely modeled on the EU. The Constitutive Act provides for an Assembly of Heads of State and Government of the Union and the secretariat is called a commission. An Executive Council of Ministers of the Union is expected to be active, as well as the Pan-African Parliament of the Union. There is also a Specialized Technical Committee of the Union; an Economic, Social, and Cultural Council; a Court of Justice; and Financial Institutions. Still, questions remain as to whether it is the best model for addressing the enormous challenges of Africa's development.

Conclusion

Nigeria's foreign policy in Africa has shown both continuities and discontinuities. Among the consistencies is the country's unalloyed focus on Africa. In this regard, decolonisation, African unity, and economic development have been central. As a good state-citizen of Africa, Nigeria has often seen its own freedom, unity, and economic progress intrinsically tied to Africa's. However, while these themes have been consistent, there have been clear discontinuities in Nigeria's interpretation of its goals, philosophies, and strategies for achieving these within the African context.

In framing an explanation, we argued that Nigeria's foreign policy has three phases: conservative, radical, and realist. We further argued that overlaps exist, particularly in transiting from one phase to another. But, more importantly, each phase is propelled by both structure and agency (*structured agency*). The chapter sought to identify the principal factors of structure and agency in each phase. It is argued that these broad phases correspond to certain activities, attitudes, and strategies of Nigeria's foreign policy in Africa. More specifically, they help to understand Nigeria's role in the formation of the OAU, its participation in the southern African Frontline States, and, finally, its role in the transformation of the OAU into the AU.

We may infer from the foregoing analysis that Nigeria's foreign policy, particularly regarding Africa, has been active and consistent. It has been driven by ideals that sometimes appear to ignore Nigeria's immediate national interest. However, there have been modifications as it has moved from one phase to another. A major challenge of policy is to find the right balance between four levels of that citizenship: (1) global, (2) regional (Africa), (3) subregional (West Africa), and (4) national. Hitherto, excessive focus has been on the regional as a result of Nigeria's economic muscle *vis-à-vis* other African countries. However, from the 1980s, the country suffered economic decline coupled with deepening political authoritarianism. Consequently, Nigeria's present foreign policy calls for a new strategy capable of employing diplomacy to enhance economic well-being and democracy at home, while pursuing the time-tested objectives of African unity, economic integration, and global solidarity.

Bibliography

Abdul-Raheem, T., 1992, "Then and Now: Seven Years of Babangida's Dictatorship," *Nigeria Now*, vol. 1, no. 5.

Advameg, 2010, "Organization of African Unity (OAU)," www.referenceforbusiness .com/encyclopedia/Oli-Per/Organization-of-African-Unity-OAU.html #ixzz0UmJGmhG9, accessed March 18, 2010.

Africa Confidential, 1992, "South Africa/Nigeria: No Longer Poles Apart," vol. 33, no. 12.

African Union, 2003, "The Constitutive Act," www.afr.ca-union.org/root/au/ aboutau/constitutive_act_en.htm

Aluko, O., 1990, "The Nationalization of the Assets of British Petroleum," in G.O. Olusanya and R.A. Akindele, eds., *The Structure and Processes of Foreign Policy Making and Implementation in Nigeria, 1960–1990*, Nigerian Institute of International Affairs, Lagos, Nigeria, pp. 375–397.

Asobie, H., 1991, "Nigeria: Economic Diplomacy and National Interest," *Nigerian Journal of International Affairs*, vol. 17, no. 2.

Asobie, H., and Ibeanu, O., 2005, "Decline, Despotism and Diplomacy: A Retrospective Appraisal of Nigeria's External Relations, 1985–1993," in D.A. Briggs, ed., *Nigeria in World Politics: Trends and Challenges*, National Institute for Policy and Strategic Studies, Kuru, Nigeria.

Browne, R., and Cummings, R., 1984, *The Lagos Plan of Action vs. the Berg Report*, Howard University Press, Washington, DC, US.

Ekundare, R., 1971, "Nigeria's Second National Development Plan as a Weapon of Social Change," *African Affairs*, vol. 70, no. 279: 146–148.

Federal Government of Nigeria, 1971, Second National Development Plan 1970–4, Federal Ministry of Information, Lagos, Nigeria.

Ibeanu, O., 1988, "Economic Crisis and Militarism in Nigeria: Dynamics of an Anti-Democratic State," in *Proceedings of the Annual Conference of the Nigerian Political Science Association*, University of Ibadan, Nigeria.

Iwuamadi, C., 2003, "NEPAD in a Globalising World," B.Sc. thesis, Department of Political Science, University of Nigeria, Nsukka.

Mwalilino, W., 2000, "An Interview with Claude Ake," *West Africa Review*, www.westafricareview.com/vol2.1/mwalilino.html, accessed March 18, 2010.

Ogwu, U. J., and Olukoshi, A., 1991, "Nigeria's Economic Diplomacy: Some Contending Issues," *Nigerian Journal of International Affairs*, vol. 7, no. 2.

Ojo, O.J.B., 1990, "The Making and Termination of the Anglo-Nigerian Defence Pact," in G.O. Olusanya and R.A. Akindele, eds., *The Structure and Processes of Foreign Policy Making and Implementation in Nigeria, 1960–1990*, Nigerian Institute of International Affairs, Lagos, Nigeria, pp. 255–274.

Olukoshi, A., 2006, "Towards an African Union Government: Envisaged Structures, Process and Roadmap," in A. Aderinwale, ed., *Africa and the Challenges of a Union Government*, Africa Leadership Forum, Ota, Nigeria.

Olukoshi, A., and Abdul-Raheem T., 1985, "Nigeria, Crisis Management under the Buhari Administration," *Review of African Political Economy*, no. 34.

Onunaiju, C., 2009, "Africa: The Dilemma of Africa Union," http://allafrica.com/stories/200907070571.html, accessed March 18, 2010.

Osuntokun, J., 2005, "Historical Background Survey of Nigeria's Foreign Policy," in J. Ogwu, ed., *New Horizons for Nigeria in World Affairs*, Nigerian Institute of International Affairs, Lagos, Nigeria.

Parker, C., and Rukare, D., 2002, "The New African Union and Its Constitutive Act," *The American Journal of International Law*, vol. 96, no. 2, pp. 365–374.

Quist-Arcton, O., 2001, "From OAU to Africa Union—Whither Africa?" Global Policy Forum, www.globalpolicy.org/component/content/article/211/44490.html, accessed March 18, 2010.

Sotunmbi, O., 1990, "From Support to a Government of National Unity to a Pro-MPLA Policy in Angola in 1975," in G.O. Olusanya and R.A. Akindele, eds., *The Structure and Processes of Foreign Policy Making and Implementation in Nigeria, 1960–1990*, Nigerian Institute of International Affairs, Lagos, Nigeria, pp. 364–374.

Stremlau, J., 1981, "The Fundamentals of Nigerian Foreign Policy," *Issue: A Journal of Opinion*, vol. 11, no. 1/2.

www.country-data.com, 1991, "Nigeria: African and Regional Issues," www.country-data.com/cgi-bin/query/r-9455.html, accessed March 18, 2010.

3

Nigeria's Role in the United Nations, the Commonwealth, and the Non-Aligned Movement

Okello Oculi

This chapter places emphasis on what has been termed the Balewa Doctrine as a guide to understanding Nigeria's activities as a member of the United Nations, the Commonwealth of Nations, and the Non-Aligned Movement. Key aspects of this doctrine include the value that Nigeria places on an activist and creative manifestation of sovereignty and national independence; the promotion of freedom, justice, and human rights, and the rejection of colonial and postcolonial governance in Africa; the primacy of peace and security within and between nations; and the promotion of socioeconomic development.

Nigeria's relations with the Commonwealth exhibit a peculiar record of bittersweet relations. In collaboration with India and Tanganyika, Nigeria in 1961 succeeded in expelling apartheid South Africa from the Commonwealth. Humiliated leaders of the racist regime in return supported Biafra in the 1967–1970 civil war (Ingelaere 2009, p. 518). Five years later, Britain's reluctance to sell arms to Nigeria may have played a role in the military leadership enacting harsh measures against Britain's economic interests as a result of its resistance to majority rule in Zimbabwe (Whiteman 2008). This legacy of dramatic diplomatic relations within the Commonwealth will be discussed.

Nigerian professionals working in specialised agencies of the United Nations and the Commonwealth often played extraordinary roles relevant to Nigeria's key areas of foreign policy. The chapter critically reviews Nigeria's diplomatic scorecard and offers recommendations for reform.

Nigeria and the United Nations

In his speech at the UN Assembly on October 7, 1960, Prime Minister Tafawa Balewa focused on a number of themes that have gained primacy in the subsequent five decades. Key was the right of Nigeria to avoid taking sides in the Cold War, though Nigeria would remain committed to the Commonwealth, as the nation "was proud to have been accepted as a member" (Obiozor 1985, p. 190). Another was the rejection of the immediate establishment of a union government in Africa, as it would not be practicable in the immediate future. However, sustained relations and consultations between states were welcome and would evolve into a political union as a "natural result."

As an early illustration of the import of Balewa's speech for future policies, his notion of the formation of regional groupings in Africa as an intermediate stage towards an African union government gave impetus to the creation in 1975 of the Economic Community of West African States (ECOWAS). In the United Nations Charter, regional groupings are assigned a significant role, and it was not out of place for Balewa to anticipate them as the future of Nigeria's foreign policy.

Third was the rejection of military coups or support for opposition parties that undermine the authority of properly chosen leaders of African states. Such measures, Balewa warned with considerable foresight, could become a major threat to peace, security, and stability in Africa (Obiozor 1985, p. 195). The value that subsequent Nigerian governments would place on playing an active role in preserving international peace and security would be evidenced by over 250,000 Nigerian troops participating in ten different peacekeeping operations between 1960 and 1995 (Ohumoibhi 2008, p. 231). For a country with a nonindustrialised economy but with the ability to support military logistics, Nigeria promoted a vital UN goal by supplying human resources. The country would also benefit by receiving additional training for military personnel.

Fourth was Balewa's preference for aid from multilateral UN agencies—deemed independent of political strings placed by major powers during the bipolar Cold War era. For instance, his government was apprehensive about accepting scholarships awarded by socialist bloc countries that could prove to be opportunities to indoctrinate Nigeria's youth with radical socialist values.

Collaborative Activities Within the United Nations

In subsequent decades Nigeria's role in the United Nations and its agencies has run on several tracks. Nigeria succeeded in winning a seat as a nonpermanent member of the Security Council during the 1966–1967 sessions in order to ensure that the body did not provide support to Biafra during the civil war. This strategic move would later enhance Nigeria's global diplomatic status as a key player in promoting the UN's commitment to achieving decolonisation and independence in southern Africa. Competing with neighbouring Niger Republic, Nigeria also contested for a seat as a nonpermanent member of the Security Council during the 1978–1979 sessions. The country's delegation won a hard-fought battle during the sixth round of voting by the General Assembly, receiving the required two-thirds majority vote. One vital vote may have come from fulfilling a promise previously made by Nigerian General Yakubu Gowon to pay salaries of civil servants of a Caribbean island country (Interview with Dr. Chijioke W. Wigwe, high commissioner of Nigeria to Kenya and Seychelles, November 16, 2006). He sees the ideology of nonalignment as a force in decline following the collapse of the ideological competition between the capitalist and socialist blocs in global politics. Accordingly, the visibility and relevance of the G-77 countries is on the increase precisely because the focus of G-77 is on material issues of economic development).

Nigeria joined non-Commonwealth leaders to expel apartheid South Africa from membership in the United Nations. Prime movers within the corridors and chambers of the UN Secretariat in New York were Ambassadors Salim Ahmed Salim of Tanzania, Leslie Harriman of Nigeria, and Ahmadu Cisse of Senegal. Salim recalled that when Abdul-Aziz Bouteflika of Algeria assumed the presidency of the General Assembly in 1974, the African Group sought and received his cooperation:

> For fifteen years an overwhelming vote by the United Nations General Assembly (in condemnation of *apartheid* in South Africa) would be interpreted by the President of the United Nations General Assembly as "a warning and moral abhorrence of apartheid." With Bouteflika as President, he assured us: "Salim I will do my duty." With votes from Africa, Asia and the Socialist Bloc, South Africa was expelled from the United Nations. The United States, Europe and two Latin American countries abstained. (Interview with Ambassador Salim Ahmed Salim, former Secretary General of the Organization of African Unity, November 6, 2009)

Permanent UN representatives of Nigeria and Tanzania were part of a larger collective effort to include Nigeria as a member of the Frontline States. Nigeria won this status through the vigorous, sustained, and significant diplomatic, financial, and military resources invested in support for the Liberation Committee of the Organization of African Unity (OAU) (Nnoli 1989, p. 262).

Nigeria was also in the forefront of diplomatic actions opposing the racist European-settler government in Southern Rhodesia (Zimbabwe) and Portuguese colonial domination in Mozambique, Angola, Guinea-Bissau, and Cape Verde; and in support of independence for South-West Africa (now Namibia). The country gave US$400,000 to officials of the South West African People's Organization to support diplomatic lobbying at the UN and $165,674 to train future officials who would administer an independent Namibia (Ohumoibhi 2008). In 1977, the Obasanjo regime hosted a joint world conference at the United Nations that committed participating countries to undertake action against apartheid. As chairman of the UN Committee for Action Against Apartheid, Ambassador Harriman alerted the Nigerian government of the UN Secretariat's interest in holding such a conference. Three themes were important to Nigeria: (1) the danger to international peace and security posed by South Africa's becoming highly militarised, including the acquisition of nuclear power; (2) rallying African support for armed struggle and liberation movements fighting apartheid; and (3) condemnation of governments (including Israel and Britain) with considerable investments in South Africa as evidenced by record arms sales to that country (Obasanjo 1990, p. 142).

General Olusegun Obasanjo's call for punitive action against "enterprises and organizations that are party to the system" of apartheid in southern Africa would be manifested in 1979 when his government nationalised British Petroleum (at a value of over 2 billion naira) as well as Barclays Bank (Whiteman 2008, p. 264). The regime also banned government ministries from awarding contracts to British firms. Barring opportunities to bid for contracts in Nigeria's booming oil economy was bound to have "a biting effect on the British economy" (Obasanjo 1990, p. 145). The ban was protected by a decree requiring its overturn to be approved by the National Assembly (Obasanjo 1990). This bilateral act was part of a wider African call for the ban of arms sales to South Africa and support for majority rule in Zimbabwe.

What has received little attention is the struggle by Nigeria's diplomats and nationals within UN agencies over policy issues. Unlike African countries that can be intimidated by donor countries' threats of cutting aid funds, Nigeria, since the post–civil war oil revenues, "can say certain things which other African countries fear to say" at policy meetings of specialised UN agencies (Interview with Augustine Aghaulor, UN Habitat, Nairobi, Kenya, November 13, 2009).

At sessions of the World Health Assembly of the World Health Organisation, Professor Eyitayo Lambo, Nigeria's minister of health, initiated many debates concerning socioeconomic issues that affect Africans' health while Professor Ransome Kuti pushed for emphasis on primary health care as more relevant for African countries (Interview with David Okello, Country Representative, World Health Organisation, Nairobi, Kenya, November 15, 2009).

Nigeria has also drawn up proposals for a collective African welfare at the UN General Assembly. As chairman of the African Union, President Obasanjo in 2003 reiterated the continent's demand for the structural democratisation of the United Nations for the benefit of fair representation for Africa's interests. He stated:

> How can the United Nations continue to perpetuate and justify a situation whereby Africa is the only continent without a *Permanent Seat* in the Security Council? In order to promote reform and democratization of the Security Council, Africa, with 53 member states, should be allocated at least two permanent seats commensurate not only with the continent's size but its track record of contributing to the maintenance of international peace and security. (Ogwu and Alli 2007, p. 40)

Attaining permanent seats for Africa in the UN Security Council would almost certainly see Nigeria as a major contender for one of the seats and would carry a collective benefit for Africa. Governing boards of the United Nations Development Programme (UNDP), UNICEF, and UNFPA are "dominated by donor countries," with developing countries having limited impact on policy decisions. A permanent seat held by Nigeria in the Security Council would augment its strength in opposing donor countries' anti-African views (Interview with Turhan Saleh, Country Representative, UN Development Programme, Abuja, Nigeria, October 23, 2009).

Some have suggested that under UN Secretary-General Kofi Annan's leadership, policymaking within UN agencies increasingly assumed a hostile North-South divide. As an example, G-77 countries collaborated with China to stalemate adoption of the UNDP's Medium-term Strategic Framework because "they felt [that] it reflected creeping conditionality and were unhappy about how much they have been consulted." Half of the thirty-six members of the UNDP Executive Board felt that emphasis on human rights and open elections were "impositions of a particular [North] view" (Interview with Turhan Saleh, Country Representative, UN Development Programme, Abuja, Nigeria, October 23, 2009). The perception that richer Northern countries exert greater control over the UN strengthens the validity of Nigeria's call for a collectivist strategic positioning of two African countries as permanent members of the Security Council.

In 2000, Nigeria took Africa's struggle against global corruption to the UN General Assembly and succeeded in its adoption of a resolution "not only condemning corruption and illegal transfer of funds abroad" but also "calling for the repatriation of such funds to their countries of origin" (Oche 2005, p. 165). The novel linking of corruption to countries that receive stolen funds imposed a responsibility and obligation for removing such funds from investment within their own economies. Notwithstanding difficulties in implementing the resolution, it lifted the convenient cover that responsibility for corruption within African countries was one-sidedly African. In response, Britain enacted legislation by which corrupt companies could be prosecuted under Section 108 and 109 of the Anti-Terrorism, Crime, and Security Act 2000. On September 25, 2009, British company Mabey and Johnson pleaded guilty to charges by the British Serious Fraud Office of bribing ministers in Ghana's National Democratic Congress government (Doudu 2009, pp. 10–11), establishing an important precedent.

Nigeria and Democratisation of the UN

Military President General Ibrahim Babangida travelled to the United Nations in 1990 to strongly advocate that Africa receive at least two seats as permanent members of the UN Security Council (Interview with A. Ghazali at Shehu Musa Yar'Adua Centre, Abuja, Nigeria, March 10, 2010). The committee of the UN General Assembly charged with drafting a resolution on reform, Open-Ended Working Group on the Question of Equitable Representation and Increase in the Membership of the Security Council, had met for over a decade in search of a consensus. African countries, however, could not agree on the option of permanent membership without veto power, a provision which South Africa and Nigeria accepted (Fasulo 2004, p. 51).

Vigorous public debate inside Nigeria over strategies for mounting an effective campaign for achieving Nigeria's election posed the challenge of determining arguments for the special contribution Nigeria would make as a permanent member. Coming decades after the collapse of apartheid and colonialism across Africa outside Western Sahara, focus shifted to placing emphasis on the potential role of culture, human resource development, and the promotion of democratic governance and justice (Gambari 2005).

Between 1978 and 1999, Nigeria's external debt grew from US$2.2 billion to $28.6 billion (Oche 2005, p. 162). General Babangida's acceptance of measures stipulated in the Structural Adjustment Programme as dictated by the Bretton Woods institutions deepened the economic crisis facing his regime. To deal with the crisis, the regime developed a strategy to link foreign policy to the promotion of Nigeria's economic interests. The notion of "economic diplomacy" was expressed by General Babangida in his speech at the UN General Assembly as he pleaded for debt relief and private investment. Olusanya (2008) links the emergence of this foreign policy thrust to seminars and lectures held at the Nigerian Institute of International Affairs (a think-tank with close ties to the presidency) between 1986 and 1990. A Nigerian voice that had stoutly and often arrogantly used the podium and committee rooms of the UN to insist that it enforce principles in its charter to benefit freedom and justice in Africa now sounded less strident.

In the late 1970s, Nigeria participated in drafting the "Law of the Sea." Chief Richard Akinjide served as chairman of the committee charged with the task. President Shehu Shagari and President Julius Nyerere of Tanzania represented Africa in inaugural talks between leaders of developed industrialised countries and those of poorer economies—what came to be known as the "North-South Dialogue." Akinjide would later support Tanzania's nomination of Salim as the OAU candidate for secretary-general of the United Nations. Salim's victory was vetoed by the United States, a bitter diplomatic event which Shagari greatly regretted.

As an advocate of the inviolability of the sovereignty of member states, Nigeria opposed Tanzania's war in Uganda and the expulsion of President Idi Amin. However, under General Sani Abacha, its own internal affairs became a target of severe criticism by the United Nations. Appeals were made not to violate the human rights of prominent prisoners Generals Shehu Yar'Adua, Obasanjo, and Chief M.K.O. Abiola. The Third Committee of the UN General Assembly passed a resolution condemning Nigeria and called on the UN Human Rights Commission to give "urgent attention" to the situation (Shehu Musa Yar'Adua Foundation 2004, p. 289).

Using public funds to pay public relations consultants for image laundering and to rescue African governments in financial crisis, the Abacha regime was able to tease out commendation from a visiting investigation team from the UN (Oyediran and Agbaje 1999, p. 325). Senior officials in the presidency affirmed to the UN team that the government would restore to the courts power to issue writ of habeas corpus, which had been terminated by Decree 14 of 1994, and that the right of appeal would be transferred from draconian special tribunals to civil courts. A 1996 UN mission stated that: "Our meetings and discussions with General Sani Abacha and others have given us the impression that the Head of State is sincere in his commitment to restore civil democratic rule by October 1, 1998" (Oyediran and Agbaje 1999, p. 324). Abacha died two years later without fulfilling the promise made to the UN team.

Nigeria and the Non-Aligned Movement

Whiteman (2008) reports that when, in August 1960, Balewa declared in a speech that nonalignment would be the anchor of Nigeria's foreign policy, it aroused considerable alarm among top British colonial officials in Nigeria, suggesting to them that he shared radical anti-neocolonial views of leaders such as Kwame Nkrumah of Ghana, Abdel Nasser of Egypt, and Surkhano of Indonesia.

However, Nigeria's commitment to the Non-Aligned Movement had not been significant among ruling circles at independence, its promotion by more radical leaders rendering it suspect to conservative leadership. British penetration of Nigeria's agencies for public socialisation, including the language of instruction in educational institutions and the media, made for a strong pro-British orientation within the political class (Akinyemi 1989). President Shagari's government ignored the legendary world heavyweight boxing champion Muhammad Ali when he visited Nigeria as President Jimmy Carter's envoy with a mission to persuade Nigeria to boycott the Moscow Olympics of 1980. Nigeria saw the boycott as part of America's Cold War offensive against the Soviet Union, though Nigeria had opposed the Soviet Union's invasion of Afghanistan because it saw the move as a Cold War measure to increase the vulnerability of NATO's access to vital oil wells in the Persian Gulf as well as naval resources in the Indian Ocean (Shagari 2001).

Bolaji Akinyemi, as President Babangida's foreign minister, was, however, not impressed by nonalignment as a policy guide and convened a conference in Lagos, Nigeria, to seek an international stamp of approval to his brainchild, "The Concert of Medium Powers." The organisation was to serve as a bridge between poor states in the South and rich states in the North, though the assembled delegates renamed the meeting a forum and dismissed it as an US-inspired plot to undermine the solidarity of the Non-Aligned Movement (Olusanya 2008, p. 175). The new body apparently excluded Tanzania and Cuba, both of which were influential in their respective regions and strong pillars within the Non-Aligned Movement.

Akinyemi reflected the leaning of his boss, of whom Prime Minister Margaret Thatcher of Great Britain commented after their meeting in 1989: "We also saw eye-to-eye about the dangers of Soviet and Cuban involvement in Africa" (Whiteman 2008, p. 267). Coming after the Murtala-Obasanjo regime's aggressive objection to US and British opposition to the Popular Movement for the Liberation of Angola in the mid-1970s and its welcoming of Cuba's military defeat of invading South African troops inside Angola, this seeming foreign policy turnaround was a major turning point in Nigeria's foreign policy (Castro 2008, p. 468).

Nigeria and the Commonwealth

Nigeria has had a record of troubled relations with the Commonwealth since October 1, 1960, when it gained automatic membership by virtue of its not having yet become a republic. In 1961 Nigeria joined with others to expel apartheid South Africa. In 1965, it broke diplomatic ground by hosting a meeting of the organisation in Lagos, setting a precedent for an organisation that had never before met outside London. Nigeria had apparently earned this right when it offered British Prime Minister Harold Wilson breathing space in negotiating with members of the Commonwealth that were bound by an OAU resolution to break relations with Britain if it did not halt the momentum of rebel leader Ian Smith's unilateral declaration for independence for Rhodesia in contempt of majority rule.

Nigeria's role in the expulsion of South Africa from the Commonwealth confirmed fears among white settler rulers across southern Africa that a new and dangerous power had arrived on the continent. Nasser's 1952 revolution in Egypt, which overthrew a pro-British monarchy in Egypt, and Sudan's independence on January 1, 1956, did not immediately raise alarm because they had both opted to stay outside of the Commonwealth. Kwame Nkrumah in Ghana had placed priority on building anticolonial movements and a momentum towards a United States of Africa. Nigeria's action was, therefore, likely to arouse counteroffensive initiatives from South Africa and its allies. Its intelligence operatives would also be expected to explore prospects for establishing vital friendships among the crop of Nigeria's military officers who served in the UN mission in the 1960–1965 Congo crisis.

Nigeria's more recent troubled relations with the Commonwealth occurred when, after being party to the 1991 Harare Declaration on principles of good political governance, it committed acts that violated its vital aspects. For example, annulment of a June 12, 1993, presidential election, which observers deemed free and fair, raised condemnation from the Commonwealth. Supporters of Social Democratic Party candidate Moshood Abiola, widely presumed to have won the election, protested in Lagos and Ibadan that their rights of speech and freedom of assembly were violated. Newspapers were banned, journalists detained, and critics assassinated. But the tipping point was the execution of Ken Saro Wiwa and nine Ogoni activists whose trial was seen as a kangaroo judicial process. Despite efforts by South Africa President Nelson Mandela to seek clemency, Saro Wiwa and his compatriots were hanged on the eve of the Commonwealth Heads of Governments Meeting in New Zealand on October 31, 1995.

Saro Wiwa had gained international visibility as an environmental campaigner against the spillage of oil and gas flaring in the Niger Delta, which destroyed agricultural lands and fisheries and polluted drinking water in many communities. Salim A. Salim, who was at the time the OAU secretary-general, reports that Mandela "did not want Nigeria suspended from the Commonwealth but Tom Ikimi [Nigeria's Foreign Minister during the Commonwealth Heads of Government Meeting in New Zealand] was determined to show that Nigeria could not be pushed around," thereby alienating even the country's friends (Interview with Salim 2009).

Following his assumption of power as an elected president of Nigeria in 1999, Obasanjo completed Nigeria's return to the Commonwealth by hosting the meeting of its Heads of State and Governments, at which the British monarch, last in Nigeria in 1956, was in attendance. Both Gowon and Shagari had invited Queen Elizabeth, but each had been overthrown by military coups before she could come.

Nigeria has attempted to assist needy members of the Commonwealth while receiving assistance from others. For example, between 1985 and 2009, Nigeria's National War College (later National Defence College) trained top military officers from Commonwealth countries Gambia, Lesotho, Mozambique, Rwanda, Tanzania, Uganda, and Zambia. By 2009, graduates of the college included the chief of army staff of Namibia and the chiefs of naval and air staff of Ghana. To underline the character of the programme as military aid, Nigeria paid the full cost of training. Nigeria has sent its own officers for training to Indian and Pakistani defence academies.

In the civilian sector, Nigeria has benefitted from the Commonwealth scholarship scheme as well as the Rhodes Scholar programme through which many Nigerians obtained higher qualifications from institutions in Commonwealth countries. Emeka Anyaoku, former secretary-general of the Commonwealth, reports that when the 1966 Lagos Conference of Commonwealth Heads of Government failed to convince Prime Minister Wilson to use force to terminate Smith's Unilateral Declaration of Independence in Rhodesia, Nigeria came up with the face-saving measure of Britain funding the establishment of a Special Commonwealth Programme of Assistance to train Rhodesian Africans to prepare for the administration of an independent Zimbabwe. In 2000 the programme sought to train 8,500 Namibians (Anyaoku 2004, pp. 67–69).

Nigeria's most positive period of relations with the Commonwealth came with the election of one of its former diplomats, Anyaoku, as secretary general. Anyaoku reports that ten years after independence, Nigeria offered Colonel Theophilus Danjuma to chair a court martial in the St. Kitts-Nevis-Anguila Commission. When Bangladesh broke away from Pakistan, Anyaoku's shuttle diplomacy across Commonwealth countries in West Africa (Ghana, Gambia, Sierra Leone, and Nigeria) and Tanzania won tentative diplomatic recognition for the new state.

In 1992 Ben Nwabueze, a professor of constitutional law, was appointed by President Arap Moi of Kenya to undertake the task of "adapting Kenya's constitution to serve the transition to multi-party elections"—a process tenaciously fought for by opposition political parties and civil society groups, but much resisted by Moi's government (Anyaoku 2004). As the regime was increasingly turning to violence against the opposition, this offered a vital path to peaceful political transition.

In 2008 former President Obasanjo intervened to resolve the post-2007 election political stalemate between Kenyan President Mwai Kibaki's ruling Peoples' National Union (PNU) and Raila Odinga's Orange Democratic Movement (ODM). Both parties were convinced that each had won the presidential election as the opposition ODM won a majority of seats in Parliament, while the ruling PNU insisted it had won the presidency. The stalemate resulted in intercommunal violence unprecedented in Kenya's postcolonial politics in which over 1,500 people died and an estimated 650,000 people were internally displaced. Obasanjo reportedly drew Odinga's attention to the fact that Kibaki had resisted pressure from those who sought intervention of the armed forces against the opposition. Such violence would have provoked temporary international condemnation but the international community would have eventually settled back to offer Kibaki diplomatic recognition after protests had died down. Odinga relented and agreed to serve in a coalition government in which he shared power with PNU as the first prime minister. That President Obasanjo, before leaving office in May 2007, had begun selling crude oil to Kenya's refinery at a concessionary price prior to the post-2007 election violence must have had a cushioning effect in his mediation talks with Kenya's warring politicians (Interview with Chijioke W. Wigwe, February 2010).

Obasanjo also introduced the novel practice of serving as "chairman-in-office." "Obasanjo made a point of actively following Commonwealth dossiers during his two years as Chairman, and it has been said that no other Commonwealth leader has visited the Commonwealth secretariat in London to talk to its staff" (Whiteman 2008, p. 271). He publicly praised the role played by British Prime Minister Tony Blair and his chancellor of the exchequer, Gordon Brown, in pushing the Paris Club of debtor nations to cancel the country's US$18 billion debt on condition that Nigeria pay $6 billion arrears of interest charges.

New Horizons

Beyond a review of the record of the last five decades it is useful to chart future policy directions. Dr. Turhan Saleh and Funmi Balogun have independently proposed that Nigeria establish dedicated funds inside UNDP, UNICEF, and other UN agencies to enable Nigerian professionals to work within these institutions in rotational schedules, thus allowing Nigeria to influence policy options on their governing boards (Interview with Turhan Saleh, Country Representative, UN Development Programme, Abuja, Nigeria, October 23, 2009; interview with Funmi Balogun, International Planned Parenthood Foundation Office, Nairobi, Kenya, November 18, 2009; Branch and Cheeseman 2009, p. 213). This would also enable Nigeria to advance its nationals using UN resources. "Such inside knowledge would, furthermore, strengthen the quality of Nigeria's contributions and provide it leverage within the General Assembly. Such funding would also enable Nigeria to insist that, if, as an example, eight people were to be recruited for the implementation of a UNDP program, 50 per cent would be Nigerians" (Interview with Balogun, 2009).

Officials who serve at Nigeria's Permanent Mission in New York work under severe limitations due to limited resources at the research and planning division of the Ministry of Foreign Affairs. Lack of a rich library at the ministry and lack of access to Internet and information technology communications also constitute serious challenges.

With perhaps the exception of the Ministry of Women Affairs, most Nigerian ministries fail to prepare working materials required by Nigeria's officials at the UN Secretariat in New York and agencies located in Vienna, Paris, Rome, and Nairobi in order to conduct deliberations and negotiations over resolutions and agenda items of various committees of the UN General Assembly. Moreover, apart from induction training at the beginning of their careers, most diplomats working in the UN and its specialised agencies find themselves without further training while having to confront increasingly sophisticated delegations from mainly non-African countries (Interview with Chijioke W. Wigwe, February 2010). Unlike other delegations that may include individuals specialised in specific fields (such as wood or genetically modified seeds) and working with dossiers prepared in coordination prior to committee sessions, Nigeria's delegations often consist of officials from diverse ministries who may meet at the conference for the first time, with agencies jostling over policy turf. These lapses deserve urgent attention as befits a country aspiring to lead Africa (Interview with Wigwe, 2009).

Under the changed post–Cold War circumstances in which the UN Security Council increasingly exercises powers that intrude into domestic governance in member countries, Nigeria's diplomats at the United Nations should give primacy to ensuring that the Security Council implements the charge to ensure peace and security and human development in the conflict-prone countries in Africa. If Nigeria gains the status of a permanent member of the Security Council, Gambari argues, Nigerian diplomats should ensure that the United Nations "provide(s) global leadership and vision in the urgent quest for alternatives to the currently dominant policies and relationships which generate inequality and sow seeds of turmoil and conflicts throughout the world" (Gambari 2005, p. 198). Nigeria's use of the Security Council to promote the realization of human development would end what appeared as loss of focus and a "one point agenda" when apartheid ended (Interview with Ghazali 2010).

Conclusion

The chapter has drawn attention to key themes in the speech on Nigeria's foreign policy by Prime Minister Balewa at the UN General Assembly on October 7, 1960, and argued that these have continued to be reflected in foreign policy paths followed by successive regimes. Major exceptions occurred during the regimes of Generals Babangida and Abacha for different reasons. General Obasanjo adopted combative relations within the arenas of the United Nations and the Commonwealth during his military regime but assumed a more conciliatory and cooperative posture as a democratically elected leader promoting significant initiatives. President Shagari scored the rare feat of restraining Nigeria's ambition to field a candidate to serve as secretary-general of the United Nations in order to support Tanzania's candidate.

Bibliography

Abimbola, L., 2009, "Nigeria's Impressive Run at UNESCO," *The Intellectual*, October.

Adebajo, A., 2008, "Nigeria's Interventions in Liberia and Sierra Leone," in A. Adebajo and A.R. Mustapha, eds., *Gulliver's Troubles: Nigeria's Foreign Policy after the Cold War*, University of Kwazulu Natal Press, Scottsville, South Africa.

Akinyemi, B., 1989, "The Colonial Legacy and Major Themes in Nigeria's Foreign Policy," in A.B. Akinyemi, S.O. Agbi, and A.O. Otubanjo, eds., *Nigeria Since Independence: The First 25 Years*, vol. X, International Relations, Heinemann, Lagos, Nigeria.

Anyaoku, E., 2004, *The Inside Story of the Modern Commonwealth*, Evans Brothers, Nairobi, Kenya.

Arinze, E., ed., 2006, *The Obasanjo Legacies: A New Nigeria in the Making*, New Jerusalem, Abuja, Nigeria.

Branch, D., and Cheeseman, N., eds., 2009, *Our Time to Eat: Kenyan Politics Since 1960*, Lit Verlag, Berlin, Germany.

Castro, F., with Ramonet, I., 2008, *Fidel Castro: My Life*, Penguin Books, London.

Dio, M., 2010, "Applying the Rotterdam Rules in Nigeria," *The Nation*, April 13.

Doudu, Cameron, 2009, "The Father of African Emancipation," *New African*, no. 488, October, pp. 18–21.

Fasulo, L., 2004, *An Insider's Guide to the UN*, Yale University Press, New Haven, CT, US.

Gambari, I., 2005, "Nigeria and the United Nations: The Pursuit of National Interest Through Multinationalism in a Changing World Order," in U.J. Ogwu, ed., *New Horizons for Nigeria in World Affairs*, Nigerian Institute for International Affairs, Lagos, Nigeria.

Garba, J., 1987, *Diplomatic Soldiering*, Spectrum Press, Ibadan, Nigeria.

Ingelaere, B., 2009, "Does the Truth Pass Across the Fire Without Burning? Locating the Short Circuit in Rwanda's Gacaca Courts," *Journal of Modern African Studies*, vol. 47, no. 4.

Marsh, D., 2009, *The Euro: The Politics of the New Global Currency*, Yale University Press, New Haven, CT, US.

Meredith, M., 2005, *The State of Africa: A History of Fifty Years of Independence*, Free Press, London.

Nnoli, O., 1989, "Nigeria's Foreign Policy and the Struggle for Economic Independence," in A.B. Agbi, S.U. Akinyemi, and A.O. Otubanjo, eds., *Nigeria Since Independence: The First 25 Years*, vol. X, International Relations, Heinemann, Lagos, Nigeria.

Obasanjo, O., 1990, *Not My Will*, University Press, Ibadan, Nigeria.

Obasanjo, O., 2005, *Standing Tall: Selected Speeches*, Diamond Publications, Lagos, Nigeria.

Obiozor, G., 1985, *Nigeria Participation in United Nations*, Fourth Dimension, Enugu, Nigeria.

Oche, O., 2005, "The Obasanjo Administration and the Diplomacy of Debt Relief," in U.J. Ogwu and W.O. Alli, eds., *Debt Relief and Nigeria's Diplomacy*, Nigerian Institute for International Affairs, Lagos, Nigeria.

Ogwu, U.J., and Alli, W., eds., 2007, *Years of Reconstruction: Selected Foreign Policy Speeches of Olusegun Obasanjo*, Nigerian Institute of International Affairs, Lagos, Nigeria.

Ohumoibhi, M.I., 2008, "A Triple Web of Interdependence, the UN, the Commonwealth and the EU," in A. Adebajo and A.R. Mustapha, eds., *Gulliver's Troubles: Nigeria's Foreign Policy after the Cold War*, University of Kwazulu Natal Press, Scottsville, South Africa.

Olusanya, G., 2008, *Memoirs of a Disillusioned Patriot*, Afremac, Lagos, Nigeria.

Oyediran, O., and A. Agbaje, eds., 1999, *Nigeria: Politics of Transition and Governance 1986–1996*, Council for the Development of Social Science Research in Africa (CODESRIA), Dakar, Senegal.

Shagari, S., 2001, *Beckoned to Serve: An Autobiography*, Heinemann, Ibadan, Nigeria.

Shehu Musa Yar'Adua Foundation, 2004, *Shehu Musa Yar'Adua: A Life of Service*, Abuja, Nigeria.

Stiglitz, J., 2009, "We Are in a Whole New Territory," *Newsweek*, April 6 and 13.

Ugboajah, C.U., ed., 2005, *Raising the Bar: Selected Speeches and Writings of Ojo Maduekwe*, Spectrum Books, Ibadan, Nigeria.

Usman, Y.B.,1979, *For the Liberation of Nigeria*, New Beacon Books, London.

Whiteman, K., 2008, "The Switch Back and the Fall Back: Nigeria-Britain Relations," in *Gulliver's Troubles: Nigeria's Foreign Policy after the Cold War*, University of Kwazulu Natal Press, Scottsville, South Africa.

4

Nigeria's Role in Democratisation: Liberia, Sierra Leone, Togo, and Equatorial Guinea

Eghosa Osaghae

D emocratisation, defined as the process by which a previously undemocratic system or regime becomes more enduringly and sustainably
democratic, is arguably one of the major defining elements of the
post–Cold War era in Africa, the rest of the Third World, and the former
Eastern Europe. Although the United States and its Western allies sought
to create—some would say impose, in view of the *regime change* condi-
tionalities that usually attend democratisation—a liberal world order by
exporting democracy to developing countries (Shaw 1997; Walt 2005), it
is misleading to analyse democratisation and democracy in straitjacket
fashion. This is because the inherent theoretical and practical benefits of
democracy have always made the system attractive: Promotion of economic growth and development, good governance, and peace and security. Indeed, adherents of the second independence school of democracy's
1980s–1990s wave in Africa argue that democratisation has mostly been
the inevitable outcome of popular struggles for freedom, accountable
governance, and material prosperity (Osaghae 2005).

One possible hypothesis from this argument, which is fairly well supported by the outcomes of democratic experiments in Africa, is that
democratisation is more likely to endure and succeed when it is propelled
and owned by local forces than when foisted by powerful external actors. It
is partly to strengthen the homegrown impetus and therefore the chances
for success that regional and subregional organisations in Africa (African
Union [AU], Economic Community of West African States [ECOWAS],
Southern Africa Development Community, Intergovernmental Authority
on Development, African Development Bank, and the Economic
Commission for Africa) as well as powerful countries such as Nigeria and
South Africa have become more actively involved in the promotion of

democracy on the continent. This is more easily seen in countries embroiled in conflict and war, which have provided an opportunity to test the popular claim that democracy offers a peaceful and enduring framework for resolving conflicts. This instrumentalist value of the democratic solution, not the altruistic allure of democracy as an end in itself, has been the most compelling reason for the roles played by powerful African states.

The purpose of this chapter is to examine Nigeria's role as a regional power in the democratisation processes in West Africa based on a comparative analysis of four contrasting cases in which the country was deeply involved: Liberia, Sierra Leone, Togo, and Equatorial Guinea. Why and how did Nigeria become involved in these countries, and what unilateral and multilateral instruments were used? What were the similarities and differences in the interventions and to what extent were they tied to Nigeria's strategic interests or to playing Africa's "big brother" role? What were the benefits, challenges, and lessons of these interventions, and what were their overall effects on the country's status as a West African and African power?

An Overview

The foregoing provides the backdrop for analysing Nigeria's role in democratisation in West Africa, which has emerged as one of the hotbeds of political instability and protracted civil wars in the post–Cold War era (Obi 2009). Between 1990 and 2008, over thirty peace accords involving ECOWAS, AU, United Nations, and warring groups were signed in the subregion. The first problem that confronts such analysis is how to reconcile inherent contradictions that attended Nigeria's promotion of democracy in Sierra Leone, Liberia, Togo, and Equatorial Guinea at a time when it was not itself democratic and was in fact as threatened by serious challenges to its statehood as the countries it sought to help. To what extent can a country, however powerful, provide commodities it does not have? What (moral) authority would a country not able to solve or manage its own conflicts have for attempting to manage conflicts in other countries?

Notwithstanding the obvious contradictions, Nigeria assumed responsibility for democratisation, albeit as a logical—and inevitable— concomitant and strengthener of conflict resolution interventions it originally initiated rather than as a direct first-line objective. This was certainly the case in Liberia and Sierra Leone where the initial objectives for the military governments at the time were to end the civil war via peacekeeping, ceasefire monitoring, peace enforcement, and peace-building and create room for negotiations and humanitarian operations. However, it was realized that no matter how effective these interventions were, it was difficult to establish enduring peace and stability without the democratic therapy. At that point, it mattered less whether Nigeria was itself democratic or not.

The situation of Equatorial Guinea and Togo was evidently different because the countries were not at war, and Nigeria had buoyed its democratic credentials through political and economic reforms. But the interventions took place within the same conflict resolution/conflict prevention/political stability framework and sought to nip the conflicts in the bud and prevent them from spreading to other parts of the subregion, which was the major lesson learnt from the earlier interventions in Liberia and Sierra Leone. From the literature, the conflict prevention genre of democratisation involves interventions through preventive diplomacy initiatives such as fact-finding missions, quiet diplomacy, diplomatic suasions and pressure, and mediation. In fact, in the case of Togo, the country was willing to take the "undemocratic" step of military intervention to bring the situation under control. As reported by a news agency, while ECOWAS was using diplomatic channels to persuade Togo's coup-makers to step down, its leading member state, Nigeria, was playing it tougher. Quoting Femi Fani-Kayode, spokesman of Nigeria's President Olusegun Obasanjo, it was reported that Nigeria did not rule out sending troops to Togo to restore constitutional order, peace, democracy, and stability in Togo and West Africa (*Afrol News* February 15, 2005).

There is, however, a more established conceptual anchor for resolving the contradictions. This has to do not only with Nigeria's status as a subregional and regional political and economic superpower, but also the fact that it provides a model of successful coexistence and diversity management in Africa (Osaghae 1999), where coexistence "describes societies in which diversity is embraced for its positive potential, equality is actively pursued, interdependence between different groups is recognized, and the use of weapons to address conflict is increasingly obsolete" (Berns and Fitzduff 2007, p. 2). As Darkwa has correctly argued, successful coexistence is a requisite for meaningful democratisation and democracy in multiethnic states: "The relationship of coexistence and democracy is in fact symbiotic. A multicultural society that values coexistence is best positioned to build sustainable democracies. Similarly, a democracy built upon a foundation of coexistence-sensitivity is poised to nurture and sustain the coexistence among the citizens it represents" (2009, p. 7). In a continent where ethnic and religious diversities underlie conflict and war and have therefore been the most potent threats to statehood, Nigeria has often found itself having to play credible leading roles in African states torn apart by ethnic and religious conflicts. A case in point is Sudan, where the country's long-standing mediation hinged on the importation of federalism and the federal character principle, which have worked relatively well as conflict management formulas in Nigeria. In the case of West African states, where exclusionary politics are well entrenched, Darkwa identifies coexistence as a key democracy requirement, which Nigeria, because of its familiarity with the challenges of diversity management, can always assist others in developing.

Having tried to resolve the seeming contradictions in Nigeria's democratisation interventions in the countries under review, we must confront the next critical question of why Nigeria intervened at all, a question that goes back to the basis of the country's foreign policy. From the literature, the answers range from the identification of a number of key principles and doctrines that give logical coherence to the country's foreign policy behavior, no matter how divergent and scattered they may be, to those that emphasise contextual exigencies, personality of head of state and managers of foreign policy including military and security personnel, and the effects of global changes. Nigerian foreign policy experts and practitioners generally favour doctrinal cohesion explanations and have listed the key principles: the country's *manifest destiny* of leadership as Africa's and the black race's most populous country, richly endowed with abundant human and material resources; national interest; Afrocentricity; and commitment to regional and global peace and stability. These terms explain the extraordinary resources deployed to the liberation of Africa from the last vestiges of colonialism in southern Africa; active participation in peacekeeping operations throughout the world; membership in key international organisations and support for concerted multilateral actions, particularly key roles in the formation of regional and subregional organisations in Africa (Organization of African Unity, AU, ECOWAS); ratification of international conventions and treaties; various forms of assistance to other African and Third World countries; and, most recently, interventions to promote peace and stability in West Africa.

Although these explanations appear self-evidently true and have demonstrably shaped the perceptions and actions of foreign policymakers, their anchor on concepts such as national interest sometimes makes it difficult to actually understand them. What exactly is Nigeria's national interest: Is it the interest of the head of state, the foreign policy elite, the intelligentsia, or the constitutive interests of civil society constituents? The national interest problematic was a major issue in Nigeria's decision to intervene militarily, initially alone and later under the aegis of the ECOWAS Monitoring Group (ECOMOG) in Liberia (and Sierra Leone as well). Many analysts attributed the action to the personal preferences of the then military president, General Ibrahim Babangida, based on his presumed friendship with Liberian President Samuel Doe (the initial plan was apparently to keep Doe in power) and the protection of alleged economic interests.

At the other end of the spectrum are the more dynamic and contextual explanations, which tend to be more discerning of the ebbs and flows as well as ambiguities, contradictions, and inconsistencies in policy. In this regard, a number of factors have been identified as shapers of policy. Foremost among these is the Nigerian civil war, which in the context of the Cold War forced a review of reliance on the Western bloc, greater attention to good neighbourliness, and the realisation that the security, stability, and development of the country is inextricably tied to relations with neighbours and the rest of the West African subregion. Second is the personality of incumbent heads of state and core foreign service personnel. Thus, under the late General Murtala Mohammed, a maverick nationalist of sorts, Nigeria pursued a radical foreign policy while, by contrast, foreign policy under Tafawa Balewa and Shehu Shagari were conservative. Third is the state of the country itself in terms of economic capacity. Clearly, the emergence of Nigeria as a major oil-producing country has enabled the pursuit of a qualitatively more ambitious foreign policy compared to the pre-oil period.

Fourth is the nature of the global political order and the pressures and demands exerted on the country. In this regard, the strong opposition of the international community to continued despotism and military authoritarian rule in Nigeria in the 1990s, out of sync with the global trend of democratic regimes, involved the imposition of sanctions and isolation of the country at a time when, ironically, one of the major propellants of the peacekeeping interventions in Liberia and Sierra Leone was the administration of Head of State General Sani Abacha, which sought to counteract its isolation by at least showing that the stability of the resource-rich West African subregion depended to a large extent on Nigeria. Furthermore, the relegation of strategic interests in African affairs by the global powers, which began with the botched US-led peacekeeping in Somalia and saw the international community failing to respond in time to deadly conflicts and wars in Africa (Rwanda, Burundi, Democratic Republic [DR] of Congo, Liberia, and Sierra Leone are clear examples), provided the opportunity for Nigeria to play the leading roles expected despite its isolation. The counter-isolation strategy worked quite well as the interventions enhanced Nigeria's role as a regional power with the economic, diplomatic, and military capability to ensure peace and stability. At the heart of this was the ECOWAS military force, ECOMOG, largely Nigerian funded and composed, which was deployed to Liberia and Sierra Leone. Although ECOMOG was not the first wholly African peacekeeping force (the credit for that belongs to the OAU peacekeeping force in Chad [1982], which was commanded by Nigeria's Major General Geoffrey Ejiga), its giant strides and successes have made it the reference point for homegrown conflict resolution and peacebuilding initiatives on the continent.

Logic of Nigeria's Role in Democratisation in West Africa

We shall now turn to the main focus of this chapter—the role of Nigeria in the democratisation processes in West Africa with Liberia, Sierra Leone, Togo, and Equatorial Guinea as case studies. To properly situate the analysis of the role, propelled in all cases by basically the same logic, we begin by interrogating the nature of the logic. The first logic is Nigeria's status as a regional power in terms of population, abundant wealth, level of development, and long history of proven leadership within and outside Africa, including material assistance to poorer countries, which gives the country enormous responsibility for the peace, security, stability, and prosperity of the subregion.

This status, consonant with the emergent *responsibility to protect* (R2P) doctrine, provides a normative framework for legitimising humanitarian interventions. According to Knight, "An important element of the R2P norm is the premise that the international community [including major powers] has a responsibility to protect innocent lives in countries where governments are either unable or unwilling to provide that protection" (2008, p. 27). It is partly on the basis of this well-acknowledged doctrine that the international community expects countries such as Nigeria to lead the region, as enunciated in Ali Mazrui's (otherwise unpopular) thesis of "benign colonialism," which advocates a kind of trusteeship system under which Africa's regional powers take full responsibility for the development and security of their "spheres of influence": South Africa for southern Africa, Ethiopia for the Horn, Kenya for East Africa, Democratic Republic of Congo for Central Africa, Egypt for North Africa, and Nigeria for West Africa (Mazrui 1994, p. 2). In an increasingly relegated Africa, whose conflicts the international community had failed to respond to promptly, it was clear that, benign colonialism or not, African regional powers were going to play more active roles in the affairs of their subregions in the post–Cold War period. They have indeed done so, mostly in the name of defending democracy and constitutional rule or preventing escalation of conflicts, which seems to be the most politically correct and acceptable justification to the global superpowers and international community at large for intervening in the internal affairs of other countries. South Africa has been particularly notable in this regard. Its roles in "stabilising" the southern African region have ranged from direct military action against Lesotho in 1995 to leading subregional interventions to defend democracy and constitutional rule in Madagascar and Zimbabwe, among others. It is often said, in the sense of leading by example, that whatever happens in or to Nigeria or whatever steps the country's leaders decide to take has implications for the region. A stable and prosperous Nigeria, it is argued, is a necessary condition for the overall peace and stability of the West African region.

By the 1990s, a number of developments in Nigeria—notably continued military dictatorship; the annulment of the 1993 presidential election, which truncated the country's democratisation process; self-succession schemes of military leaders; increased human rights abuses; and repression of opposition groups (one of whose most notorious was the execution of Ken Saro-Wiwa and other Ogoni minority activists in 1995)—were incongruent with the evolving globally acceptable norms of statecraft and governance, threatening Nigeria's claim to leadership as a regional power. The country came increasingly under the *regime change* agenda of global powers and the international community, which took the form of imposition of sanctions, isolation of the Nigerian government, and threats of suspension from major international organisations.

Coming at a time when the country was already fully involved in the ECOMOG peacekeeping operations in Liberia and in the unraveling Sierra Leonean conflagration, one would have expected a reaction from Nigeria, but instead the government of General Sani Abacha stepped up the ECOMOG operations, especially in Sierra Leone. One plausible explanation for this unexpected response is that Nigerian leaders saw the noble roles the country was playing in ending conflict and war in the West African region as a way of reasserting its influence and showing its indispensability, which it hoped might persuade the international community to end Nigeria's isolation. The strategy worked fairly well to show the international community, initially reluctant to get involved in the complex West African conflicts, that no matter how bad the situation was in Nigeria, its role in West African and African affairs could not be ignored. It was partly for this reason that, notwithstanding Nigeria's virtual pariah state status, the United Nations joined forces with the Nigeria-led ECOMOG in peacekeeping operations in Liberia and Sierra Leone. The situation improved after Nigeria successfully transited to democratic rule in 1999 and exploited every opportunity to redeem and consolidate its image and status as a regional power and win back the confidence of the global powers. The latter provided the impetus for interventions in the democratisation processes in Togo and Equatorial Guinea.

Despite its significant internal problems, which have arguably limited its ability to function as a credible regional power, Nigeria has performed creditably well in providing leadership in the region. The country's readiness to provide leadership, sometimes at great cost and sacrifice, is due largely to the realisation by Nigerian leaders that whatever happens in the region also has serious implications for the country's own stability and development. It is not surprising that Nigeria has taken responsibility for leadership considering such factors as the close historical, cultural, economic, and religious ties between groups in the nation and rest of the region; the large Nigerian immigrant populations in several countries that have suffered discrimination and repatriation over the years; the large population of West African immigrants in Nigeria; the multinational character of rebel and militant groups that underlies the multiplier effect and diffusion of conflict and war in individual countries; and the devastating effects of cross-border crimes (smuggling, robbery, human trafficking, and hard drugs) and proliferation of small arms and refugee flows. Even so, it took the Nigerian civil war and more recently the interconnectedness between the violent anti-state conflicts in the oil-rich Niger Delta and the civil wars and political conflicts in Liberia, Sierra Leone, Ivory Coast, Guinea-Bissau, and Equatorial Guinea to persuade Nigeria of the region's strategic importance. These events and developments showed how vulnerable the country could be in the face of a hostile West Africa, given the widespread opposition to its perceived dominance and the deep suspicions that often attend its regional initiatives.

Indeed, the greatest challenge Nigeria has faced in asserting its leadership role is the deep-rooted opposition to its perceived dominance and overbearing power, especially by the francophone countries and their former colonial master, France. Such opposition has sometimes taken dramatic forms, such as the refusal of Togolese authorities to grant landing clearance to an aircraft carrying an advance party of President Olusegun Obasanjo's mediation team in 2005 and, before then, the refusal of

Ivorien authorities to allow a contingent of the Nigerian air force that was sent at the outbreak of civil war in that country. It is instructive that the initiative to form ECOWAS came after the bitter diplomatic lessons of the civil war, including the support for Biafra by Houphouet Boigny's Ivory Coast—indeed, the initiative was calculated to ameliorate hostility towards Nigerian leadership—or dominance—especially from francophone countries and France. With the exception of Togo, which supported Nigeria all the way and was part of a joint ministerial committee that toured West Africa to seek support, almost all francophone West African countries opposed Nigeria's ECOWAS initiative.

In addition, President Senghor of Senegal advocated the extension of West Africa to include Zaire (now Democratic Republic of Congo) to counteract Nigeria's domination of the region. The continued emphasis on encouraging regional consensus within ECOWAS in responding to conflicts within individual countries informed the recourse to a regional peacekeeping force in Liberia and Sierra Leone, and regional mediation groups in Togo and Niger, even when it was evident that the force was largely a Nigerian affair and that, in the case of Togo and Niger, the country could act unilaterally. This emphasis therefore may be interpreted as deliberate efforts to assuage fears of domination and the hostility that has often attended the country's leadership. Thus, although it already had troops in Liberia (a fact this author, who was on official secondment to Liberia at the time, was privileged to know), Nigeria proposed the formation of a regional peacekeeping force.

The second logic is the coupling of democratisation with conflict resolution, post-conflict peacebuilding, and good governance in the post–Cold War reforms paradigm. The prospects for enduring *settlement* and peace, as the experience of countries such as South Africa shows, are far brighter when a framework exists that at a minimum guarantees constitutional rule; inclusion; equity; consensus building; participation; access to justice; human rights; free, fair, and peaceful elections; and accountable governance. Therefore, as Nigeria quickly realised, peacekeeping and peace enforcement were necessary but not sufficient to bring about lasting solutions in Liberia and Sierra Leone. Democratisation, which went beyond holding elections to include coexistence and the institutionalisation of conflict management instrumentalities, was required to consolidate the gains of peacebuilding. As pointed out earlier, Nigeria had the credentials to manage these aspects of democratisation even at a time when it was itself in the throes of a difficult democratisation process. The democratisation-conflict resolution logic also applied to the Togolese and Equatorial Guinea situations except that, this time, Nigeria's primary concern was to prevent the political crisis that engulfed the two countries from throwing the region into another round of deadly war. The crisis that followed Togo President Gnassingbé Eyadema's death could easily have degenerated into civil war with region-wide consequences due to the large population of Togolese opposition leaders in exile across the region and historical tensions between Ghana and Togo on account of cross-border affinities of members of the Ewe ethnic group split between the two countries. Interventions in Equatorial Guinea were more related to the protection of Nigeria's strategic resource interests but ultimately had to do with applying the democratic solution to political conflict and instability.

This logic is complemented by institutional and multilateral advocacy and support for democratisation as a facilitator of good governance, which became an integral part of foreign aid and donor support packages and was embraced by African regional bodies. One of the lynchpins of African advocacy was the outlawing of unconstitutional changes of government, rightly identified as an important factor in the dysfunctionality of the postcolonial state in Africa (Souare 2009). Key instruments in this respect include the Lome Declaration on the Response to Unconstitutional Change of Government, which was adopted by African Heads of States and Governments in July 2000; the African Charter on Democracy, Elections and Governance adopted in Addis Ababa, Ethiopia, in January 2007; and the Constitutive Act of the AU, which seeks to partner with Regional Economic Communities in the execution of these instruments in their regions. Largely because of its vast experience in peacebuilding and democratisation support, ECOWAS took the lead in terms of the AU act through its Protocol on Democracy and Good Governance, which was ratified in December 2001.

The Lome Declaration and Addis Ababa Charter specified five situations as constituting instances of unconstitutional change of government:

1. Military coup d'etat against a democratically elected government
2. Intervention by mercenaries to replace a democratically elected government
3. Replacement of democratically elected government by rebel movements and dissident groups
4. Refusal by an incumbent government to relinquish power to the winning political party after regular, free, and fair elections
5. Any amendment or revision of the constitution or legal instruments, which is an infringement on the principles of democratic change of government

The essence of these charters, declarations, and conventions is that they legitimise the roles played by regional powers such as Nigeria, especially when such roles take place within the ambit of regional organisations as was done with ECOWAS. Nigeria's armed intervention initiative could further be justified under the May 1983 ECOWAS Protocol on Mutual Assistance on Defence, which provided for collective armed intervention in the event of aggression against any member state that constituted a threat to the entire community, armed conflict between two or more member states, or internal conflict with proven external instigation and support. It is instructive that President Doe requested military assistance from ECOWAS on the basis of this protocol.

To tie the elements of this framework together, it may be said that Nigeria's intervention in the democratisation processes in West Africa in general was first and foremost a function of its historic leadership role in the region. It was a role that assumed greater significance with the advocacy and facilitative roles assigned to regional bodies and powers by international and regional bodies on the one hand and the neglect of African conflicts by the international community in the post–Cold War period on the other. The roles were further propelled by the tendency of protracted conflicts and civil war in West Africa to assume region-wide significance and engulf the entire region. Major factors in this regard were the diffusion of politically salient ethnic affinities across artificial boundaries created by colonialism and the formidable communities of exile opposition leaders and militants, which had been forced out of their countries by despotic regimes that held sway in West Africa from the 1970s through 1990s. The Liberian civil war, which was prototypical of the growing tendency, had the character of a regional war not only because various rebel forces were composed of recruits from all over West Africa but also because the civil wars that subsequently erupted in Sierra Leone, Ivory Coast, and Guinea-Bissau were either directly or indirectly connected with the Liberian situation. Then, of course, there was the emergence of democratisation as an instrument of conflict resolution and a justification for external (in this case regional) power intervention in the internal affairs of other countries. If Nigeria was going to provide the regional leadership traditionally assigned to it, it had to be at the vanguard of these various movements.

This provides the framework for analyzing Nigeria's role in the democratisation processes in Liberia, Sierra Leone, Togo, and Equatorial Guinea. As will be seen, although the essence of democratisation in all cases was conflict resolution and peacebuilding, they nevertheless presented different dynamics and peculiarities, which can broadly be classified into three analytical categories based on the nature of the democratisation antecedents and Nigeria's role in them. In the first category, to which Liberia and Sierra Leone belonged, democratisation was a concomitant of peacebuilding and post-conflict stability, which was embraced from the point when the peace process needed to be consolidated. In the second category, which comprises Togo and Equatorial Guinea to a large extent, democratisation was embraced as a conflict-prevention instrument to halt a deterioration of the extant political crisis and conflict into war. In the first and second categories, the immediate objective was regional stability, peace, and security, although, as was pointed out earlier, Nigeria has recognized since its own civil war that its peace and security are closely tied to those of the region. The third category is Equatorial Guinea, in which democratisation was also necessitated by conflict resolution considerations, but had more to do with the furtherance and protection of Nigeria's strategic oil interests in the Gulf of Guinea, especially in the aftermath of the complicated border dispute with Cameroon over the oil-rich Bakassi peninsula. We shall now turn to an analysis of each case.

Liberia

Liberia is Africa's oldest republic, having declared its independence in 1847. Although it is widely regarded as a former colony of the United States, Liberia was never formally colonized, having been established as a resettlement colony of freed slaves repatriated from America. Throughout the years, Liberia remained essentially an uncompleted and contested state, a situation that nurtured endemic political violence that finally culminated in civil war throughout the 1990s. The core issues were:

- the apartheid regime in the country that included the Americo-Liberians, as repatriated freed slaves were known, together with slaves freed on the Atlantic (so-called Congo men) and migrants (mostly freed slaves) from neighbouring Sierra Leone who occupied the coastal counties as citizens, and the indigenous (upcountry, hinterland) peoples and territories as subjects rather than citizens;
- the monopoly of power by the True Whig party of the Americo-Liberians and exclusion of the indigenous Liberian populations from the political, economic, and social mainstream to such an extent that those at the boundaries with Ivory Coast, Guinea, and Sierra Leone

were virtually stateless (though, through a colonial-type process of assimilation, a few indigenous Liberians were admitted into the privileged ranks); and
• the repressive character of political control.

In 1980, Master-Sergeant Samuel Doe led a few other noncommissioned officers in overthrowing the Americo-Liberian "dynasty" in a bloody coup that saw the execution of several leaders of the *ancien regime* and the fleeing into exile (mostly to the United States) of the new opposition elements. Coming at a time when military intervention was on the decline in a vastly democratised West African region, the coup was roundly condemned by ECOWAS leaders. President Shehu Shagari of Nigeria led a walkout of leaders at an ECOWAS meeting attended by the Liberian military leader. Doe subsequently exploited the soft belly of the Cold War to entrench himself in power. He devised a democratic transition programme that returned him as elected president in 1985 in an election that was purportedly massively rigged. Having legitimised his hold on power in the increasingly impoverished country, Doe proceeded to replace Americo-Liberian hegemony with exclusionary and ultra-repressive indigenous Liberian rule that revolved around his Krahn ethnic group and pushed more Liberians, including progressives who supported the historic overthrow of True Whig oligarchy, into exile. Doe's despotism did not however go unchallenged by opposition leaders in exile who used bases in neighbouring Guinea, Sierra Leone, and Ivory Coast to launch attacks on Monrovia.

The initial attacks were led by Doe's fellow coup plotter and former deputy, Thomas Quiwonkpa, who was believed to enjoy the support of powerful Americo-Liberians who sought to return to power. The ferocious opposition finally unraveled in December 1989 when Charles Taylor's National Patriotic Front of Liberia (NPFL) invaded the country in a bid to overthrow Doe. The origins and composition of the NPFL, whose forces trained in Libya and Burkina Faso and included dissidents from virtually every West African country, made it a threat to the peace and security of the entire West African region (some analysts saw it as an extension of Libya's attempts to gain control of the region). The linkage of the NPFL with the civil war in Sierra Leone, Ivory Coast, and Guinea-Bissau, as well as the protracted conflicts in Guinea (the home base of the Mandingos who controlled the ULIMO-J [United Liberation Movement of Liberia–Johnson] and ULIMO-K [United Liberation Movement of Liberia–Koroma] rebel forces) and the dangers inherent in refugee movements throughout the region, showed how far the NPFL threat potential could go. This fact made it easier for Nigeria to garner support from other countries for the formation of ECOMOG.

The NPFL offensive plunged the country into a protracted civil war that lasted until the close of the 1990s. Contrary to what many expected, the killing of President Doe by a splinter group of the NPFL, led by Prince Yormie Johnson, complicated the war, which at one time involved over six fighting forces and splinter groups, including the Armed Forces of Liberia. During that time, the NPFL and Taylor, its leader, remained the dominant (rebel) force and claimant to power. But the reluctance of ECOWAS leaders, especially Nigerian, to allow Taylor to have his way, because of the many atrocities and war crimes he was alleged to have committed, was backed by ECOMOG's offensives against the NPFL and prolonged the war. Taylor was a major factor in the civil war that had erupted in Sierra Leone with Foday Sankoh's Revolutionary United Force (RUF) as the main protagonist. Many of those enlisted by RUF had been trained by the NPFL, and Sankoh was a known protégée of Taylor, with whom he perpetrated the blood-and-arms-for-diamonds trade.

Taylor was also allegedly involved in the plundering of Liberia's resources as well as the illegal small arms trade that was threatening to turn the entire West African region into a theater of war. In spite of these, it was clear that the civil wars could not be resolved without Taylor realizing his inordinate ambition to be president, which he did following general elections held in 1997 (with Nigerian backing). But as Taylor's short-lived rule came under serious opposition from various rebel forces, which threatened to plunge the country into another round of war in 1999, a deal struck with him to go into voluntary exile in Nigeria paved the way for the signing of the Comprehensive Peace Agreement in August 2003. Under the terms of the agreement, all former warring factions, including government forces, became involved in a postconflict process of disarmament, demobilisation, reintegration, and rehabilitation. The interim government headed by Charles Gyude Bryant under the guidance of the UN Mission, ECOWAS, and other international community actors organised elections in October/November 2005. The election of Ellen Johnson-Sirleaf as president, which was the conclusion of what we have termed the democratisation concomitant of conflict resolution and peacebuilding, finally brought to an end more than ten years of protracted conflict and war.

The story of the Liberian civil war and its ultimate resolution is also the story of Nigeria's most direct and successful regime change intervention in the internal affairs of another country. Nigeria is said to have spent over US$5 billion and its soldiers constituted over 75 percent of the military personnel involved in the war. The casualty figures remain unknown but are estimated at several thousand. Nigerian soldiers were first deployed to Liberia early in 1990, apparently to defend Doe's government, and later formed the bulk of ECOMOG, which undertook peacekeeping, peace enforcement, and peacebuilding operations under Nigeria's auspices. Nigeria was also involved in—in fact, led—virtually all peace talks, negotiations, and elections that produced the interim national governments headed by Professor Amos Sawyer, President Taylor, interim President Bryant, and finally President Johnson-Sirleaf. Although Nigeria was the prime mover of interventions to bring peace, democracy, and stability to Liberia, its actions were more multilateral than unilateral and were validated within the framework of ECOWAS and later the UN.

One significant aspect of Nigeria's role in Liberia was that it achieved its primary objective of regaining the confidence of the international community as a regional leader. The ECOMOG initiative in Liberia and Sierra Leone was applauded as a model of African peacekeeping interventions, and Nigeria's support for democratisation was taken as an indication of the country's commitment to the promotion of political and economic reforms, though the intervention was quite unpopular at home. Many Nigerians criticized it as an act of personal aggrandisement on the part of General Ibrahim Babangida (who moreover was said to be a close friend of Samuel Doe) and General Abacha. Support for ECOMOG was seen as an act of hypocrisy because, while Nigeria was promoting peace, stability, democracy, and security abroad, the country faced unresolved conflicts, repression, human rights abuses, and increased poverty occasioned by continued military dictatorship at home. It was therefore not surprising that one of the first steps taken by the civilian government of Olusegun Obasanjo after its inauguration in 1999 was to order the return of Nigerian soldiers from Sierra Leone (the remaining soldiers served under the UN mission).

Sierra Leone

The history of Sierra Leone is similar to that of Liberia, having started out as a British colony for the resettlement of freed slaves, some of whom migrated to Liberia. Although a system of structural inequalities did not become as fully entrenched as was the case in Liberia, the country nevertheless suffered from the excesses of exclusionary one-party rule for most of its history. The origins of the protracted political crisis, which engulfed the country in the 1990s and ultimately resulted in civil war, lay in the emergence of a mostly youth-based radical opposition movement in the country that sought to terminate the more than twenty-three-year rule of the All People's Congress Party.

This was the context within which the RUF, led by Foday Sankoh, invaded the country in March 1991. While the government of General Joseph Momoh was battling the rebels with the aid of Nigerian troops, Captain Valentine Strasser toppled the government. In January 1996, Brigadier J.M. Bio replaced Strasser and, following pressure from Nigeria and other powers to immediately restore democratic rule, organised elections that were won by the Sierra Leone People's Party, with Ahmed Tejan Kabbah emerging as president. The spectre of instability, however, continued, and, in May 1997, Johnny Paul Koroma led another group of officers to overthrow Kabbah. While the civil war in Liberia was already beginning to take its toll on the political scene in Sierra Leone, as previously indicated, a good number of Sierra Leonean dissidents were enlisted and trained by Charles Taylor's NPFL. These formed the bulk of the RUF, which, under the leadership of Sankoh, invaded Sierra Leone from its Liberian base in 1991 to launch a civil war that was declared officially over in January 2002 after a complicated process of negotiated settlement. Although the invasion was targeted at the overthrow of the government of President Joseph Momoh, the RUF had to confront ECOMOG, not only because the peacekeeping force had established military bases in Sierra Leone (the Nigerian air force used the Lungi airport for its operations in Liberia) but also because the RUF connection with the NPFL was perceived to be the first movement of the NPFL's regional extension. Indeed, based on Charles Taylor's open boast that countries that facilitated ECOMOG's operations would taste the bitterness of war, it was believed that the RUF attack was part of the NPFL's strategy to break ECOMOG's launching pads. So, to realize one of the immediate objectives for setting up ECO-MOG—namely to safeguard the collective security of the region—the force had to also take on Sierra Leone. It was in this capacity that it warded off several rebel attacks and reversed the coup of May 1997 by members of the Sierra Leonean army, restoring President Kabbah to power. A ceasefire was brokered in July 1999, after which Sankoh was arrested, and the UN mission in Sierra Leone, backed by ECOMOG, organised elections in May 2002.

Nigeria is widely hailed as the benefactor of Sierra Leone's "liberation" and democratisation. Soon after the RUF invasion of 1991, the Nigerian Forces Assistance Group, which was administratively under ECOMOG but controlled from Nigeria, was deployed to the country under an extant Status of Forces agreement. The reluctance of Nigeria's allies, especially Ghana, to get involved in another prolonged operation like Liberia meant that, although the peacekeeping force in Sierra Leone was administered by ECOMOG, it was a wholly Nigerian contingent, and Nigerian soldiers played heroic roles in the wars. In 2000, the Nigerian government arrested and detained Sankoh and helped to restructure the Sierra Leonean military, in acknowledgment of which General Maxwell Khobe, commander of the Nigerian contingent, was appointed chief of defence staff. Nigeria's role in Sierra Leone was, however, far from unilateral, as it had the backing of ECOWAS and OAU (later AU), as well as the UN, which imposed an arms embargo on Sierra Leone and passed a resolution in October 1997 supporting ECOWAS's intervention. The contact group composed of the foreign ministers of Nigeria, Ghana, Guinea, and Ivory Coast, set up by ECOWAS to negotiate peaceful settlement with the military junta that overthrew President Kabbah, approved use of force as a last resort. The carrot-and-stick diplomacy paid off when an agreement to hand over power and restore democratic rule by April 1998 was signed in Conakry, Guinea, in October 1997 between ECOWAS and the Koroma junta. Nigeria was also fully involved in the diplomatic manoeuvres that complemented military intervention. Ambassador Olu Adeniji, who later became the country's foreign minister, served as the UN special representative in Sierra Leone and was a prime mover of the peace accord signed in 2000 that produced a government of national unity.

Togo

By 2005, when President Gnassingbe Eyadema died, he had been in office for thirty-eight years, making him one of Africa's longest-serving leaders. During those years, Togo suffered under one party dictatorship and a regime of gross human rights abuse that swelled the ranks of opposition leaders, many of whom, like Sylvia Olympio, lived abroad. The country had a chequered history of democratisation that, among others, saw the transmutation of Eyadema from military head of state to civilian president, having seized power in a coup in 1967, and the convening of a sovereign national conference, which was the dominant mode of democratic transition in francophone Africa in the early 1990s. Togo also came under the scrutiny of La Francophonie, the group used by France to persuade its former colonies to embrace political and economic reforms, including democratisation. The failure of Togo to respond appropriately to internal and external pressures, which heightened fears that the country could easily fall prey to the protracted conflicts and civil wars that swept through West Africa in the 1990s, led to the suspension of aid by the European Union in 1993. Togo thereafter made efforts to improve its human rights record and relations with the opposition, but the country remained largely undemocratic.

These were the circumstances under which President Eyadema died in 2005. Following his death, the military, led by General Zachari Nandja, chief of staff, unexpectedly set aside the constitutional succession provision for the speaker of the National Assembly to take over and instead installed Eyadema's son, Faure Gnassingbe, as president (Banjo 2005). This action was rejected outright by the opposition and international community and met with spontaneous street protests and riots, which were violently suppressed by the army and police. Unable to withstand the concerted pressure for long, military authorities were forced to organise elections, which were allegedly manipulated to favour Gnassingbe, who was declared winner. That declaration began a new crisis which was only resolved through power-sharing negotiations between Gnassingbe and the opposition brokered by Nigeria and ECOWAS.

Let us now turn to Nigeria's role in the Togolese democratisation struggles, which on balance were largely pro-democracy, positive, and progressive. Togo has a history of cordial relations with Nigeria, which has facilitated close formal and informal economic ties. The military government of General Yakubu Gowon was particularly close to Eyadema, who was Nigeria's greatest supporter in the formation of ECOWAS in 1975. By the time the constitutional and political crisis that followed Eyadema's death broke out in 2005, Nigeria had already regained its voice as a credible regional power. It had not only successfully steered the peacebuilding and democratisation processes in Liberia and Sierra Leone, but the country's economy was booming once again, making it possible for Abuja to offer material assistance to Ghana and other countries. Most of all, the country had itself become a thriving democracy.

These qualitative changes enhanced the country's leadership roles in the transformation of the OAU to the AU and the adoption of NEPAD as an instrument of good governance and economic development. Ironically, one of the key levers of the AU's pro-democratisation initiatives, the Declaration on the Framework for an OAU Response to Unconstitutional Change of Government, which opposes the overthrow or replacement of democratically elected governments by military coup d'etat, mercenaries, dissident groups, or rebel movements, was adopted in Lome, Togo, in July 2000 and was invoked in the AU's declaration of military intervention in Togo as unconstitutional. Article 23(5) of the African Charter on Democracy, Elections and Governance of 2007, otherwise known as the Addis Charter, further opposed "Any amendment or revision of the constitution or legal instruments, which is an infringement on the principles of democratic change of government" (African Charter on Democracy, Elections and Governance of 2007). Under Nigeria's leadership, the profile of ECOWAS as an agent of conflict resolution, peacebuilding, and collective security (anchored on the Protocol on Democracy and Good Governance of the Economic Commission of West African States 2001) had grown tremendously, and this gave it the needed verve to engage in first-line mediation in any country where a crisis was brewing. Nigeria used these platforms quite well in its democratisation engagements, especially as President Obasanjo was chairman of ECOWAS and the AU in 2005.

Following early-warning signals learnt from civil wars in the region, the potential of the Togolese crisis to unravel into a civil war was high. In the new, conventional wisdom, the most appropriate response to the situation was to nip it in the bud, using democratisation as the arrowhead. This was exactly what Nigeria did. The initial attempt by Obasanjo to intervene both as Nigerian president and chairman of ECOWAS (and AU) was rebuffed as the aircraft conveying his advance party was refused landing rights in Lome. This did not, however, deter Nigeria, which assumed a tough posture on the issue, including the recall of the country's ambassador and the contemplation of military intervention and economic sanctions. The ECOWAS mediation committee, which included Nigeria's foreign affairs minister Olu Adeniji (and the foreign ministers of Ghana and Niger), was also talking tough, threatening imposition of sanctions and expulsion, while at the same time exploring various diplomatic channels. Finally, military authorities bowed to this intense pressure, apologised to Nigeria over the aircraft incident, and agreed to hold elections. The violent eruption that followed the declaration of Faure Gnassingbe as president again brought Nigeria fully back in. This time, Nigeria facilitated the negotiation of a power-sharing (government of national unity) deal between Gnassingbe and the main opposition leaders in Abuja, which calmed the situation and enabled Togo to embark on a peaceful process of democratic growth.

Equatorial Guinea

Nigeria's role in Equatorial Guinea was markedly different from that of Liberia, Sierra Leone, and Togo. While its actions in the latter countries were mediated by multilateralism involving ECOWAS, AU, UN, and others, in Equatorial Guinea they were more unilateral and propelled by mutually shared strategic interests. Guinea, which shares the resource-rich Gulf of Guinea with Nigeria, as well as Angola, Gabon, Cameroon, Congo, and Sao Tome and Principe, has had mixed relations with Nigeria. Initially, the spats were over the welfare of the large population of Nigerian workers in Equatorial Guinea, which at various points suffered periodic harassment, discrimination, deportation, and expulsion that elicited the vehemence of the Nigerian media and citizens who advocated invasion and annexation of the tiny country a la *pax Nigeriana* (Obadare 2001).

Three closely related factors further increased the strategic importance of Equatorial Guinea to Nigeria. First was the fact that Nigeria's territorial waters are located in the South Atlantic basin, making it rely almost exclusively on seaborne trade for its economic health (Ogwu 2004). Second was the vulnerability of Equatorial Guinea to external interventions, which mostly took the form of attempts by mercenaries or foreign-sponsored elements to overthrow the government. One such case involved British mercenaries who were arrested in Zimbabwe, and another involved militants allegedly from Nigeria's Niger Delta. The danger inherent in Guinea's vulnerability was fully dramatised in 1988 when it was reported that the apartheid regime in South Africa, against which Nigeria led the larger African struggle for liberation, planned to establish a military base in Equatorial Guinea. The involvement of Pretoria in attempts by Argentina and Brazil to organise a South Atlantic Treaty Organization to cover coastal areas, including the Gulf of Guinea, was another cause for worry that led Nigerian foreign affairs managers and intellectuals to advocate a counter organisation to be led by Nigeria and Brazil.

The third factor was the discovery of oil in Equatorial Guinea in the late 1980s (it became sub-Saharan Africa's third largest oil producer after Nigeria and Angola), which attracted even greater foreign interest as the new scramble for Africa and African resources got fully under way. With the uncertainties that surrounded oil supplies from the Middle East in the aftermath of the Gulf War, the attention of the United States turned to Africa and, in particular, the Gulf of Guinea, which it had declared "ungoverned territory" because of the lawlessness that permitted piracy and other maritime crimes on the high seas. (It is projected that African sources will account for one-quarter of total US oil supplies by 2015; in 2005, the United States derived 15 percent of its oil from the Gulf of Guinea.) Citing Jack Child, Joy Ogwu (2004) provides the basis for dubbing the Gulf of Guinea ungoverned territory: "The South Atlantic is a strategic vacuum involving large ocean areas with relatively low military presence by either superpowers or local littoral states. The value of the eastern portion of the South Atlantic has grown considerably with the increasing use of its sea level by tankers bringing Middle East oil to European and US markets." The controversial deployment of a US Africa Command, AFRICOM, to the Gulf further heightened Nigeria's anxieties. With Nigeria's oil industry in turbulence—threatened internally by the unrelenting war waged by aggrieved groups in the Niger Delta and externally by the loss of the oil-rich Bakassi peninsula to Cameroon—the country had to take its relations with Equatorial Guinea much more seriously. The strategic nexus between the Gulf and Nigeria's Niger Delta crisis on the one hand and the overall stability of West Africa on the other was clearly articulated by President Obasanjo in an address at a meeting of the Gulf of Guinea Energy Security Group in Abuja in September 2006:

> The objective [in setting up the group] was to provide a forum for collaborative efforts . . . to map out modalities for energy security and orderly development of the Niger Delta in a climate of peace as part of the purpose of making the Gulf of Guinea a haven of peace, security, stability, and predictability. The forum was therefore conceived by Nigeria as a forerunner of wider strategies that may be employed in other countries. . . . The initiative became imperative in recognition of the importance of the Gulf of Guinea to the attainment of sustainable socioeconomic development of the West African sub-region and the sub-region's increasing contribution to oil requests of the world (*The Guardian,* September 8, 2006, p. 43).

Other responses included a proposal to set up a joint force, the Gulf of Guinea Guard Force (presumably to counter the US AFRICOM), and the establishment of the Gulf of Guinea Commission on Peace, Stability and Management of Oil Resources, as well as a joint commission and agreements with Equatorial Guinea on maritime boundary (to prevent another Bakassi situation) and several joint oil exploration and production ventures.

The other aspect of Nigeria's stability-enhancing interest and influence in Equatorial Guinea, which assumed greater significance after Nigeria's return to civilian democracy in 1999, was support for the country's political stability and democratisation. This was against the backdrop of Guinea's long history of one-party, one-man dictatorships; coups; mercenary activities; and overall political instability. Francisco Nguema, its first president after independence in 1968, was toppled by Teodoro Mbasogo Obiang following a bloody coup d'etat in 1979. A new constitution that gave extensive powers to the president was adopted in 1982. A key instrument of Nigeria's policy in Equatorial Guinea was support for constitutional rule, elections, and other democratic processes. In 2007, when the country's stability was once again threatened by another mercenary-led coup, this time involving people suspected to be militants from Nigeria's Niger Delta, Nigeria was in the forefront of condemning the attempted infraction of the constitutional process. The complicity of Nigerian elements was promptly denied, and Nigeria's foreign affairs minister, Ojo Maduekwe, employed shuttle diplomacy overtures to reassure and protect the Equatorial Guinea government. Overall, in contrast to Liberia, Sierra Leone, and Togo, Nigeria's role in Equatorial Guinea has been more strategic and economic, though it was also increasingly clear that these could not be pursued without promoting and protecting democracy as an instrument of stability.

Conclusion

The lessons and benefits of Nigeria's role in democratisation are fairly obvious. First, it strengthened the appreciation of the recursive relationship between democracy and conflict resolution, which necessitated the building of capacity in this area both for peacekeeping forces and the foreign policy establishment. But this did not apply to Nigeria alone, as ECOWAS also entrenched democratisation and good governance as instruments of conflict resolution and peacebuilding. Second, the interventions showed Nigeria as a promoter and defender of democratisation, including peaceful coexistence, free and fair elections, constitutional rule, and conflict resolution. Third, it restored and enhanced Nigeria's status as a credible regional power, which increased its influence within regional and international organisations. Finally, the role served as a surety for Nigeria's own continued democratisation as, increasingly, the strength of its voice and ability to influence events in other countries depended on the extent to which it remains a thriving and stable democracy.

Bibliography

Banjo, A., 2005, "Constitutional and Succession Crisis in West Africa: The Case of Togo," *African Journal of Legal Studies*, vol. 2, no. 2, pp. 147–161.

Berns, J., and Fitzduff, M., 2007, "What Is Coexistence and Why a Complementary Approach?" *Coexistence International Working Paper*, Brandeis University, Waltham, MA, US.

Darkwa, L., 2009, "Focus on Coexistence and Democracy Building in West Africa," *Coexistence International Working Paper*, Brandeis University, Waltham, MA, US.

Knight, W.A., 2008, "Disarmament, Demobilization, and Reintegration and Post-Conflict Peace-Building in Africa: An Overview," *African Security*, vol. 1, no. 1, pp. 24–52.

Mazrui, Ali, 1994, "Recolonisation or Self-Colonisation? Decaying Parts of Africa Need Benign Colonization," *International Herald Tribune* (Pretoria), August 4, p. 2.

Obadare, E., 2001, "Constructing Pax Nigeriana? The Media and Conflict in Nigeria-Equatorial Guinea Relations," *Nordic Journal of African Studies*, vol. 10, no. 1, pp. 80–89.

Obi, C.I., 2009, "Economic Community of West African States on the Ground: Comparing Peacekeeping in Liberia, Sierra Leone, Guinea Bissau and Cote D'Ivoire," *African Security*, vol. 2, nos. 2–3, pp. 119–136.

Ogwu, J., 2004, "The Strategic Importance of South Atlantic and the Gulf of Guinea," *The Comet* (Lagos), August 20, p. 39.

Osaghae, E.E., 1996, *Ethnicity, Class, and the Struggle for State Power in Liberia*, CODESRIA (Council for the Development of Social Science Research in Africa), Dakar, Senegal.

Osaghae, E.E., 1999, "Democracy and National Cohesion in Multiethnic African States: Nigeria and South Africa Compared," *Nations and Nationalism*, vol. 5, no. 2, pp. 259–280.

Osaghae, E.E., 2005, "The State of Africa's Second Liberation," *Interventions: International Journal of Postcolonial Studies*, vol. 7, no. 1, pp. 1–21.

Shaw, M., 1997, "The State of Globalization: Towards a Theory of State Transformation," *Review of International Political Economy*, vol. 4, no. 3, pp. 497–513.

Souare, I.K., 2009, "The AU and the Challenge of Unconstitutional Changes of Government in Africa," *ISS Paper* 197, Institute for Security Studies, Johannesburg, South Africa.

Walt, S.M., 2005, "In the National Interest: A New Grand Design for American Foreign Policy," *Boston Review*, vol. 30, no. 1, pp. 6–10; and critical responses/rejoinders by R. Falk, J.S. Nye, N. Chazan, M. Mamdani, et al., pp. 11–24.

PART 2

PROMOTING PEACE

5

Nigeria's Global Role in Peacekeeping: From the Congo Through Lebanon to Bosnia Herzegovina

Julie G. Sanda

A cursory look at Nigeria's involvement in the global arena since independence in 1960 shows that an activist anticolonialism posture has been a distinguishing factor. Pursued under the "Africa as centre-piece" banner, Nigeria was in the forefront of anticolonial and liberation struggles on the continent. A natural corollary to this pursuit became its activism in the arena of global security, specifically peacekeeping. Although peacekeeping *per se* is not a term mentioned in the Charter of the United Nations, it has become a major instrument of conflict resolution for the UN and a major plank in Nigeria's external relations within and outside the African continent. Born in the Cold War era and steeped in the power politics characteristic of that era, peacekeeping has evolved from its traditional conception as a military operation to cover a plethora of activities, which include a wide range of police, civilian, and humanitarian roles. Consequent upon these developments, *peace support operations* (PSO), a more encompassing term, is now commonly employed.

From the Congo in 1960 to date, Nigeria has been involved in more than forty peacekeeping missions worldwide in both military and police roles. It has also contributed senior civilian leadership in a number of these operations. Due to an increasing demand for peacekeepers worldwide, thus stretching global resources, Nigeria's largely good record and willingness to serve over the years has resulted in increasing demand for its personnel. Peacekeeping has provided the country with a "major redeeming point" in the global community. According to Agwai:

> The commitment to global peace has continued to define Nigeria's foreign policy since her independence in 1960. And nowhere is it more evident

than in Africa which has remained the cornerstone of her foreign policy. Today, Nigeria is the leading peace-keeping nation in Africa and has shown tremendous leadership in all regional and continental efforts in conflict management. (2010, p. 2)

The prestige accruing from such efforts has boosted the country's leadership credentials and is often cited in diplomatic circles as a qualifying factor for a permanent seat on the UN Security Council.

While Nigeria's contributions have to a large extent been well received externally, on the domestic front there has been growing criticism or questioning of the rationale for such extraordinary human and material investment, particularly when the benefits accruable do not seem commensurate with that investment. Moreover, there is a perception that Nigeria's generosity is increasingly being taken for granted. Existing literature consists largely of personal accounts of individual peacekeepers (Ayuba 2006), academic perspectives on the Economic Community of West African States Monitoring Group (ECOMOG) (Vogt 1992), historical accounts and military perspectives dealing with operational matters (Oni 2002; Ogomudia 2007; Jonah and Zabadi 2009), and others raising policy matters (Alli 2009; Iliya 2009). One common thread in the literature is a querying of the national or strategic interest served by pursuing an active peacekeeping role globally.

It is against this background that this chapter addresses the following questions: What is Nigeria's motivation for participating in global peacekeeping? Are there strategic national interests being served? How can Nigeria's involvement be organised and better managed for maximum results and benefit for Nigeria and its citizens? What is the future of peacekeeping and Nigeria's role? To answer these questions, we suggest that: (1) the poor coordination and absence of cooperation between policymaking actors (institutions and individuals) account for the lack of a well-defined, clearly articulated national interest as far as peacekeeping is concerned; and (2) the lack of a strategic approach to peacekeeping has continued to rob Nigeria of tangible and intangible benefits. Nigeria's participation in UN operations in the Congo, Lebanon, and Bosnia-Herzegovina provide the backdrop for our investigation.

Definitions and Mandates

The surplus of activities that make up a PSO (or peace operation, according to the Brahimi Report, Panel on United Nations Peace Operations 2000) has increased tremendously since its early days. The issue of definition has been subjected to considerable academic debate by critics of both peacekeeping theory and its practice (Durch 2006, p. 7). We will therefore simplify the matter by adopting definitions developed by the UN.

Traditional peacekeeping, which emerged in the early years of the UN, was born in the Cold War climate. Little wonder that it emphasised the principles of consent, neutrality, and impartiality, and was either a peacekeeping or observer mission. The latter involved military observers deployed to keep the peace where there is peace to keep—that is, where a ceasefire had been agreed upon while the requisite diplomatic and political moves towards resolving the conflict were being conducted. A peacekeeping operation would separate belligerents within determined zones, thus creating space for resolution. A PSO is a complex multidisciplinary, multifunctional, and multidimensional operation covering a range of activities that include peacemaking, peacekeeping, peace enforcement (see Capstone Doctrine, UN Department of Peacekeeping Operations 2008), and peacebuilding.

This does not mean that all activities are necessarily part of any one operation. Peacemaking involves diplomatic action to facilitate resolution by bringing belligerents to a negotiated agreement. Peacekeeping is essentially a military affair to maintain peace where a ceasefire has been agreed and makes room for other elements, civilian and police, to engage in the mission area. In peace enforcement, coercive measures are utilised to ensure there is a peace to keep, and peacebuilding is a long-term process wherein measures are employed to build national capacities after security elements have been rolled back to ensure that a relapse to conflict is averted (UN Department of Peacekeeping Operations 2008, pp. 17–20). Today most UN-mandated missions are multidimensional, thus allowing space for manoeuvre. By definition a multidimensional UN peacekeeping operation would have a direct political role in efforts to resolve the conflict and is often mandated by the Security Council to provide good offices or promote national political dialogue and reconciliation (Figure 5.1).

A mandate is the legal authorisation for a peacekeeping operation issued by the mandating organisation, in this case the UN. It is derived from relevant articles in the UN Charter, even though the Security Council does not specifically refer to any article in articulating a mandate for any mission. The UN argues that to force such a rigid compartmentalisation would create difficulties for countries contributing troops and/or partners providing training (UN Department of Peacekeeping Operations 2008, p. 14). However, it is useful for analytical purposes and helps in clarifying what a mission can or cannot do, according to the

Figure 5.1   Linkages in a Peace Support Operation

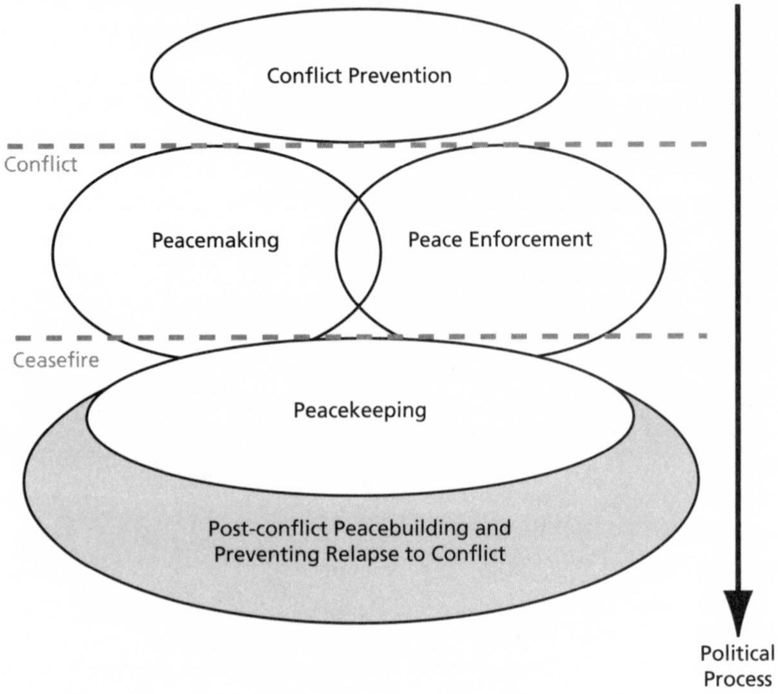

Source: UN Department of Peacekeeping Operations 2008, p. 10.

UN charter. Thus Chapter VI deals with pacific settlement of disputes, allowing for preventive diplomacy; Chapter VII deals with enforcement action; and Chapter VIII allows for involvement of regional arrangements. It was the provision of Chapter VI that gave the legal basis for traditional peacekeeping.

As the scope widened, the UN found legitimisation in the other articles and gave expression to its role of maintaining international peace and security. The invention of the peacekeeping tool allowed it to circumvent antics of the superpowers deployed in checkmating each other by using the veto against the employment of the collective security principle. The issue of mandate is critical to the deployment and tasking of a mission and to its success. A mandate can either strengthen the hand of a commander/mission or seriously limit the latitude for action, thus risking at times the lives of peacekeepers and the community it is there to protect or serve. When the Rwandan genocide occurred, a UN mission was on ground but its mandate did not allow it to stop the violence. Similarly, in Kosovo, Bosnians were massacred in UN-protected areas. The UN Security Council has in such cases been accused of playing politics at the expense of the people at risk (Mbanefo 2005, p. 14). UN politics are such that the five veto-wielding powers in the Security Council determine how a mandate is defined for any mission. Since 1999, the Security Council has placed the protection of civilians more firmly on its agenda, resulting in four resolutions on the matter (United Nations 2009). The latest of these, Resolution 1674 (United Nations 2006, p. 11) has tried to ensure that a "protection of civilians" mandate provides clear guidelines and gives enough flexibility for missions to interpret the best course of action in the circumstance. Africa is the largest client of UN peacekeeping initiatives in an era where Western nations are no longer keen to send large numbers of foot soldiers to keep the peace where theatres of war have been bloody and intractable.

The Beginning:
Operations des Nations Unies au Congo (ONUC)

As the conceptual framework for Nigeria's foreign policy emerged, it came to be identified as a commitment to Nigeria, Africa and Africans, and the United Nations. It is within this context that Nigeria became involved in the Congo crisis in the 1960s at two levels: diplomatic and then with the deployment of its military assets as part of ONUC. As Chibundu (2009) and Akinyemi (1986) have noted in different contexts, the decision to enter the Congo crisis was born of a happy coincidence of both governmental policy and nongovernmental demands. However, in the early stages of the crisis, there was little or no concern in Nigeria, a situation Akinyemi attributes to the preoccupation of government and political parties with internal issues. As he explains, following the federal elections of 1959, political parties were faced with internal reorganisation, and the country at large was preparing to celebrate independence in October 1960. The UN decision to intervene in the Congo was a welcome development in some circles, but at the governmental level a still cautious Prime Minister Tafawa Balewa said he was studying the situation when he gave his maiden speech at the UN General Assembly, during which the Congo was a major issue. A fifteen-member Conciliation Commission already decided upon by the UN before Balewa made his proposal for a fact-finding mission was formed on November 5, 1960 (with Nigeria as a member), comprising members of the Afro-Asian group that had contributed military and administrative personnel to the Congo.

On the political and diplomatic front, Nigeria also served on the UN Advisory Committee on Congo, the Secretary-General's Congo Club, and later chaired the Congo Conciliation Commission barely a month after joining the UN. Even when the House of Representatives in Nigeria tabled a motion of censure against the UN, Balewa defended Nigeria's continued support, well aware of the shortcomings of the world body, because "we must all agree that it is the only body which can do such work" (Akinyemi 1986, p. 58). When the death of Congo's prime minister Patrice Lumumba triggered strong anti-UN sentiments in the country, Nigeria's support for the UN was unwavering.

Nigeria's support for Dag Hammarskjold as UN secretary-general was not necessarily transferred to all UN decisions on the Congo. For example, Nigeria lodged a complaint against Rajeshwar Dayal, head of the UN mission in Congo, mirroring the complaint of many African countries that eventually led to his removal. Dayal was replaced with a duo that included a Nigerian, Francis Nwokedi, and a Ghanaian. As chair of the Conciliation Commission, Nigeria became deeply involved in the resolution of the Congo crisis. Thus, the path was paved for the Nigerian government to agree to the UN request to send troops to the Congo. The first batch of Nigerian Army troops sent to ONUC under the command of Lt. Col. Aguiyi Ironsi was two-batallion strong, comprising 5th Infantry Battalion with engineers, signals, and medical services elements. The 4th Infantry Battalion joined following a request for additional troops under the command of Lt. Col. Price. Nigerian soldiers operated mainly in Kivu, Kasai, North Katanga, and Leopoldville provinces (Sani 2009, p. 5). By the end of the mission a total of approximately 5,000 Nigerian Army personnel had served in the Congo in rotation over four years (Ogomudia 1997, p. 116). As many as sixteen officers and men of the Nigerian Army were decorated for their courageous acts in the Congo, and Ironsi was appointed force commander in January 1964 "partially in recognition of Nigeria's contribution" (ibid, p. 116). From this first outing in 1960, Nigeria has become a major troop-contributing country, not only to the UN but also to the African Union (AU) and ECOWAS operations, playing major and even pioneering roles in Chad and Liberia. These two operations, perhaps more than others, are testimony to the pride of place PSO has in Nigeria's foreign policy.

Following the successful deployment in the Congo, the Nigerian Army helped out in Tanganyika in 1964 under a bilateral arrangement between Nigerian authorities and then Prime Minister Julius Nyerere. In Okoosi-Simbine's assessment, the Congo operation put "Nigeria on the world map and has kept Nigeria in world view since then, earning it early world recognition and respect" (2004, p. 149). However, from 1967 to 1970, Nigerian troops were locked in a bloody civil war, during which the strength of the Nigerian Army grew from about 7,000 to 200,000 at the end of the war (Sani 2009, p. 8).

United Nations Interim Force in Lebanon

In 1978, Nigeria deployed to Lebanon, contributing a total of 7,000 troops rotated in nine battalions to the United Nations Interim Force in Lebanon (UNIFIL), and featured the third largest infantry in the operation, which lasted from 1978 to 1984. The Nigerian contingent was, however, withdrawn in 1983 following the second invasion of southern Lebanon by Israeli forces, which put Nigerian troops in the line of hostilities (Ogomudia 1997, p. 119). The Nigerian contingent included the Navy; its sealift capability was deployed in November 1982 "when she sailed a Landing Ship Tank (LST) NNS Ambe from Lagos to Beirut and participated" (Akintola 2007, p. 77). The LST had a personnel strength of ninety men and four officers in the mission.

Because the Nigerian troops often came under direct attack, Nigeria suffered losses in this operation, including three personnel—Capt. Oweh, Lance Corporal Mohammed Tanko, and Signalman Enahoro (Ogomudia 1997, p. 118)—ammunition, and equipment though the mission operated under rules of engagement, in which the use of arms was highly constrained. Eventually the Nigerian government elected to cut its losses in the ever-worsening security environment and pulled its troops out in 1983 (Oluyemi-Kusa 2007, p. 148; Albert 2007, pp. 170–173). Scholars differ in their analysis of this decision. While Ekoko (cited in Albert 2007, p. 173), for example, saw it as a lost opportunity for maximising gains of that outing, Albert (2007) supports the decision, citing US withdrawal from Somalia as a case in point. The military adviser to the UN secretary-general at the time of the Lebanon operation made a damning revelation that buttresses Albert's stand: UNIFIL was given "a mandate it could not fulfill: to escort the powerful Israelis out and to restore the authority of the disintegrating Lebanese government" (Rikhye 1993, p. 9).

Nigeria's involvement with the Lebanon crisis, like the Congo before it, was not limited to security aspects. Nigeria was engaged at the political and diplomatic level and was emboldened to condemn Israel and the Western nations that appeared to support Israeli occupation of southern Lebanon. The peacekeeping mission was, however, an entirely military operation, as defined by its mandate. A military historian posits that "Nigeria's overall national interest might have influenced her enthusiastic response. . . . Nigeria saw the need to pay back Israel in the same coin considering her role during the Nigerian civil war when she openly supported the secessionist cause, for whatever reason" (Oni 2002, p. 16). To Ogomudia, Nigeria's involvement in UNIFIL was both "a means of fulfilling an international obligation under the UN Charter (and) also a foreign policy objective" (1997, p. 118).

In the 1990s the Nigerian military became even more involved in PSO, the high point being the ECOMOG deployment to Liberia. An essentially humanitarian intervention, ECOMOG was soon to engage in enforcement action as it became evident that there was no peace to keep in the classic peacekeeping sense. As at February 2010, Nigeria had 4,968 officers and personnel in PSO worldwide with 1,609 in Liberia and 3,305 in Darfur. The highest-ranking Nigerian is Lt. Gen. C.I. Obiakor, chief military adviser to the UN secretary-general, who has been serving in that capacity since 2008 (*Daily Trust* 2010).

United Nations Mission in Bosnia and Herzegovina

According to Durch, when the UN looked at Bosnia-Herzegovina in mid-1992, it saw the Congo—"an experience never to be repeated" (1993, p. 8). The UN Operation in Congo (ONUC) had set a precedent for coercive action—what is now known as peace enforcement—and it came with disastrous consequences. The United Nations Mission in Bosnia and Herzegovina (UNMIBH), essentially a police operation, comprised the International Police Task Force (IPTF) and UN Civilian Office. The Nigeria Police Force (NPF) was part of the IPTF, to which it deployed a total of 110 personnel in Sarajevo, commanded first by Simeon Midendu and then Godwin Obi (Nwolise 2004, p. 172). The sterling performance of the police, first in Congo and then in Namibia (1989–1990) where the NPF contingent was rated the best (Nwolise 2004, p. 135), increased the demand for NPF personnel. In both missions, police peacekeepers received accolades and medals for their accomplishments. Thus, when the UN decided to dispatch an International Police Task Force to Bosnia-Herzegovina, Nigerian police were sought as peacekeepers.

Since then, the scope of police roles in peacekeeping has increased considerably, as has the participation of NPF. Not only does the NPF contribute civil police officers, it is also a pioneer and foremost Formed

Police Unit (FPU) provider since the UN Mission in Liberia (UNMIL) in 2004. An FPU is a composite police unit with an executive mandate— that is, a "fully armed unit saddled with . . . law enforcement and other allied duties in the mission area" (Okiro 2009, p. 152). Police in PSO is a growth area, and NPF has not lagged behind in this development. With a total of 108 women peacekeepers in 2007, one of the highest worldwide, the NPF policy is to attain "a minimum of 15% women representation in all deployments" (Owohunwa 2007, p. 290).The NPF today manages PSO matters in a full-fledged department under the DIG Operations. As at June 2009, it was composed of a total of 616 personnel, including officers, deployed in operations all over the world. Of this, 245 are members of FPUs in Haiti and Liberia, while 371 are police monitors in both UN and AU missions. The areas of deployment are: Haiti (UN Stabilization Mission in Haiti)—129; East Timor (UN Integrated Mission in Timor-Leste)—57; Kosovo (UN Interim Administration Mission in Kosovo)—20; Liberia (UNMIL)—142; Sierra Leone (United Nations Mission in Sierra Leone)—4; Sudan (UN Mission in Sudan)—57; Cote d'Ivoire (UN Operation in Côte d'Ivoire)—4; Afghanistan—1; and Burundi—1. Similarly, 201 NPF personnel, including officers, are deployed in Sudan (African Union/United Nations Hybrid Operation in Darfur [UNAMID]) as police monitors (NPF 2009).

Civilian Dimensions

A multidimensional PSO also involves civilian actors. Whereas Nigeria has an impressive record as a major contributor of troops and police, its record on the civilian side has neither been consistent nor appreciable. No doubt Nigerians such as Ambassadors Olu-Adeniji and Shola Omoregie, who have headed missions in Liberia and Guinea-Bissau, respectively, have held high-profile positions. So also has Ambassador Baba Gana Kingibe, who headed the African Union Mission in Sudan as special representative of the chairperson of the AU Commission. Most recently Professor Ibrahim Gambari has been appointed to the highest office in a UN mission as the UNAMID joint special representative. Often such appointments are made in recognition of a country's contribution in a particular mission. However, on the whole, Nigerians serving at various levels in a civilian capacity in PSO have largely deployed either as international civil servants seconded to the UN as contract staff hired directly to the mission concerned or as UN volunteers. Yet the civilian dimension is another key growth area for PSO globally, given the increasing involvement of UN and regional organisations in peacebuilding-related activities.

The UN indicates that within five to ten years a postconflict state has a high probability of relapse into civil war if left unchecked (UN Department of Peacekeeping Operations 2008, p. 22). This is the finding on which it has hinged the development of multidimensional peacekeeping. The AU and ECOWAS have adopted a similar approach in developing their capacities for conflict management. As both organisations develop their intervention mechanisms, the African Standby Force (ASF) and its ECOWAS counterpart, several opportunities abound especially in the civilian dimension. In what follows, we consider matters arising from Nigeria's role in PSO over the years.

PSO in Nigeria's Strategic Matrix

A subject of popular discourse is that of Nigeria's gains and losses in PSO. Bamalli's view is that the Nigerian Armed Forces are the better for the exposure gained in PSO; it has brought "immense improvement in the training, exposure and education of the Nigeria Armed Forces . . . [and] collectively enhanced the profile of the . . . nation as a whole" (2009, p. 253). On the other hand, there are those who argue that the practice of the military profession is watered down by the regular involvement of Nigerian troops in peacekeeping. One source (a serving senior military officer in Defence Headquarters) explains that regular combatant soldiers learn how to defend themselves offensively and defensively and avoid such losses as were suffered in Liberia and Sudan, for example (Interview with Senior Military Officer [Maj-Gen], March 2010, Defence Headquarters, Abuja).

In peacekeeping, however, the use of force is based on the rules of engagement allowed for the mandate, and this can only be in self-defence or for the protection of civilians, as the mandate allows (United Nations 2006, 2009). Similarly, Agwai clarifies thus:

> The principles employed in conventional warfare do not apply in PSOs for the obvious reason that in PSOs you have no defined enemy. Although the principles of war may be employed during Peace Enforcement (PE) operations, their application is guided by more stringent rules of engagement (ROE). (2010, p. 6)

General I.D. Pennap, chief of operations at Defence Headquarters, in a telephone interview, explains further that "the persistent and continuous use of soldiers in peacekeeping reduces their effectiveness in combat operations. . . . Peacekeeping generally is a police duty just like internal security operations" (Interview with Major-General I.D. Pennap, April 22, 2010, Abuja, Nigeria). He admits, however, that ongoing retraining of troops to update and bring them up to required standards would mitigate any negative effect.

Nigeria's engagement in ECOMOG has also received vociferous criticism, given the magnitude of resources expended. Although actual financial expenditure in ECOMOG is controversial, former president Olusegun Obasanjo (Oluyemi-Kusa 2007, p. 153) suggests a figure of approximately $US8 billion while Brigadier Gen. I. Sani, director of peacekeeping operations, Army Headquarters, quotes $US10 billion (Sani 2009, p. 8). Nigeria, the backbone of the operation that lasted over a decade, provided "12 combat battalions, an air squadron . . . apart from the loss of lives of officers and soldiers and equipment" (Sani 2009, p. 8). It is estimated that over 800 soldiers lost their lives in that operation and were said to have been brought back and buried in the night "to avoid public outcry and panic" (Malu quoted in Oluyemi-Kusa 2007, p. 153).

Oni argues that the figure of 800 is but one single instance of mass burial, stating further that "existing official but restricted documents on NIGCON [Nigerian contingent] operations in Liberia and Sierra Leone show a gross underestimation of the total picture" (2002, pp. 252–253). Be that as it may, in the assessment of another former head of state, Abdulsalami Abubakar, "Nigeria can claim a fair share of the glory for peace that is enjoyed in Sierra Leone today." He then admits that over 70 percent of ECOWAS troops and 80 percent of funds were provided by Nigeria and that Nigeria "lost economically by this." He nevertheless concludes that "Nigeria has gained a lot . . . [it is] now recognized as a sub-regional superpower and respected in the international community at both AU and the UN" (Abubakar 2009, p. 195). Undertaken in the spirit of "Responsibility to Protect," Nigeria's action also served as a precursor to the development and emergence of this international norm. Malu admits that "without Nigerian involvement and leadership, it is doubtful that the peace could have been achieved" (2009, p. 174).

The gains derivable from peacekeeping are both tangible and intangible. While some accrue directly to the individual peacekeeper, others are systemic and institutional. For example, individual soldiers receive allowances, which contribute to the family's welfare, as well as awards, which are personal. However, Nigerian soldiers allege they have been shortchanged by commanders, as the case of the "Akure 27" illustrates. Twenty-seven soldiers protesting illegal diversion of their allowances were convicted of mutiny in 2009. Officers who served in ECOMOG operations also recount similar experiences. A logistics officer who served in the NIGCON Depot in Liberia in the mid-1990s recounts in an interview (April 22, 2010) that on several occasions rations from home arrived in a condition unfit for human consumption. Soldiers often were forced to stretch their meagre allowances of $150 a month to feed themselves. Oni corroborates this: "It was not an uncommon experience to find acute shortages in the rations meant for troops either as a result of perishable supplies that had gone bad or inadequate supplies" (2002, p. 248).

No doubt the situation has improved considerably, and the economic gains accruable are significant to the extent that soldiers actually lobby to be deployed on missions, particularly UN missions. Since the ECOMOG days, the Nigerian Armed Forces have progressively instituted self-regulating measures to improve the welfare of personnel and conditions under which they are deployed in international engagements. But overall these can hardly compensate for the extraordinary sacrifices the nation continues to make for global peace. Agwai sums it up thus:

> In spite of our long years of participation in peacekeeping, experience has shown that Nigeria has not capitalized on her human and material contributions to the UN. Even though economic considerations have not been the motivation behind Nigeria's contribution . . . nothing stops her from benefitting from such efforts as some countries are known to be doing at the moment. In order to achieve this goal Nigeria has to her ability to take part in Peace Support operations (PSO) both in quality and level of participation. (Agwai, 2010)

In the words of another seasoned Nigerian peacekeeper,

> Nigeria is known for its robust peace keeping capability operations and its preparedness to sacrifice for Africa. We should not continue to partake in peace operations as we have in the past and are still doing without pausing to go into self introspection in order to come up with firm standards, principles or procedures that would guide us in choosing to participate or not [sic] in future PSOs, based on our beliefs, culture, political expediency, our foreign policy thrust and our national and security interests and even our economic standing. (Iliya 2009, p. 2)

The pertinent questions arising from this are: What is the national interest and how is it to be determined? Iliya asks further, "How would the protection of the national interest affect our choice to . . . participate in Peace Support Operations or not?" (Iliya 2009, p. 8). Alli, while agreeing with the imperative of defining a national objective identified as socioeconomic development, however, cautions that it is imperative for the nation to review its approach . . . in such a manner that would not jeopardize the maintenance of global peace and the achievement of the national goal of socio-economic development (2009, p. 23).

He advises further,

> Nigeria should stop any unilateral peacekeeping activity and seek at all times the collective burden-sharing and UN approved and sponsored approach to peace support operations. At the same time Nigeria should ensure that Standby Force arrangements already decided upon by the AU and the ECOWAS are operational and available for deployment for peace support operations. (2009, p. 24)

The complexity of contemporary PSO has opened it to a wider array of actors, institutions, opportunities, and training because PSO is a growth area in the nation's defence and police sectors. The training curricula used in the National Defence College and Nigerian Army Peacekeeping School are based on UN standardised modules and conform to international standards and best practice. Nigerians are slowly becoming accustomed to opportunities available for civilians in PSO, and Nigeria is beginning to contribute to global efforts at knowledge production for use by the PSO industry within the UN system and beyond. These include doctrine development, training standards and manuals, and operational procedures. None of this has happened as a result of deliberate systemic or national effort, though nations that have a well-planned system have received recognition and, beyond that, have gained a seat at the table where the agenda for the ever-burgeoning PSO industry is set.

One glaring area in which Nigeria has failed to maximise the gains of PSO is in the area of logistics, specifically contingent-owned equipment holdings. The UN reimburses contributing countries for providing equipment according to a specified Table of Equipment. According to former UNAMID Force Commander General Agwai:

> If Nigeria has 10 APCs and they stay in Darfur for one month, that is US$ 60,000. Multiplied by one year, you get a total of US$ 720,000 on the 10 APCs [armoured personnel carriers] alone. . . . When it comes to this, you are actually making money. I have evidence to prove that there are countries today that are virtually running their military, particularly the army, based on their investments in the UN. All what you need to do is invest. . . . If a battalion is equipped to meet UN standards, each battalion will fetch you a minimum of US$ 1.2 million a month. But if you don't invest, you cannot get anything. And that is the problem we are having in the third world, particularly in Nigeria. (*Afrique en Ligne* 2009)

General Joseph Owonibi, a former UNMIL force commander, corroborates these points. In an interview (March 24, 2010) he said countries that have well-organised national systems have more to show for their PSO efforts. He cited examples of the largest troop-contributing countries—India, Pakistan, and Bangladesh—as able to deploy within a month if need be, once the necessary groundwork is completed.

With regard to policy and decisionmaking for PSO, the lines of communication are not very clear in Nigeria. There is also lack of coordination and consultation among key agencies involved with PSO, resulting in lack of information and leakages in the decisionmaking process. At independence, foreign policy was the direct responsibility of the prime minister; as the first external relations minister, he was actively engaged with the decisions of the day. When a minister (Jaja Wachuku) was appointed to that portfolio, the prime minister remained personally and closely interested in foreign affairs. The office and person of the prime minister were major players in foreign policy decisionmaking and, more specifically, in the decision to participate in the Congo operation. So also was the Parliament of the day. Nigeria's decision to involve itself in the Congo hinged on the nature and dynamics of the federal system, its pulls and tugs, as manifested in the First Republic. The political parties had views, well publicised, on events unfolding in the Congo and the role of the UN in containing the situation. They also had strong views on the government's handling of the circumstances. We know this because debates were held in the public sphere with events of that time well documented and information accessible.

Over the years the circle of decisionmaking has become smaller and the flow of information has become more restricted, as has the sphere of public discourse. The growing involvement of the military in peacekeeping and the constricting of the policy and decisionmaking space is largely a factor of military rule, though it is yet to change much under civil rule since 1999. Military rule and increasing requirements for security aspects of peacekeeping combined to facilitate Nigeria's increasingly active posture in peacekeeping. An army general, Joseph Garba, was external affairs minister when Nigeria sent a large contingent to Lebanon. At the time of UNMIBH, the Nigeria Police had honed its skills in modern peacekeeping with the Namibian experience, where it acquitted itself well, returning with accolades and international applause. The demand for Nigerian peacekeepers was on the increase, and it was considered a matter of pride to be asked to send troops and/or police. The army, particularly, and later police came to be represented in UN Headquarters, in the

Department of Peacekeeping Operations (DPKO). This made the line of communication between DPKO and troop- and police-contributing countries more direct. The usual process is for a peacekeeping-related request for troops or police to be made to the Ministry of Foreign Affairs (MFA) through Nigeria's Permanent Mission to the UN in New York and sometimes directly from UNDPKO to MFA (depending on the matter at hand). It is then passed onto the Ministry of Defence (MOD), especially where it relates to security requirements. However, a senior government official alleged that Nigeria's representatives in New York have on occasion made commitments without necessarily consulting MOD about the situation on ground. Requests for very senior appointees have also on occasion been made directly from the UN secretary-general to the president. Although this is in the nature of high-level international politics, it further distorts channels of communication down the line.

In terms of coordination, a senior police officer who had worked in the office of the inspector-general of the Nigerian police confirmed that in current practice police authorities make decisions independent of military authorities and vice versa, because each is acting within its area of professional competence and with little, if any, direct political guidance (Interview with Senior Police Officer [Assistant Commissioner of Police], February 2010, Lagos).

The question therefore arises as to how political and strategic guidance for these decisions is derived and how subsequent actions are fed into the foreign policy decisionmaking process. The principle that dictates that an army should not send itself to war applies in peacekeeping. An army does not serve itself but its political authority, and so the decision to deploy military assets to peace operations outside the shores of Nigeria should be subjected to wider consultation among stakeholders, particularly the legislature, whose role in this process is constitutionally defined.

Nigeria's Defence Policy (2006, pp. 21–22) makes provision for peacekeeping, and the Nigeria Police routinely considers peacekeeping part of its operational mandate. If peacekeeping is indeed within the purview of foreign policy, the missing link in this policy area remains the MFA. So far, the ministry's involvement is limited. According to Prof. Bola Akinterinwa, then special assistant to the minister of foreign affairs, the MFA relies on concerned ministries, departments, and agencies to carry on with external relations in their sphere of competence and keep MFA informed of their activities (Interview, March 10, 2010, Abuja, Nigeria). This may be connected with the dearth of specialist officers in the Foreign Service today. However, reporting back is not always done, thereby hampering coordination efforts. The situation continues to rob the country of a coordinated and integrated national system for managing PSO.

The Imperative of a PSO Policy

What is required is a policy that articulates a shared, comprehensive, and strategic vision; addresses the complexity of the global environment and the demands of modern PSOs; determines interests to be served in each operation; and provides a framework for determining which operations to participate in. Moreover, peacekeeping today has grown much more complex than the military and police operations of yesteryears. The civilian and humanitarian dimensions are yet to be taken on board in Nigeria's articulation of possible areas for peacekeeping participation. PSO is today a multifarious industry encompassing high-level politics, extensive financial contributions, economic opportunities, training activities, international discourse, knowledge production, and partnerships spanning many of these areas. Participation is not restricted to field personnel but includes headquarters staff, finances, diplomacy, intelligence, civilian and humanitarian staff, logistics, administration, doctrine, and policy development. A comprehensive policy would encompass these dimensions and more while providing a guide as to what kinds of missions Nigeria would be interested in and why, as well as the nature and extent of its involvement.

The proposed policy would be an instrument for better governance of Nigeria's external relations and make for greater transparency in the way Nigeria's human and material assets are expended in pursuit of global peace and security. It would also be a guide for oversight and serve to institutionalise PSO practise in Nigeria, giving it coherence. The country's contributions should be formally incorporated and given a more focused expression by Nigeria's official voice on the foreign scene, principally the president and key MFA officials. Undoubtedly, the PSO policy would be an overarching *policy within policy*, embedded within the nation's foreign policy as a well-articulated document that would facilitate coordination. Concerned authorities and agencies would then draw on it to develop their own institutional and professional guidelines. To that end, the presidency working closely with ministries of Foreign Affairs, Police Affairs, and Defence should lead the process of participatory policy formulation.

At the operational level it would also be useful to establish a dedicated coordination unit within MFA in which liaison officers from the police and military would serve to assist the flow of information and processing of documents and information across stakeholders. There is a precedent for this in the First Republic during which a military liaison officer served in the then Ministry of External Affairs. Perhaps now more than ever, such a function is required. The National Defence College has played a coordinating role and has been in the forefront of harnessing and galvanising the nation's interests for maximum utilisation of assets for PSO, especially in the area of education and training and contributing to the continuous global discourse. This position should be formalised in the proposed PSO policy. The military and increasingly the police have garnered much experience, expertise, knowledge, and documentation in the area of peacekeeping, which are unmatched by any single agency. Harnessing these in the most realistic manner will greatly benefit Nigeria and Nigerians.

Conclusion

In this era of transition to democracy, Nigerians are increasingly asking what the benefits are of the country's various forays into peacekeeping. They raise this query not because they expect direct personal gain but because they see the country being criticised on the international scene in spite of enormous sacrifices in the promotion of global peace (Alli 2009) and lost opportunities to gain more mileage than it has so far. As Nigeria marks fifty years of independence on October 1, 2010, it is essential that we plan for the next fifty years. In the specific area of peacekeeping, this should begin with a strategic review and assessment of the past and a long hard look at the world and where it is headed as well as where Nigerians want to position themselves in that future. It is likely that Nigeria will continue to engage in international PSOs. What is required is an approach that would maximise the experience and expertise of the past fifty years and ensure they yield tangible results in the pursuit of well-articulated national objectives. In this regard, it is recommended that as a first step the presidency do the following:

- Convene a PSO Committee comprising military and police professionals, civil servants, academics, the media, and other relevant stakeholders to advise on the best options for documenting the last

fifty years of the nation's contributions to global peace and security in the specific area of peacekeeping.
- Institute a standing interagency committee for the purpose of consultation and coordination on PSO matters until the system is able to fashion the appropriate institutional response to PSO.
- Initiate a consultative process for formulating a PSO policy.

Bibliography

Abubakar, A.A., 2009, "Peacekeeping in West Africa: the Nigerian Experience," in G.J. Jonah and I.S. Zabadi, eds., *Peace Support Operations in the New Global Environment: The Nigerian Perspective*, National Defence College, Abuja, Nigeria, pp. 177–195.

Afrique en Ligne, 2009, " 'Nigeria May Review Peacekeeping Operations'— Defence Minister," www.afriquejet.com/news/africa-news/nigeria-may-review-peacekeeping-operations-defence-minister-2009081133232.html, accessed March 23, 2010.

Agwai, M.L., 2010, "Nigeria's Military Capacity for Regional and Global Peace Support Operations," lecture presented to participants of National Defence College Course 18, Abuja, Nigeria, March 30, 2010.

Akintola, A.L., 2007, "The Nigerian Navy in Peace Support Operations since 1960," in A. Ogomudia, ed., *Peace Support Operations, Command and Professionalism: Challenges for the Nigerian Armed Forces in the 21st Century and Beyond*, Gold Press Limited, Ibadan, Nigeria, pp. 68–87.

Akinyemi, B., 1986, *Foreign Policy and Federalism—The Nigerian Experience*, 2d ed., Macmillan Nigeria Publishers Limited, Lagos, Nigeria.

Albert, I.O., 2007, "Epochs and Lessons of Nigeria's Participation in International Peace Support Operations," in A. Ogomudia, ed., *Peace Support Operations, Command and Professionalism: Challenges for the Nigerian Armed Forces in the 21st Century and Beyond*, Gold Press Limited, Ibadan, Nigeria, pp. 164–189.

Alli, W.O., 2009, "Nigeria in Global Peace Support Operations: The Imperative for New Strategic Vision," presented at "Nigeria in Global Peace Support Operations," Nigerian Defence Academy, Kaduna, Nigeria, July 19–23.

Ayuba, B., 2006, *Kalemie: Memoirs of a UN Military Observer in the Democratic Republic of Congo,* Blessed Oresanya Limited, Lagos, Nigeria.

Balewa, Sir Abubakar Tafawa, 1960, "Nigeria at the UN Maiden Speech," www.nigeriaunmission.org/index.php?option=com_content&view=article&id=86&Itemid=78, accessed March 23, 2010.

Bamalli, N. 2009, "Peace Support Operations of the United Nations Mission in Sierra Leone (October 1999–December 2005)," in G.J. Jonah and I.S. Zabadi, eds., *Peace Support Operation in the New Global Environment: The Nigerian Perspective*, National Defence College, Abuja, Nigeria, pp. 231–254.

Bellamy, A.J., Williams, P., and Griffin, S., 2004, *Understanding Peacekeeping*, Polity Press, Cambridge, MA, US.

Chibundu, V.N., 2009, *Foreign Policy with Particular Reference to Nigeria: (1961–2008)*, Spectrum Books Limited, Ibadan, Nigeria, pp. 127–130.

Daily Trust, 2010, "5000 Nigerian Troops Serving in Peacekeeping Missions," http://news.dailytrust.com/index.php?option=com_content&view=article&id=13530:5000-nigerian-troops-serving-in-peacekeeping-missions&catid=1:latest-news&Itemid=119, February 2, accessed April 22, 2010.

Durch, W.J., ed., 1993, *The Evolution of UN Peacekeeping: Case Studies and Comparative Analysis*, Henry Stimson Center/St. Martin's Press, New York, US.

Durch, W.J., with T.C. Berkman, 2006, "Restoring and Maintaining Peace, What We Know So Far," in W.J. Durch, ed., *Twenty First Century Peace Operations*, United States Institute of Peace, Washington, DC, US, pp. 1–48.

Eze, O., 2009, "Nigeria in International Peace Support Operations: Trends and Policy Implications," presented at "Nigeria in Global Peace Support Operations," Nigerian Defence Academy, Kaduna, Nigeria, July 19–23.

Iliya, S., 2009, "Nigeria in Global Peace Support Operations—The Need for a Realistic Policy Framework," presented at "Nigeria in Global Peace Support Operations," Nigerian Defence Academy, Kaduna, Nigeria, July 19–23.

Inamete, U.B., 2001, *Foreign Policy Decision-making in Nigeria*, Rosemont Publishing and Printing Corporation, New Jersey, US.

Jonah, G.J., and Zabadi, I.S., eds., 2009, *Peace Support Operations in the New Global Environment: The Nigerian Perspective*, National Defence College, Abuja, Nigeria.

Malu, S.V.L., 2009, "ECOMOG: A Peacekeeping Operation in Perspective," in G.J. Jonah and I.S. Zabadi, eds., *Peace Support Operations in the New Global Environment: The Nigerian Perspective*, National Defence College, Abuja, Nigeria, pp. 159–175.

Mays, T.M. 2002, *Africa's First Peacekeeping Operation, the OAU in Chad, 1981–1982*, Praeger Publishers, Westport, CT (US) and London.

Mbanefo, A.C.I., 2005, "United Nations and World Peace," presentation to participants of National War College Course 13, Abuja, Nigeria, February 28, p. 14.

Ministry of Defence (Nigeria), 2006, *National Defence Policy*, Abuja, Nigeria.

NPF (Nigeria Police Force), 2009, http://nigeriapolice.org/peacekeeping/67-peacekeeping-section.html written June 21, 2009, accessed March 8, 2009.

Nwolise, O.B.C., 2004, *The Nigeria Police in International Peace-keeping Under the United Nations*, Spectrum Books Limited, Ibadan, Nigeria.

Ogomudia, A., 1997, "International Peace-keeping: The Nigerian Experience," in C.A. Garuba, ed., *International Peace and Security, the Nigerian Contribution*, National War College Press, Abuja, Nigeria, pp. 111–127.

Ogomudia, A., ed., 2007, *Peace Support Operations, Command and Professionalism: Challenges for the Nigerian Armed Forces in the 21st Century and Beyond*, Gold Press Limited, Ibadan, Nigeria.

Okiro, M., 2009, "The Nigeria Police in Peace Support Operations." in G.J. Jonah and I.S. Zabadi, eds., *Peace Support Operations in the New Global*

Environment: The Nigerian Perspective, National Defence College, Abuja, Nigeria, pp. 143–155.

Okoosi-Simbine, A., 2004, "Nigerian Army in United Nations Peace Support Operations in Africa," in J.W.T. Gbor, ed., *The Nigerian Army in Global Security*, Megavons (West Africa) Ltd., for Nigerian Army, Lagos, pp. 125–154.

Oluyemi-Kusa, D., 2007, "Sacrifices of the Nigerian Nation, and Armed Forces in Peace Missions Since 1960," in A. Ogomudia, ed., *Peace Support Operations, Command and Professionalism: Challenges for the Nigerian Armed Forces in the 21st Century and Beyond*, Gold Press Limited, Ibadan, Nigeria, pp. 137–163.

Oni, S.K., ed., 2002, *The Nigerian Army in ECOMOG Operations: Liberia and Sierra Leone*, Sam Bookman Publishers for Nigerian Army Education Corps and School, Ibadan, Nigeria.

Owohunwa, I., 2007, "Nigeria Police in International Peacekeeping Operations," in S.E. Arase and P.O.I. Iheanyi, eds., *Policing Nigeria in the 21st Century*, Spectrum Books Ltd., Ibadan, Nigeria, pp. 287–295.

Panel on United Nations Peace Operations, 2000, *Brahimi Report*, A55/305–S/2000/809, United Nations, New York.

Rikhye, I.J., 1993, *Military Adviser to the Secretary General, UN Peacekeeping and the Congo Crisis*, Hurst and St. Martin's/International Peace Academy, London and New York.

Sanda, J.G., 2009, "Peace Support Operations (PSO) Training and Research at the National Defence College, Nigeria," in G.J. Jonah and I.S. Zabadi, eds., *Peace Support Operations in the New Global Environment: The Nigerian Perspective*, National Defence College, Abuja, Nigeria, pp. 255–274.

Sani, I., 2009, "Nigeria Army Contributions and Achievements in Support of Peace and Global Security," unpublished.

Uhomoibhi, M.I., 2008, "A Triple Web of Interdependence: The UN, the Commonwealth and the EU," in A. Adebajo and A.R. Mustapha, eds., *Gulliver's Troubles: Nigeria's Foreign Policy after the Cold War*, University of Kwazulu Natal Press, Scottsville, South Africa.

UN Department of Peacekeeping Operations, 2008, *Peacekeeping Operations: Principles and Guidelines* (Capstone Doctrine), Department of Field Services. United Nations, New York.

United Nations, 2006, Security Council Resolution S/RES/1674, www.r2 pasiapacific.org/documents/UN1674.pdf, accessed April 21, 2010.

United Nations, 2009, Report of the Security Council on the Protection of Civilians in Armed Conflict, S/2009/277, New York, http://caccessddsny.un.org/doc/undoc/gen/no9/343/97/pdf/no934397.pdf, accessed 22 April 2010.

Vogt, M.A., ed., 1992, *The Liberian Crisis and ECOMOG: A Bold Attempt at Regional Peacekeeping*, Gabumo Publishing Co. Ltd., Lagos, Nigeria.

Zabadi, I.S., 1997, "The Expanding Nigerian Role in Africa's Peace and Security," in C.A. Garuba, ed., *International Peace and Security, the Nigerian Contribution*, National War College Press, Abuja, Nigeria.

6

Nigeria's Role in Peacekeeping in Africa: ECOMOG, Chad, Liberia, and Sierra Leone

Andrew Okolie

This chapter focuses on Nigeria's role in regional peacekeeping, peacemaking, and peace enforcement. This is distinct from its global participation in UN peacekeeping operations discussed in Chapter 5. Peacekeeping and peacemaking around the world, especially on the African continent, are areas in which Nigeria is justified in taking pride. Nigeria's peacekeeping and peacemaking role in Africa has a long history dating back to the early 1960s when Nigerian troops and police were deployed in the Congo during the country's political crisis, sadly culminating in the assassination of Patrice Lumumba and the assumption of power by Mobutu Sese Sekou. Since then, Nigeria has sent peacekeepers to Lebanon, Liberia, Sierra Leone, Bosnia-Herzegovina, Somalia, Sudan, and Rwanda. Although there have been sporadic reports of problems, they have not been significant enough to lead to an abrupt end of Nigeria's peacekeeping operations anywhere.

Nigeria's involvement in peacekeeping, especially in Africa, is a logical policy corollary to the commitment of its leaders to African independence from colonialism and foreign domination, its sense of itself as the regional power with a determination to keep other nations from exercising strong influence in what it considers its sphere of influence, and, above all, its consideration of what constitutes its national (especially national security) interest. This may explain why Nigeria's commitment to peacekeeping in Africa has hardly wavered even during severe economic and political strains under varying administrations. Even when the Nigerian government was most isolated diplomatically by the international community in the 1990s, peacekeeping remained a vital link to the world.

Nigeria's peacekeeping record on the continent includes operations in Chad, Liberia, Sierra Leone, Somalia, and Sudan. This chapter, however, concentrates on Nigeria's role in peace support operations in Chad, Liberia, and Sierra Leone—peacekeeping/peacemaking/peace enforcement operations in which Nigeria was the prime mover or initiator and closely tied to its position as a preeminent power in Africa, especially in the West Africa subregion. These operations forcefully define Nigeria's image as a major contributor to global security and clearly mark its contributions in that regard. They also demonstrate the challenges and limits of Nigeria's peacekeeping capabilities as well as embody important lessons for Nigeria and the African and global communities.

Chad

Peacekeeping in Chad resulted from the political crisis that followed the country's independence, culminating in a coup d'état in 1975 (believed to have had French support) during which the country's first president, Francois (later Ngarta) Tombalbaye, was assassinated. Nigeria was uncomfortable with what it considered the meddling of France and Libya in Chad, its neighbour to the northeast, and was motivated by the desire to thwart attempts by foreign powers to exercise influence in what Nigeria considered its natural sphere of influence.

After the assassination of Tombalbaye, his successor Felix Malloum faced a Libya-sponsored civil war throughout his tenure in office from 1975 to 1979, and, in 1977, Libya seized a piece of Chadian territory, the Aozou Strip. In 1979, rebel forces attacking from the north, with Libyan backing, brought down the Malloum regime. However, as there was no cohesive regime to replace it, given the factionalization of the opposing forces, a Nigerian force of approximately 800 soldiers intervened to restore order. The intervention sent a strong message about Nigeria's readiness to intervene in the region when it deems a conflict has the potential to either produce a humanitarian disaster or affect its national interests.

Nigeria's peacekeeping deployment followed efforts to reconcile rival Chadian factions that were attacking each other. Its offer to mediate in the crisis led to two summits in Kano, Nigeria, between March and April 1979; the unilateral formation of a Union Government in Chad on April 29, 1979, by some of the factions; a conference in Lagos, Nigeria, in May 1979, which the Union Government shunned; and another conference in Lagos in August of the same year (Yar'Adua 1979). The second

Lagos conference produced a Transitional Government of National Unity with Goukouni Oueddei as president, Abdulkader Kamogue as vice president, and Hissen Habre as defence minister. Delegates also agreed to the withdrawal of French troops and their replacement by an African force (James 1993, p. 140). In 1980, the crisis worsened as Libya sent troops to support Oueddei, who was being challenged by Habre, himself backed by the French, whom Libya saw as a major threat to its interests. In March 1980, Habre seized the capital, N'Djamena.

Nigeria commenced peacekeeping operations in Chad in 1979 but was outmanoeuvred by the French and their client, Habre, with the United States supporting them from the sidelines. Nigerian peacekeepers returned in 1982, however, as the dominant component of the Organization of African Unity (OAU) peacekeeping presence in Chad in the wake of a so-called agreement by Libya and Chad to merge, a ploy by Libya's Qaddafi to maintain influence in the country (Kingibe 2009; James 1993, p. 140).

Nigeria's intervention was motivated by the desire to prevent the influx of refugees into the country through its northeast border with Chad, as well as its determination not to allow a hostile government in Chad, as relations had been strained from clashes over Lake Chad. The Lake Chad Basin supports the livelihood of many Nigerian communities, and both countries planned to explore for oil there (James 1993). Nigeria was also interested in halting what it considered Libyan expansionism and limiting what it saw as French meddling in the West African region, having perceived France as its main rival in the contest for influence in the subregion. However, France and Nigeria, as well as the United States, were worried about Gaddafi's radicalism and had a common interest in curtailing Libyan expansion. Shehu Musa Yar'Adua, chief of staff in Olusegun Obasanjo's military government, headed Nigeria's mediation efforts in the conflict, and summed up Nigeria's position as follows:

> The Chadian conflict contains all the germs of the disease of instability which . . . threaten every one of us. Chad has an unhappy colonial past and has since independence been bedevilled by divisions along tribal, religious and ideological lines . . . it is the primary responsibility of Chadians to solve their own problems . . . but we also feel our obligation to find an African solution to an African problem. (Farris and Bomoi, 2004, p. 142)

The Chadian operation was the first case of subregional peacekeeping by Nigeria in which it was the initiator of the operation and deployed troops and personnel to carry it out. The intervention also exposed Nigeria's limitations. By many accounts, it was a disastrous experience for Nigeria as its inexperience in the geopolitics of the Cold War and its diplomatic and operational inadequacies became glaringly manifest (Berman and Sams 2000; Adisa 1996; Aguda 1996; Ndiaye 1996; Imobighe 1996). The lessons learnt helped to guide subsequent peace support operations in the West African subregion.

Ambassador Baba Gana Kingibe, a former career diplomat, and former Nigerian ambassador to Greece and Pakistan, explained that when Nigeria discovered that it could not operate from N'Djamena, due to the hostility of the government there, it approached the United States for logistical support. But the United States appeared reluctant and continued to stall while Habre consolidated his hold on power. Apparently, Nigeria did not understand that US interests were different from its own. The United States was more concerned with Libyan expansionism and therefore seemed more comfortable with Habre in power (Kingibe 2009). And Nigeria became further involved in an unwinnable situation with no clear exit strategy. In fact, one of the important lessons of the Chadian experience was the need not to go it alone in the subregion while being more sensitive to linguistic as well as colonial and geopolitical divides in West Africa. According to Kingibe (2009), this notwithstanding, the intervention announced Nigeria's arrival on the regional peacekeeping stage. The sight of Nigerian military planes, piloted by Nigerians, landing in Chad with troops and equipment sent a powerful message to the French and others in the international community that Nigeria was determined to be a key player in conflict management and stabilizing efforts in the subregion, and would strive to protect its national interests.

ECOMOG: Liberia and Sierra Leone

While Nigeria's initial peacekeeping intervention in Chad was largely unilateral, its interventions in Liberia and Sierra Leone through the Economic Community of West African States Monitoring Group (ECOMOG) were multilateral, as Nigeria worked with other member states of the Economic Community of West African States (ECOWAS) to form a collective response to the security and humanitarian challenges posed by conflicts in those countries. It was the first such action by a subregional organisation in Africa, relying principally on its own personnel, money, and military materials to manage three conflicts in West Africa: Liberia, Sierra Leone, and Guinea-Bissau between 1990 and 1998 (Adebajo

2002, p. 1). The declared objective included the establishment of an interim government in Liberia, which would exclude all warring parties, and the supervision of elections that would produce a popularly elected government in Liberia (Aguda 1996; Essuman-Johnson 2009).

Later the ECOMOG mandate changed from peacekeeping to peace enforcement and included a mandate to:

- Disarm and demobilize the various warring factions
- Conduct and observe elections
- Rehabilitate and reintegrate soldiers into local communities
- Restructure and reform security forces
- Oversee transitional civilian authorities (Adebajo 2002; Turk 2000; Olowo-Ake 1996)

Background to the ECOMOG Interventions

On April 12, 1980, a group of noncommissioned officers of the Liberian Armed Forces, led by Master-Sergeant Samuel Doe, staged a military coup that overthrew the Liberian government and assassinated President William Tolbert. The coup appeared to be a reaction to the political dominance and marginalisation of indigenous Liberians by the Americo-Liberian elite, rising social discontent, and political repression both in the military (such as poor housing conditions) and in the broader Liberian society. Social discontent culminated in the riots of April 14, 1979, protesting an increase in the price of rice (Johnson 1996; Vogt 1993; Hutchful 1999; Essuman-Johnson 2009). The coup, at least temporarily, brought to an end the political dominance of the Americo-Liberians, which began with the founding of the country by former US slaves in 1847.

Doe, who became president following the coup, soon imposed a reign of terror on Liberians, especially those in the opposition, resulting in an insurgency by the National Patriotic Front of Liberia (NPFL) led by Charles Taylor. Said to be supported by Libya, Ivory Coast served as the launching pad for Taylor's forces while training took place in Burkina Faso. This would have implications for attempts at a peaceful settlement as those countries resisted ECOMOG intervention (James 1993; Johnson 1996). The rebels recorded quick military successes and posed a real possibility of capturing Monrovia, the capital, when ECOMOG intervened. As a result, Taylor regarded ECOMOG as an enemy during much of the Liberian conflict.

The ECOMOG intervention followed several failed mediation attempts in the crisis by Nigeria and other members of ECOWAS. Taylor remained adamant and intransigent, refusing to attend or participate in peace initiatives and ignoring agreements that were reached, including reneging on his own commitments. Despite controlling two-thirds of the country, he could not win militarily because of ECOMOG (MacQueen 2002, p. 174). Other factions were to emerge, as benefits began to accrue to Taylor as a result of his military victories, including recognition as a major player and control of economic resources in the areas under his troops' control. The proliferation of factions further complicated and undermined the peace effort.

The Liberian conflict appears to have been an important factor leading to the conflict in Sierra Leone, which saw ECOMOG intervening. The monopolisation of political power by a one-party state, political repression, and rising social discontent ultimately led to a military coup by Captain Valentine Strasser that overthrew the government of Joseph Momoh in April 1992.

By the 1980s, illegal and unofficial mining had led to significant declines in government revenue for the ineffective, corrupt, and central one-party regime led by President Siaka Stevens, who handed over power to General Momoh. By 1995, the country's infrastructure and key institutions had virtually collapsed.

The Sierra Leonean war, which erupted in 1991, occurred for two related reasons: the control of diamond mining and an attempt by Taylor to undermine ECOMOG in neighbouring Liberia. The war was started by a group called the Revolutionary United Front (RUF), founded by an ex-soldier, Foday Sankoh, and radical ex-student leaders and lecturers who were thrown out of the universities in the 1980s after a series of protest actions. It also included Liberians and Burkinabes, who received training in Libya. Initially the insurrection was popular, as it articulated grievances of the masses. But internal squabbles led to the elimination of intellectual leaders such as Abuh Kanu and Rashid Mansaray, resulting in Sankoh becoming the undisputed leader.

When Strasser led a group of soldiers who stormed the State House in 1992 demanding unpaid wages, Momoh panicked and fled. Strasser seized power and proceeded to recruit street kids and criminals into the army, raising the size from 3,000 to 10,000. He also contracted foreign mercenaries to help push back rebels already controlling vast areas of diamond-rich territory who were marching on Freetown, the capital. Strasser's successor, Ahmad Tejan Kabbah, involved other mercenary outfits, which fought alongside ECOMOG to restore peace in Sierra Leone.

ECOMOG'S Challenges

ECOMOG interventions were difficult indeed. The group was designed to monitor (and perhaps bring to an end) numerous post–Cold War conflicts that were particularly brutal and protracted. While Cold War insurgencies had clear ideological undertones or political agendas, these post–Cold War conflicts had none, other than capturing power and economic resources. Due to the complexity of their interests and support networks, the conflicts also often resisted external pressure. For instance, when ECOMOG intervened in 1990, the Liberian state had virtually collapsed; warring factions were splintering and proliferating; and the most powerful faction, Taylor's NPFL, opposed ECOMOG's intervention, condemning it as a Nigeria-led attempt to deny it the political fruits of its military labour. Taylor kept his promise to attack ECOMOG troops when they landed in Liberia.

The missions severely tasked Nigeria's diplomatic, logistical, and military strength and capacities. There were legitimacy questions, linguistic and geopolitical divisions and rivalries, and operational challenges. In economic terms the timing of the interventions were inauspicious. From the beginning, it was questionable as to whether ECOMOG had the mandate and legitimacy to intervene, given that ECOWAS was merely an economic grouping. Mutual security protocols that would have allowed ECOWAS to anticipate crises had not been implemented. Linguistic and geopolitical problems in the area further compounded matters. The francophone countries, with loyalty towards France, saw Nigeria as trying to impose its will (James 1996; Essuman-Johnson 2009; Hutchful 1999; Adebajo 2002). France continued efforts to undermine and displace Nigeria as the subregional power, while Libyan efforts to exercise influence in the region were opposed by Nigeria and the West.

At some periods in the Liberian and Sierra Leone conflicts, Ivory Coast, Burkina Faso, Ghana, and Nigeria were accused of taking sides rather than remaining impartial or neutral mediators. Therefore, the closeness of regional actors to the conflict societies, while providing the advantage of depth of knowledge of issues and locales, also posed serious challenges. The perception that they were too interested in the outcomes required international intervention to resolve the conflict (Hutchful 1999; Dorn 1998; Adebajo 2002; Vogt 1996; Adisa 1996; Johnson 1996).

With regard to economic resources to prosecute intervention, the subregion and the rest of Africa (indeed the entire Third World) were reeling in economic crises and structural adjustment imposed by multilateral financial institutions in response to the international debt crisis. Most countries in the subregion could not afford the cost of peacekeeping operations, which left Nigeria, itself in severe economic crisis, to shoulder much of the burden. As a result, Nigeria was the main contributor of personnel and equipment and the driving military and diplomatic force behind ECOMOG. The force began with 3,500 troops in August 1990, and, by mid-January 1993, troop strength had reached 16,000, of which 12,000 (75 percent) were Nigerians. Nigeria also provided 90 percent of funding for ECOMOG during much of the war in Liberia from 1990 to 1994 (Adebajo 2002, pp. 48 and 55; Vogt 1996, p. 307).

Military challenges included obsolete equipment and poor logistics, training, and interoperability, made worse by language differences. The field force was virtually independent of the political directorate (ECOWAS), making political control of troops and commanders difficult. And ECOMOG had no reliable allies for peace, including the factions and their sponsors/sympathisers. Agreements were made and broken with ease, resulting in a stalemate that led to the invitation of the OAU and UN, which then brought legitimacy, impartiality, and international pressure that helped end the conflicts.

There were other challenges. For example, the ECOMOG troops, including Nigerian units, did not have adequate doctrine (i.e., training inclusive of equipment that an army or force requires to fight the next war or conduct the next operation). The Liberian operation also exposed inadequacies of battlefield necessities, such as maps, intelligence, and communications equipment (Aboagye 1999; Interview with Hassan Mamman Lai, March 11, 2010).

The capture and killing of Doe and his guards at ECOMOG headquarters on September 9, 1990, as well as negative media reports of ECOMOG looting and illegal trade, dampened troop morale. The killing of Doe raised serious unresolved questions about ECOMOG neutrality and possible complicity. So did changing political fortunes in Sierra Leone. For instance, the Sierra Leonean contingent to ECOMOG was supportive of Strasser's coup (for promising to end the conflict in Sierra Leone and continuing with ECOMOG participation) and openly demonstrated that support, to the embarrassment of the Nigerian contingent. But it did not have the same enthusiasm for President Kabbah, who replaced Strasser in March 1996, and it openly supported Major Johnny Paul Koromah's coup of May 1997. The divergence of interests between Sierra Leonean and Nigerian troops dampened the morale of the entire force (Aboagye 1999, p. 161).

Poor accommodation, poor feeding (with soldiers individually buying and cooking their own meals), poor transport, and corruption (including soldiers using ECOMOG vehicles for private commercial transport) were other critical issues that undermined the mission (Aboagye 1999, pp. 162–166). A senior Nigerian diplomat who served in Liberia during part of the ECOMOG operation said that ECOMOG had been supplied with motorcycle helmets rather than military steel helmets and also with rotten tomatoes, rotten fish, and sand-filled garri (cassava flour) because of corruption in the procurement process. In his words, "ECOMOG operations have been presented as a huge success story, but there were too many scandals involving contractors and commanders" (Interview, March 24, 2010). According to Stephen Ellis (2006), one of the most egregious examples of corruption by ECOMOG in Liberia was the total removal of the Buchanan iron ore processing machinery for onward sale while the Buchanan compound was under ECOMOG control.

Nigeria has long been ridiculed in UN peacekeeping operations for ill-equipping its troops. In addition, salaries and allowances have not been promptly paid. In January 2008, the UN threatened to deactivate the two Nigerian Contingent (NIGCON) battalions serving in the UN Mission in Liberia (UNMIL) on account of inadequate equipment, which resulted from Nigeria's failure to implement the memorandum of understanding (MoU), which it signed before deploying the troops. The UNMIL headquarters had called the inadequacy of logistics of Nigerian troops a "disappointment," adding that the country had "failed to meet UN-Nigeria MoU on equipping its troops with the right calibre of military and peace-keeping equipment" (Taiwo 2009). In fact, Nigeria was reported to have been losing US$1.2 million monthly for deploying a battalion that was equipped below UN standards for peacekeeping. For example, an armoured personnel carrier earns a country US$6,000 per month if equipped to UN standards. The chief of training and operations, Defence Headquarters, Major General Ishaku Pennap, acknowledged to a reporter that "We also discovered that before now, our troops were deployed without First-Aid kits. We are now deploying each peacekeeper with the First-Aid kits" (Taiwo 2009).

There were other problems. Nigeria did not deploy a full complement of forces, and troops were often inadequately prepared for deployment. Staffing was also poor. For instance, rather than the UN standard battalion ratio of 800/25 (i.e., 800 troops to 25 officers), Nigeria's ratio was often 200/5 or 500/10. One of the troop commanders in both Liberia and Sierra Leone reported that he received only a twenty-four-hour notice to lead troops to Liberia. "I was writing soldiers' names in the aircraft after we had departed," he said (Interview, April 2, 2010). This is contrary to the minimum of six months' training required for troop buildup (combining different categories of troops: combat, medical, engineering, carpenters, masons, etc.), concentration, briefing, mission statements, rules of engagement, international passports, vaccination cards, physical checks, and next-of-kin arrangements, including payments. He also disclosed that, rather than being based on merit, troop and commander selections were sometimes influenced by nepotism (with soldiers producing notes from senior officers and prominent Nigerians asking that they be included in the missions). One consequence was that many Nigerian soldiers died because of commanders' carelessness. For example, both the commander and a retired senior diplomat who worked at the Nigerian mission in Liberia at the time confirmed that many Nigerian soldiers died at Tubmanburg because they were participating in illegal diamond mining (Interview, April 2, 2010).

Despite these shortcomings, Nigeria's participation and leadership of ECOMOG was on the whole extremely beneficial to conflict-ridden countries and the subregion and is acknowledged as an important contribution to addressing global concerns of peace and security.

Reasons for Success

The ECOMOG interventions were largely successful due mainly to the political will and doggedness of ECOWAS members, particularly Nigeria. For humanitarian and self-interest reasons, the regional body could not abandon the campaign midstream. Second, the interventions combined three phases of conflict resolution: peacekeeping, peacemaking, and peace enforcement, altering the mandate of field forces as developments on the ground dictated. In Liberia, for instance, ECOMOG operations, in relation to carrying out the group's mandate, were largely informed by response to the security situation on the ground. Where it encountered violence against its troops (e.g., when its troops were attacked on landing) or opposition to ECOWAS decisions, it engaged in peace enforcement. Otherwise it followed traditional peacekeeping principles such as fairness, firmness, neutrality, mediation, and negotiation (Aboagye 1999, p. 158; Vogt 1993). ECOMOG found it expedient to enter into alliance with factions in the Liberian conflict, such as the Independent National Patriotic Front of Liberia and the

Armed Forces of Liberia, but it later disarmed the former when the situation warranted. This flexibility derived from the decoupling of the military from the political directorate.

Nigeria's dominance and determination to succeed helped to make possible the disengagement of the military from diplomatic operations. While this weakened political control of the troops, it made military operations more cohesive and decisive than the fractious politics of ECOWAS allowed. The ability to sustain the Nigeria-led military pressure was critical in ending the Liberian conflict and minimizing humanitarian costs.

Ironically, the authoritarian hold that the key ECOMOG governments (Nigeria and Ghana) had on their populations helped them to sustain ECOMOG military operations. In fact, when the Banjul Accord (with the demand for free and fair elections as a component) paved the way for ECOMOG intervention in 1990, key ECOMOG countries such as Ghana and Nigeria were under military rulers who were resisting the demand for elections by their own civil societies. As Eboe Hutchful (1999, p. 12) explains:

> The ability of the ECOMOG countries, and Nigeria in particular, to sustain the almost indefinite support of the force in a period of critical economic and fiscal difficulty at home, could only be explained in terms of the existence of authoritarian political structures, which did not permit any political debate on, oversight of or accountability towards these actions.

But this authoritarian hold also ensured that human security, in the sense of human and political rights, was undermined in the conflict societies. Their military character partly explains why ECOMOG remained primarily a military venture with little of the accompanying civilian activities that have become associated with peacekeeping, including policing, human rights monitoring, humanitarian activities, and the establishment of administrative structures in liberated areas. It is also possible that the financial drain of ECOMOG interventions may have worsened social discontent in leading countries such as Nigeria and led to more pressure by civil society for military rulers to relinquish power. Thus, while the political processes in Nigeria helped to shape ECOMOG interventions, peacekeeping also helped to shape political processes in Nigeria (Hutchful 1999, p. 3). The irony was not lost on Nigerian civil society when Nigeria's military rulers claimed to promote democracy in the subregion while obstructing it at home. This contradiction motivated civil society activists to argue that military rulers in Nigeria might produce a domestic version of the Liberia or Sierra Leone crisis.

Benefits of ECOMOG/Nigeria's Leadership

The ECOMOG intervention helped to save lives and restore democracy in Liberia (1995) and Sierra Leone (1998). Ports, power stations, communication facilities, roads, and bridges were revitalized in the two countries, paving the way for stabilisation in the subregion and mobilisation of international donor support for the war-torn countries (Adebajo 2002). Much credit goes to Nigeria. Thirty thousand refugees were repatriated in addition to thousands more who found refuge and protection in the areas under ECOMOG control (Aboagye 1999, p. 210).

Nigeria's diplomatic contributions were equally significant. A key long-term achievement of ECOMOG under Nigeria's leadership was the region's consensus on matters of regional security. In the past, ECOWAS paid lip service to regional security, and the 1981 treaty was never implemented. Indeed, member states had heretofore displayed cynical disregard for regional security, as seen in the way francophone countries aided the invasion of Liberia and deliberately frustrated peace initiatives (Hutchful 1999, p. 15; Vogt 1993 and 1996; Aminu 1996).

Nigeria also helped to expand the concept of peace support operations in a manner that weakened the principle of noninterference in the internal affairs of member states, a principle behind which leaders have historically hidden while perpetrating acts of internal repression that might threaten the entire region. When, on May 25, 1997, a military coup overthrew the newly installed democratic government in Sierra Leone, Nigeria reacted by using its Navy to bombard Freetown and followed up a year later with an invasion. The coup plotters were removed by force, and Nigeria was accused of interfering in the internal affairs of a member state of ECOWAS. Critics claimed that the situation that prompted the intervention was materially different from the armed insurrection by RUF. Then ECOWAS Secretary-general Abass Bundu, who had supported intervention in Liberia, now argued against the Nigerian intervention in Sierra Leone (Hutchful 1999, p. 15). Ghana also did not appear to be favourably disposed to Nigeria's intervention; it sent troops but claimed they were only meant to evacuate Ghanaian citizens.

ECOWAS countries unanimously agreed that the coup was unacceptable and should not stand. Fears were again raised about Nigeria's unilateralism. But the unanimity in rejecting the coup indicated an expansion of the concept of regional security and what might justify intervention. The issues thrown up by this, as well as the civil war in Guinea-Bissau in which ECOMOG did not commit troops (Senegal and Guinea did), were dealt with in December 1998 at the Fourth Extraordinary Summit of the

ECOWAS Heads of State and Government held in Lome, Togo. The summit approved the establishment of a subregional mechanism for conflict prevention, management and resolution, and subregional security. A July 1998 meeting of experts in Banjul, Gambia, drafted a set of proposals for such a mechanism for approval by the Heads of State meeting in Ouagadougou, Burkina Faso, in October. Among the proposals were that "though the organization [ECOWAS] was established for the primary purpose of economic integration of the region, economic development can only be effectively pursued in a secure and stable environment" (Hutchful 1999, p. 16). Also, while the provisions for intervention would not extend to "internal situations that are sustained and maintained from within," it would apply to situations in which an internally driven conflict threatens to generate a humanitarian disaster, pose a serious threat to peace and security in the subregion, or erupted "following the overthrow or attempted overthrow of a democratically-elected government" (Hutchful 1999, p. 16). Clearly, the member states of ECOWAS had realized that conflict was not helpful and that internal anarchy could lead to regional political instability as a result of Nigeria's initiatives and diplomacy.

In December 2009, the ECOWAS Chiefs of Defence Staff meeting in Freetown approved the ECOWAS Standby Force (ESF) brigade structure and composition. This, according to ECOWAS, would boost the commission's participation as a major stakeholder in the African Union (AU) exercise designed to test the operational readiness of the African Standby Force (ASF), comprising the standby forces of the continent's Regional Economic Communities. According to Hassan Mamman Lai, a brigadier general and ESF chief of staff, the ECOMOG model was essentially copied for the ASF and ESF. The 1999 ECOWAS Mechanism for Conflict Prevention, Management and Resolution formed the basis for the AU continental equivalent, resulting in regional arrangements for the standby force by the various regional economic groupings (Interview, with Lai, March 11, 2010).

The 6,500-strong ESF includes a Main Brigade and a Task Force, which can deploy in fourteen days instead of the thirty days previously planned in conformity with AU standards. A provisional approval to the Main Brigade structure and composition was earlier given at the June 2009 meeting in Ouagadougou. Defence chiefs also agreed to consider, at their next meeting, details on the operations of the Committee of Chiefs of Security Services, including police, gendarmerie, customs, and immigration services (*Leadership* 2009, p. 16).

Nigeria's experience with ECOMOG and other peacekeeping operations encouraged it to work hard at the continental level to provide impetus to the establishment of the ASF but also the African Union Non-Aggression and Common Defence Pact. The operating mechanism of the latter came into force in January 2010 with a treaty adopted during the Fourth Ordinary Session of the Assembly of Heads of State and Government of the AU held in Abuja, Nigeria, in January 2005. According to AU Commission Chairperson Jean Ping, it was expected to provide "more speedy attention and stronger deterrent signals" to the numerous conflict situations in Africa (Obayuwana 2010).

In making these contributions to ECOMOG interventions, Nigeria has incurred enormous costs. Due to lack of transparency, it is difficult to state with any degree of certainty the financial cost. Estimates have ranged from $US8 billion to $US12 billion (Oluyemi-Kusa 2007; Atoyebi 2007). Although some of the cost came back to Nigeria in terms of ECOMOG contracts, it still represented a huge sacrifice during severe budgetary constraints at home resulting from the collapse of oil prices.

An unfortunate consequence of employing ECOMOG veterans to pacify Niger Delta militants who had taken up arms to fight for a greater share of oil revenues from the region is that many of those light arms are believed to have come from ECOMOG operations (Hutchful 1999, p. 14).

Peacekeeping may also have helped prolong military rule in Nigeria by moderating pressure from the international community for political liberalisation in the country. The ECOMOG mission, for instance, helped Nigeria's military rulers ward off the threat of more severe international sanctions against their regimes. While some sanctions were imposed, Nigeria still sold oil to its traditional customers; regime officials continued to travel around the world, and their assets were never frozen. By demonstrating their indispensability in peacekeeping in a region that the West was retrenching from militarily, the regimes were able to avoid complete diplomatic isolation (Adebajo 2002). Peacekeeping also helped Nigeria to establish itself as the hegemonic power in the subregion.

Reasons for Nigeria's Participation in Peace Support Operations in Africa

A set of reasons explains each case of Nigeria's participation in peacekeeping in Africa. Some have adduced the personal interest of Nigeria's rulers, while Nigerian leaders point to national interest, humanitarian considerations, and regional stability as reasons for intervention. For example President Ibrahim Babangida had this to say:

[In] a sub-region of 16 countries where one out of three West Africans is a Nigerian, it is imperative that any regime in this country should relentlessly strive towards the prevention or avoidance of the deterioration of any crisis which threatens to jeopardise or compromise the stability, prosperity and security of the sub-region. . . . We believe that if [a crisis is] of such level that has the potentials to threaten the stability, peace and security of the sub-region, Nigeria, in collaboration with others in this sub-region, is duty-bound to react or respond in appropriate manner necessary to . . . ensure peace, tranquillity and harmony. (Babangida 1990)

Certainly Nigeria's interventions through ECOMOG cannot be said to have been solely motivated by the pursuit of national interest. Perhaps this partly explains the lack of followup or "peace dividends" some critics say Nigeria never realizes.

National interest alone cannot explain the shift from the government's opposition to Samuel Doe in the pre-Babangida period to its support for Doe during the Babangida regime. It does not explain why Taylor was prevented from taking Monrovia only to later promote a settlement that put him in power years later, thus prolonging the conflict. The personal interest of rulers, such as Babangida's (and Ghanian President Rawlings's) friendship with Doe, was also important. Doe, in fact, visited Nigeria and personally appealed to Babangida to intervene to save his regime. He may also have received a planeload of arms apparently delivered by Brigadier General David Mark (Vogt 1993; Hutchful 1999; Aguda 1996). A retired senior Nigerian diplomat indicated that the position of Nigeria's foreign ministry at the time was that the country had no business intervening in Liberia and that Nigeria lacked credibility in trying to prevent someone from seizing power with force. "In fact, a good number of Ministry staff took leaves of absence at the time hoping that the Liberian crisis would be over by the time they returned," because they did not want to be posted there (Interview, April 2, 2010).

Apart from personal motives, economic motives have also been identified as reasons for Nigeria's intervention. These included an agreement to exploit the Bong iron ore mine in Liberia to feed Nigeria's Ajaokuta steel mill, which would have been jeopardised in the event of Doe's removal. According to this view, ECOMOG was used as a multilateral veneer for what were clearly Nigeria's unilateral objectives. Nigeria's leaders, however, defended their participation on the grounds of consistency with a national peacekeeping tradition and humanitarian grounds of saving lives.

Although both partially true, reasons for Nigeria's participation are more complex than either position allows. These may be broken down into two broad categories: objective and subjective conditions. It is important to note that factors that may not have influenced the decision to intervene or participate may have played a role in sustaining or prolonging the participation. The objective conditions include Nigeria's size, population (a fifth of Africa's population), resources (richest in the subregion), the size of its military (the largest in Africa), and colonial experience (which makes it wary of allowing external powers free rein in the subregion). As for the subjective condition, in a world dominated by a handful of global powers, projecting regional power status was more feasible for Nigeria than claiming world power status or projecting global power.

Another subjective reason was the Nigerian government's fear of the so-called domino effect—that is, destabilisation spreading from hot spots to other countries in the subregion, thereby threatening regimes, including Nigeria. Nigerian military leaders have historically inveighed against coups in the region by radical junior military officers. Thus when Jerry Rawlings, a flight lieutenant, overthrew a regime of senior military officers in Ghana and executed many, the Obasanjo government cut off oil supplies to Ghana in order to put pressure on the Rawlings regime. Also, when Doe seized power in Liberia, the Shehu Shagari civilian government barred Doe from attending the OAU Heads of State meeting in Lagos and coordinated a move to deny him succession as chairman of the OAU (Vogt 1993, p. 198). Punitive action was again taken against the Rawlings regime when he staged his second coup in 1981. But relations with Doe improved when Babangida came to power in 1985 (Vogt 1993; Hutchful 1999). As Hutchful explains, reactions of Nigerian governments likely derive from "the desire of the ascendant Nigerian bourgeoisie to act as a conservative bulwark of stability in the region [as well as] the anxiety of its military wing to avoid a repetition of the traumatic uprising of their own ranks in July 1966" (1999, p. 7).

Additionally, Taylor's civilian insurgency raised concerns that render Nigeria's intervention in terms of Babangida's friendship with Doe inadequate. The defeat of any official army by civilian insurgents (as in Uganda) would potentially undermine military prestige in the subregion. Babangida reportedly emphasised this element in speeches to his military commanders at the initial stages of the intervention. This seemed to have been particularly frightening, given the rapidity of advances by Taylor's NPFL and Sankoh's RUF in Liberia and Sierra Leone, respectively. The known presence of dissidents from other West African countries in Taylor's army created concerns that Taylor (and his Libyan sponsors) had wider regional interests and that other West African states could follow once Liberia and Sierra Leone fell (Hutchful 1999).

There was also concern over the possible influx of refugees and the pressure it would put on resources as well as its potential destabilising effect (Vogt 1993 and 1996; Aminu 1996; Johnson 1996; Adisa 1996). Babangida stuck to the humanitarian line in his public defence of the mission:

> Nigeria has no territorial ambition in Liberia or anywhere else. We are in Liberia, because events in the country have led to the massive destruction of property, the massacre by all the warring parties of thousands of innocent civilians including those of foreign nations, women and children some of whom had sought sanctuary in the churches, mosques, diplomatic missions, hospitals and under Red Cross protection, contrary to all recognized standard of civilized behaviour and international ethics and decorum. . . . [S]hould Nigeria and other responsible countries in this sub-region stand and watch the whole of Liberia turned into one mass graveyard? (Johnson 1996, p. 290)

Another reason for Nigeria's participation in peace support operations is external pressure, especially from the United States (e.g., Chad, Liberia, and Sierra Leone). Enormous external pressure was brought to bear on Nigeria by Western countries, especially the United States, to send peacekeeping troops as they became increasingly unwilling to send troops to Africa following the humiliation of US troops in Somalia. Currently, in 2010, the United States is mounting pressure on Nigeria to send troops to Somalia where the state has clearly failed and factional fighting has turned the country into a failed state. Although the Nigerian government has publicly said it would commit troops, it is unclear that it is willing to send troops to that chaotic and extremely dangerous situation. This was not helped by US refusal to allow the Islamic Courts Union, which seemed to have the potential to restore peace in Somalia, to assume power when it controlled most of the country's territory, including the capital, Mogadishu. In retrospect, it may have been better to have a government to hold accountable rather than the current chaotic and lawless situation in Somalia.

In addition to the personal interests of Nigeria's rulers and military commanders, evidenced by the personal friendship of Babangida and Doe, some soldiers and commanders were allegedly involved in the illicit diamond trade, particularly in Sierra Leone. Indeed, ECOMOG was accused of deliberately prolonging the conflict because of this illicit gain. In a letter to the UN, the Indian general who commanded UN forces in Sierra Leone, Vijay Jetley, made strong allegations against Nigerian military commanders, a charge vehemently denied by Nigerian commanders. He alleged that the Nigerian army was "interested in staying in Sierra Leone due to the massive benefits they were getting from the illegal diamond mining." He further accused commander Mohammed Garba and the UN Secretary-general's Special Representative Oluyemi Adeniji, both Nigerians, of undermining the UN mission and making Nigerian interests "paramount even if it meant scuttling the peace process" (*Washington Post* 2000). ECOMOG troops have also been accused of removing economic assets from Liberia, to the extent that the phrase ECOMOG came to be translated by local critics as "Every Car or Movable Object Gone" (Cleaver 1998; Turk 2000). While the illicit trade was certainly not a reason for intervening, it may have helped to prolong the conflict.

Whatever the truth may be, the lesson here is that troops need to be well equipped, their welfare assured, and discipline enforced. Another important reason for Nigeria's participation seems to be a way to keep the military busy, diverting ambitious officers away from plotting coups. General Sani Abacha was said to have used ECOMOG assignments to rid himself of troublesome units and officers, many of whom were subsequently retired at the end of their posting (Hutchful 1999).

Peacekeeping also served as income augmentation for the military as an institution and for serving personnel in times of austerity and shrinking budgets. It is difficult to reduce military spending when commitments are being made for peacekeeping. In addition, payments by the UN to participating governments, such as Nigeria's for peacekeeping operations, help to subsidize military spending in times of severe budget cuts. Seen in this light, peacekeeping becomes a form of low-wage labour export. Allowances paid to the troops and civilians on peacekeeping missions have become an important source of income, leading to intense lobbying by soldiers and police officers for peacekeeping duties. Ibrahim Gambari, Nigeria's former foreign minister and permanent representative to the UN, recalled asking Nigerian police officers in Yola, Nigeria, in December 2009 why they were so good outside Nigeria but terrible at home. Their commander responded that if they get in Nigeria what the UN gives them—decent uniforms, boots, and generous allowances that are paid promptly—they would be as good officers inside Nigeria.

The practice of giving better reward to troops on foreign assignments has a long history. As Saliu Ibrahim notes, with respect to Nigeria's first peacekeeping operation:

The Nigerian troops were enthusiastic in service in the Congo and one of the reasons was the special allowances that they were paid while serving there. In addition to his normal pay, a soldier was entitled to a daily UN allowance, a Nigerian special Overseas allowance, an additional allotment for his family and an allowance in lieu of leave he was unable to take while in the Congo. Taken all together these meant that a private soldier whose normal monthly pay was less than 10 pounds sterling might receive up to £26.7s.6d a month in allowances. Higher ranks receive considerably more. (1993, p. 87)

On Ghanaian troops' participation in the UN Interim Force in Lebanon (UNIFIL), General Emmanuel Erskine, a former Ghanaian army commander, noted:

"Op Sunrise" [Ghana's peacekeeping mission in Lebanon] undoubtedly helped to improve the living standards of our troops. For once they could afford freezers, cookers, hi-fi systems, television sets and all sorts of household items normally too expensive for them. A corn-milling machine—known to the Ghanaian troops as a "knicker-knocker"—became the status symbol for all troops on "Op Sunrise." Almost every soldier bought one, either to use commercially, or to sell. (Hutchful 1999, p. 13)

The ECOMOG operations, which did not receive significant UN financial support and therefore were not that well endowed, saw troops helping themselves to resources in their theatres of operation.

Peacekeeping and Nigeria's National Interest

Many critics of Nigeria's foreign policy have focused on what they regard as Nigeria's inability or unwillingness to leverage its peacekeeping role in its relations with countries in the region, especially the beneficiaries of its peacekeeping efforts. It is, therefore, important to examine this claim in some detail. An informed attempt at identifying Nigeria's national interest would include the following:

- Stability in the region and the promotion of greater regional cooperation
- Prevention of refugee exodus from conflicts
- Keeping foreign troops (national armies and mercenaries) out of the region
- Developing markets for investments, goods, services, and labour

While peacekeeping has given Nigeria its best international polish, it is, paradoxically, also a metaphor for Nigeria's numerous failings at home—lack of planning; short attention span on critical issues of national development, including foreign policy; and the impact of over-reliance on oil revenues (leading to a lack of real interest in exploring markets for investment and export by Nigerian businesses).

Many Nigerian critics liken Nigeria's enormous peacekeeping sacrifices to Santa Claus (Father Christmas) gifts given as pure charity, without expectation of returns. Some blame the country for not having a strategy and follow-up actions; others accuse the African beneficiaries of Nigeria's largesse of ingratitude toward Nigeria. Such sentiments flare up particularly when any of those countries or their peoples take actions deemed inimical to the interests of Nigerians, including those living in those countries. Examples include the 2008 violent attacks on foreigners, including Nigerians, in South Africa and the appointment of a Rwandan general, Patrick Nyamvumba, to lead the African Union/United Nations Hybrid Operation in Darfur (UNAMID), in place of a Nigerian. Although material and diplomatic gain may not dictate or inform Nigeria's participation in peacekeeping operations, it is Nigeria's position that it is unfair to miss out on such opportunities where they exist just because of Nigerian leaders' and diplomats' inattentiveness or lack of strategy and preparedness and that countries should duly reciprocate Nigeria's gesture by treating Nigerians well and conceding important multilateral leadership positions.

The Nigerian government's stated objectives and preparations for peacekeeping operations must be reviewed in order to see the extent to which they are designed to fit with Nigeria's national interest as outlined. Major General Suraj Abdurrahman, then director of policy, Nigerian Armed Forces, in a presentation at a seminar organised by the Austrian Blue Helmet Association, noted that Nigeria's objective in its peacekeeping efforts in Africa, especially West Africa, is neither financial reward nor international accolades. Rather its expected reward is simply *peace* (Abdurrahman, 2006).

In the area of training, for instance, it is interesting to note that the curriculum of predeployment training does not seem to include doctrine on national interest. According to Abdurrahman,

> The curriculum outline for the (pre-induction training) program includes the organization and composition of peace-keeping forces, peace-keeping concepts, geo-political briefs on the host country, code of conduct and the mission mandate. Additionally, instructions on laws of war, humanitarian

assistance and cooperation with NGOs, operational and non-operational safety measures are included. There is also a 2-day package on humanitarian international law conducted by the ICRC.

That the Nigerian government does not systematically pursue its national interests through peacekeeping may be connected to the authoritarian manner in which decisions about Nigeria's participation in peacekeeping/peacemaking have been made. In none of these cases was Nigeria's participation subjected to systematic public debate and scrutiny. To be sure, there were commentaries in the mass media but they were no substitute for debate within institutions of democracy, such as the Parliament. Thus, key decisions were made within military circles. Indeed, Nigerians have not really been consulted by their leaders on whether the country should participate in these operations, which have cost many Nigerian lives and enormous resources. Funding for missions has likewise not been subjected to debate and public scrutiny. Legislative oversight and scrutiny, even under civilian governments, are seen as an irritant by the executive; under the military it was nonexistent.

With regard to decisionmaking and governance generally, the Nigerian people have had little input in Nigeria's participation in peacekeeping and, as a result, there is little accountability. Operations have not been funded by taxation to any significant degree but by oil rents from which the people are alienated. Demands for accountability have been feeble at best and have largely been ignored by successive Nigerian governments. In this context it is more likely that Nigerian governments would pursue the ad hoc personal and political interests of those in power rather than articulate and pursue the key national interests previously identified.

Conclusion

Without doubt, Nigeria has been instrumental in bringing about peace in Africa, especially in the West African subregion. Yet, this has come at great cost to Nigeria, both in financial, human resource, and social terms. Reasons for Nigeria's participation and leadership in peace support operations in Africa are varied and cannot be tied to one particular factor. While personal relationships among leaders are important in foreign policy, the factors shaping Nigeria's peacekeeping contributions are multifaceted. These include the need to prevent humanitarian disasters, the need for political stability in the subregion, and for the avoidance of the so-called domino effect of conflicts spreading to other areas, including Nigeria, as well as domestic and international pressures to intervene.

It can be said that Nigeria has shouldered these burdens simply because it could. Its geographic location in a region with much smaller, less-endowed countries makes it difficult for Nigeria to avoid international and sometimes domestic pressures to intervene to prevent or reduce humanitarian disasters and to help end conflict and stabilise the region. In the ECOMOG operations, that effort was sustained despite severe economic difficulties at home, largely because Nigeria was under military rule with little accountability. Also important was the weak political control of military commanders from ECOWAS, allowing commanders more flexibility to adapt to evolving situations on the ground.

However, such interventions could be better thought out in the future. There is little doubt that Nigeria's intervention prevented Charles Taylor from achieving a military victory. Yet after the enormous human and material losses, a settlement was reached that put Taylor in power. This raises serious questions as to whether the intervention, which may have prolonged the war, actually cost more lives than it saved. According to Christopher Turk:

> Ultimately, ECOMOG`s success was less in peace-keeping, since the fighting may well have been more prolonged and heavy than if it had not intervened. The ECOMOG operation was, in reality, an ambiguous exercise in attrition, sustained by Nigeria's willingness to accept heavy material costs which succeeded largely because of eventual compromises made bilaterally between the then Nigerian President, Sani Abacha, and Charles Taylor which gave Taylor much of what he sought. (2000, p. 13)

But just as foreign policy often reflects domestic policy, disorganisation and poor political leadership at home are reflected in peacekeeping operations. There is often little strategic thinking and planning for leveraging the enormous goodwill that comes from peace support sacrifices to further national interests.

There is certainly a need to address some of the key issues thrown up by Nigeria's experiences with peacekeeping. These include the need to mobilise other countries in support of peace support operations rather than acting unilaterally; to plan well and develop clear-cut objectives for going in with a plan to exit; to select troops and commanders on merit; and to train, equip, and reward troops in order to keep their morale high, including articulating and familiarising troops with Nigeria's national interests and objectives in each given operation. There is also a critical need for the country's political and diplomatic leaders to clearly understand the geo-political interests and ideological leanings of international actors so as to better understand how to respond to given international situations based on the likely interests of those actors.

Some of these issues are already being addressed through the ECOWAS Standby Force/African Standby Force, currently being put together by the ECOWAS and AU. Hassan Lai is confident that a great deal of work has gone into the ESF with donor support to ensure that Nigerian troops will no longer go into peace support operations unprepared and ill-equipped (Interview, March 11, 2010). But more needs to be done. Above all, given Nigeria's size and resources relative to other countries in the subregion, it is likely that Nigeria will continue to shoulder the bulk of the burden of peacekeeping whenever peace is threatened in West Africa. It is critical, therefore, that the country invest in preventive diplomacy, in particular helping to prevent crises from degenerating into humanitarian catastrophes. Nigeria should use its influence to promote good governance, democracy, and human rights in the subregion and indeed Africa. This means that it must do the same at home so as to have the moral authority to do it elsewhere.

It is also important to reexamine the concept of peacekeeping by regional actors who are often closer to conflict societies than nonregional actors. They may have a better understanding of underlying issues in the conflicts and may deploy troops quicker than is typical of the UN. However, their closeness may also work against peace efforts as they may have a stake in the outcomes of conflicting parties. The conflicts in Sierra Leone and especially Liberia fell into such a category, with key regional actors demonstrating biases and, in some cases, undermining peace efforts for much of the period. While it is likely that the UN will continue to rely on regional organisations for peacekeeping, especially in Africa where the appetite for Euro-US troop deployment for peacekeeping is declining, it is important that regional peacekeeping is carried out under close UN supervision and with the injection of troops from outside the affected region. There should not be different peacekeeping standards for different regions. Global peacekeeping should continue to be a UN responsibility.

Bibliography

Abdurrahman, S., 2006, "Peace Support Operations in Africa: A Perspective from Nigeria," presented at a seminar organized by the Austrian Blue Helmet Association, Vienna, Austria.

Aboagye, F.B., 1999, *ECOMOG: A Sub-regional Experience in Conflict Resolution Management and Peace-keeping in Liberia*, Sedco Publishing, Accra, Ghana.

Adebajo, A., 2002, *Building Peace in West Africa: Liberia, Sierra Leone, and Guinea Bissau*, Lynne Rienner Publishers, Boulder, CO, US.

Adisa, J., 1996, "The International Community and Peace-keeping in Africa," in M.A. Vogt and L.S. Aminu, eds., *Peace-keeping as a Security Strategy in Africa: Chad and Liberia as Case Studies*, Fourth Dimension Publishing Co., Enugu, Nigeria, pp. 160–183.

Aguda, A., 1996, "The Concept of Sovereignty and Non-Interference in the Internal Affairs of States and the Phenomenon of Peace-keeping Forces in Africa," in M.A. Vogt and L.S. Aminu, eds., *Peace-keeping as a Security Strategy in Africa: Chad and Liberia as Case Studies*, Fourth Dimension Publishing Co., Enugu, Nigeria, pp. 204–218.

Aminu, L.S., 1996, "Peace-keeping and Humanitarian Relief Operations: The Chad and Liberian Cases," in M.A. Vogt and L.S. Aminu, eds., *Peace-keeping as a Security Strategy in Africa: Chad and Liberia as Case Studies*, Fourth Dimension Publishing Co., Enugu, Nigeria, pp. 100–118.

Atoyebi, Olayinka, 2007, "Vital Statistics on Nigeria's Military Participation in Peace Support Operations Since 1960," in A. Ogomudia, ed., *Peace Support Operations, Command and Professionalism: Challenges for the Nigerian Armed Forces in the 21st Century and Beyond*, Gold Press Limited, Ibadan, Nigeria, pp. 190–199.

Babangida, I., 1990, "The Imperative Features of Nigerian Foreign Policy and the Crisis in Liberia," *Contact*, vol. 2, no. 3 (November 1990), from C. Turk, 2000, "'Every Car or Moving Object Gone': The ECOMOG Intervention in Liberia," *African Studies Quarterly*, vol. 4, no. 1 (February 2000), http://web.africa.ufl.edu/asq/v4/v4i1a1.htm, accessed January 31, 2010.

Berman, E.G., and Sams, K.E., 2000, *Peace-keeping in Africa: Capabilities and Culpabilities*, United Nations Institute for Disarmament Research, Geneva, pp. 220–221.

Cleaver, G., 1998, "Liberia: Lessons for the Future from the Experience of ECOMOG," in O. Furley and R. May, eds., *Peace-keeping in Africa*, Ashgate, Aldershot, UK, p. 232.

Dorn, A.W., 1998, "Regional Peace-Keeping Is Not the Way," in *Peace-keeping and International Relations*, vol. 27, no. 2, July–October, Pearson Peace-keeping Centre, Nova Scotia, Canada, p. 1.

Ellis, S., 2006, *The Mask of Anarchy*, New York University Press, New York, US.

Essuman-Johnson, A., 2009, "Regional Conflict Resolution Mechanisms: A Comparative Analysis of Two African Security Complexes," in *African Journal of Political Science and International Relations*, vol. 3, no. 10, pp. 409–422.

Farah, Douglas, 2000, "Internal Disputes Mar UN Mission: Power Struggle Cripples Troops in Sierra Leone," *Washington Post*, September 10, p. A-01.

Farris, J., and Bomoi, M., eds., 2004, *Shehu Musa Yar'Adua: A Life of Service*, Yar'Adua Foundation, Abuja, Nigeria.

French, H.W., 1997, "A Muscular Nigeria Proves a Flawed Peacekeeper," *New York Times,* June 26.

Hutchful, E., 1999, "The ECOMOG Experience with Peace-Keeping in West Africa," in *Wither Peace-keeping in Africa*, Monograph No. 36, April, Institute for Security Studies, South Africa, www.iss.co.za/pubs/monographs/no36/ECOMOG.html, accessed December 15, 2009.

Ibrahim, S., 1993, "Nigeria's Participation in United Nations Operations in the Congo ONUC) 1960–1964," in M.A.Vogt and A.E. Ekoko, eds., *Nigeria in International Peace-Keeping 1960–1992*, Michigan State University Press, Ann Arbor, MI, US, pp. 71–93.

Imobighe, T.A., 1996, "The Analysis of Political Issues Raised by OAU Peace-Keeping in Chad," in M.A. Vogt and L.S. Aminu, eds., *Peace-keeping as a Security Strategy in Africa: Chad and Liberia as Case Studies*, Fourth Dimension Publishing Co., Enugu, Nigeria, pp. 241–259.

James, I., 1993, "Nigeria in OAU Peace-keeping in Chad: Historical and Political Analysis," in M.A. Vogt and A.E. Ekoko, eds., *Nigeria in International Peace-Keeping 1960–1992*, Michigan State University Press, Ann Arbor, MI, US, pp. 129–142.

James, I., 1996, "The Role of ECOWAS in Peace-keeping in Liberia," in M.A. Vogt and L.S. Aminu, eds., *Peace-keeping as a Security Strategy in Africa: Chad and Liberia as Case Studies*, Fourth Dimension Publishing Co., Enugu, Nigeria, pp. 321–341

Johnson, B., 1996, "Peace-keeping in Liberia: A Liberian Experience" in M.A. Vogt and L.S. Aminu, eds., *Peace-keeping as a Security Strategy in Africa: Chad and Liberia as Case Studies*, Fourth Dimension Publishing Co., Enugu, Nigeria,, pp. 280–303.

Leadership, December, 16, 2009, p. 16.

Kingibe, B. 2009, Contribution to Methodology workshop organized by the Shehu Musa Yar'Adua Centre, Abuja Nigera, October 15.

MacQueen, N., 2002, *United Nations Peacekeeping in Africa Since 1960*, Longman, London.

Ndiaye, T.M., 1996, "Legal Questions Raised by the Peace-Keeping Operations in Chad and Liberia, in M.A. Vogt and L.S. Aminu, eds., *Peace-keeping as a Security Strategy in Africa: Chad and Liberia as Case Studies*, Fourth Dimension Publishing Co., Enugu, Nigeria, pp. 219–238.

Obayuwana, O., 2010, "African Common Defence Pact Comes into Force," *The Guardian,* January 4.

Olowo-Ake, A., 1996, "ECOMOG and Eurocorps: Models of an African Strategic Peace Equation? An Independent Study for the Organization of African Unity (OAU) and the Economic Community of West African States (ECOWAS) Proposing the Establishment of Sub-Regional Peace-Keeping Mechanisms for the Management of Defence and Security Challenges in Africa," presented to HE Edward Benjamin, executive secretary of ECOWAS, June 1, Lagos, Nigeria.

Oluyemi-Kusa, D., 2007, "Sacrifices of the Nigerian Nation, and Armed Forces in Peace Missions Since 1960," in A. Ogomudia, ed., *Peace Support Operations, Command and Professionalism: Challenges for the Nigerian*

Armed Forces in the 21st Century and Beyond, Gold Press Limited, Ibadan, Nigeria, pp. 137–163.

Sowole, J., 2009, "Nigeria: Mutiny—27 Soldiers Get Life Sentence," *ThisDay* (Lagos), April 16.

Taiwo, J., 2009, "Nigeria: Peace-Keeping: Ending the Embarrassing Trend," *ThisDay* (Lagos), October 12.

Turk, C., 2000, "'Every Car or Moving Object Gone': the ECOMOG Intervention in Liberia," *African Studies Quarterly*, vol. 4, no. 1 (February), http://web.africa.ufl.edu/asq/v4/v4i1a1.htm, accessed January 31, 2010.

Vogt, M.A., 1993, "Nigeria in Liberia: Historical and Political Analysis of ECOMOG," in M.A. Vogt and A.E. Ekoko, eds., *Nigeria in International Peace-Keeping 1960–1992*, Michigan State University Press, Ann Arbor, MI, US, pp. 195–215.

Vogt, M.A., 1996, "Analysis of the Political Issues Raised by Peace-keeping in Liberia," in M.A. Vogt and L.S. Aminu, eds., *Peace-keeping as a Security Strategy in Africa*, Fourth Dimension Publishers, Enugu, Nigeria, pp. 304–320.

Yar'Adua, S.M., 1979, "Opening Remarks at the Resumed Conference on Chadian Crisis held in Lagos, Nigeria, August 1979 by the Chief of Staff, Supreme Headquarters, Major-General S. M. Yar'Adua," unpublished from the Yar'Adua personal collection, Yar'Adua Centre Library, Abuja, Nigeria.

PART 3

PROMOTING REGIONAL INTEGRATION AND ECONOMIC DEVELOPMENT

7

Nigeria, ECOWAS, and the Promotion of Regional Integration in West Africa

Hamid Bobboyi

Nigeria's foreign policy has undergone a series of transformations, in focus and tempo, in the last fifty years. From the sedate and cautious days of the Tafawa Balewa regime, through the combative years of the Murtala–Obasanjo era, to the difficult—and some may add painful—years of International Monetary Fund politics and diplomacy under the Babangida regime, these changes were patently reflective of the complex matrix of Nigeria's socioeconomic and political landscape and the varying fortunes of the international environment.

Despite these transformations, the promotion of regional integration and development has remained one of the cardinal objectives of Nigeria's foreign policy. As far back as October 8, 1960, when Prime Minister Sir Abubaker Tafawa Balewa addressed the United Nations General Assembly on the occasion of Nigeria's admission as the ninety-ninth member of the august body, he identified "the promotion of African unity" and "the creation of the necessary conditions for the economic, political, social and cultural development of Africa" as two of the guiding principles of Nigeria's engagement with the world (Otubanjo 1989, pp. 1–11). These principles were reaffirmed by subsequent governments and reformulated under different guises, including the geometric Afrocentrism of the Murtala-Obasanjo regime, to suit the exigencies of the time and temperament of their leaders (Garba 1987; Gambari 1989).

The continuity in Nigeria's quest for regional integration and development, despite occasional incongruities, engendered one of the nation's major foreign policy triumphs. The coming together of fifteen Heads of State and Government on May 28, 1975, in Lagos, Nigeria, to append their signatures to the treaty establishing the Economic Community of West African States (ECOWAS) was a glowing tribute to Nigeria that

127

brought to a successful conclusion years of hard work and diplomacy under the leadership of General Yakubu Gowon. This chapter discusses the crucial role Nigeria played in the formation of ECOWAS, assesses its achievements and the challenges facing it, and proffers recommendations for enhancing Nigeria's role in moving ECOWAS forward.

The Context

The broad contours of ECOWAS's evolution have been fairly well established, as has the theoretical basis and conceptual problems of a customs union and trade liberation framework within the West African subregion (Akinyemi et al. 1984; Gana 1989; Bappah 2007). However, this discourse by its very nature has tended to obscure basic elements of the socioeconomic and political context of Nigeria's role in the formation of the subregional organisation and the essence of Nigeria's participation in this challenging exercise. First, the strategic position of Nigeria in West African is evident. With 52.48 percent of the population of the subregion and ample material endowments at its disposal, Nigeria, even at its passive moments, is an indispensable element in the subregional equation. The ECOWAS Report of 2008 dispassionately observed:

> A careful examination of the economies and population of the ECOWAS Member States shows that ECOWAS is a good model of regional economic integration in which the strong and weak co-exist to foster socioeconomic development on a large scale. Nigeria is the dominant economy in the region accounting for 62% of the regional GDP in 2007. Given the size of the Nigerian economy in relation to its neighbours, it is expected that Nigeria will continue to play its leadership role, within the frame-work of solidarity, in fostering sustainable regional economic development. (ECOWAS Commission 2009a, p. 24)

The second contextual element that deserves mention relates to the bitter experiences of the civil war, which ravaged the nation from 1967 to 1970. The civil war tested Nigeria's resilience and reaffirmed its belief in the triumphant ethos of unity and solidarity, reconciliation, and the imperative of mutual coexistence. But the civil war was not only a test of Nigeria's strength, it was also a test of the resilience of solidarity and good neighbourliness in West Africa. Although France threw its weight behind the Biafran cause, it was only President Felix Houphouet-Boigny of Cote d'Ivoire and President Emile Derlin Henri Zinsou of Dahomey (now Benin Republic) who broke ranks with their West African compatriots to support the dismemberment of Nigeria (Nwolise 1989, p. 206). Others, including Benin Republic after 1969, stood their ground and gave varying degrees of support to Nigeria's federal government and its head of state, General Yakubu Gowon. It is probable that the cordial relationship between General Gowon and the president of Togo Republic, General Gnassingbe Eyadema, might have emerged during this trying period in Nigeria's history. As Nwolise pointed out, the latter was active in preventing weapons smuggling into Biafra and "seized the aircraft used for gun-running to Biafra which crash-landed on his territory and handed over to the Nigerian Government millions of Nigerian Pounds found in it" (1989, p. 206).

Third, Nigeria's confident outlook, coming out of the civil war experience, was further reinforced by a bourgeoning economy predicated on a sharp rise in oil revenues beginning in 1971. Income from the export of oil, which stood at US$104 million in 1968, jumped to US$1,337 million by 1971. With the oil embargo in 1973, this figure was to reach US$8,513 million by 1974, constituting approximately 92.6 percent of Nigeria's export earnings and 82.1 percent of total revenue (Akindele 1988, p. 75). The era of the petrodollar economy had properly begun and Nigeria had the financial wherewithal to put action to word in the pursuit and realisation of the cardinal objectives of its foreign policy, particularly the promotion of regional integration and development.

It should also be added that the dramatic rise in oil prices in the first half of the 1970s, of which Nigeria was a major beneficiary, had the effect of bringing into sharp focus the unfair and exploitative relationship that existed between primary commodity producers and the industrialised countries and, indeed, exposed the frailties of the prevailing international economic order. The dominant rhetoric of international economic discourse within the developing world was fair trade, and this was pursued with vigour at the United Nations General Assembly, the UN Conference on Trade and Development, Economic Commission for Africa, and other forums (Adedeji 1984). Equally clear was the realisation that developing countries would have to act together and form stronger economic and trade blocs to extract better terms of trade and meaningful development assistance from the industrialised countries. The term *collective self-reliance*, ambiguous as it may seem, had become a doctrine, and its significance could not have been lost on West African leaders when they established ECOWAS.

Nigeria and the Formation of ECOWAS

Although the doctrine of collective self-reliance had been an active part of the regional agenda since the 1960s, efforts to bring about a West

African subregional group that would actualise it were disjointed and self-defeating. There are two major perspectives on this historical epoch. First is the francophone perspective, which focuses on the efforts of France's former West African colonies to come together as a politico-economic group in the subregion. The first important arrangement in this direction was the formation of the Union Douarniere Entre Des Etats De L'Afrique Occidentale (UDAO), or the Customs Union of West African States, a pre-independence contraption meant to consolidate French neo-colonial dominance over its former colonies. The UDAO arrangements were, however, short lived, and, in 1966, a new treaty was signed in Paris for the establishment of the Union Douarniere Des Etats De L'Afrique De L'Ouest (UDEAO). Customs arrangements under UDEAO lasted a little longer but virtually collapsed in 1972 to give way to the emergence of the Communaute Economique De L'Afrique De L'Ouest on April 17, 1973, at the height of consultations to form ECOWAS (Gana 1989; Ezenwe 1984; Bappah 2007).

The second perspective, largely ignored by scholars, is one that focuses on the broader effort to enhance economic cooperation and development across the colonial divide, a perspective that may provide a better understanding of the dynamics of economic relations in West Africa and indeed the foundation of ECOWAS. According to Adebayo Adedeji, Nigeria's commissioner for economic development under the administration of General Gowon and his chief policy adviser on West African integration:

> The first attempt to achieve collective self-reliance in West Africa was made in November 1963 when a conference on industrial harmonization in the sub-region was held here in Lagos. This was followed, in Niamey, by a conference on economic co-operation in October 1966. At a similar conference at Accra, in April 1967, an agreement on the Articles of Association of a proposed Economic Community in West Africa was signed. Under this framework, an Interim Council of Ministers was established with the task of preparing a draft treaty for the proposed community. The Interim Council held its first meeting in Dakar [Senegal], in November 1967, when it was agreed that the inaugural meeting of the proposed community should take place at the level of the Heads of State or Government. (1984, pp. xxiv–xxv)

Adedeji also pointed to another effort, this time by the Organization of Senegalese River States, that resulted in a summit of West African Heads of State at Monrovia, Liberia, in April 1968 and the signing of a protocol establishing the West African Regional Group. The summit mandated Nigeria and Guinea to prepare priority studies on areas of cooperation, while Liberia and Senegal were tasked with preparing a draft treaty and protocol for a customs union. "Later in the year," Adedeji stated,

Officials of the Governments of Nigeria and Guinea met to prepare the studies which were submitted to the then fourteen West African States pending their consideration by the Interim Council of Ministers. Unfortunately, this body never met. Consequently, neither the priority studies nor the draft treaty and protocol on the Customs Union were considered, let alone adopted. This was the standstill in which West Africa found itself until April 1972, when Heads of State of Nigeria and Togo decided to revive the process of achieving economic co-operation in the sub-region and accordingly mandated their ministers and officials to work out the framework and strategy of such co-operation. (1984, p. xxiv–xxv)

The processes initiated by the Nigeria–Togo Project took three years to come to fruition. Having participated in several failed integration projects, the two parties were fully conversant with the socioeconomic and political cleavages of the subregion and the gargantuan challenges that lay ahead. They began with extensive consultations, and a joint Nigerian–Togolese Ministerial Delegation, led by Professor Adedeji, visited the independent West African states between July and August 1973. They also adopted a pragmatic approach with modest and realistic goals for the new community. This entailed pursuing limited objectives capable of early realisation as well as having an open-door policy "to enable all the countries in the sub-region to become members of the community if and when they were ready" (Adedeji 1984). On December 14, 1973, Nigeria and Togo were finally able to submit their proposals to a meeting of ministers from the fifteen West African states in Lome, Togo, where the basic principles for ECOWAS's creation were agreed upon. Ministerial meetings to examine the draft treaty were subsequently held in Accra, Ghana, in February 1974, Monrovia in January 1975, and in Lagos in May 1975 (Adedeji 1984, p. xxv; Okwuosa 2009, p. 2). It was these spirited efforts that paved the way for the Lagos Summit and the signing of the ECOWAS Treaty by the fifteen West African heads of state on May 28, 1975.

Despite quick ratification of the treaty by many member states—by June 23, 1975, seven states had ratified the treaty—ECOWAS could not properly take off until November 1976 when the West African heads of state signed, in Lome, the relevant protocols to the ECOWAS Treaty. These include protocols relating to

- Definition of the concept of goods originating from ECOWAS member states
- Fund for Co-operation, Compensation and Development of ECOWAS, now called ECOWAS Bank for Investment and Development

- Re-exportation within the ECOWAS of goods imported from third countries
- Contribution of member states to the ECOWAS budget
- Assessment of revenue loss by member states as a result of trade liberalisation within the economic community (Adedeji 1984, p. xxv–xxvi; Okwuosa 2009, p. 2; Irele 1990, pp. 127–221).

It was also in November 1976 that Lagos was adopted to host the secretariat of ECOWAS, while Lome was chosen as the headquarters of the ECOWAS Fund. In January 1977, the first executive secretary of ECOWAS, Dr. Abubakar Diaby-Ouattara of Cote d'Ivoire, was appointed, and when he reported for duty in March 1977, it could be said that ECOWAS as an organization had properly taken off (Okwuosa 2009).

ECOWAS and Its Institutions

Despite the time it took for member states to build consensus on key protocols, ECOWAS has been able to evolve over the last three decades as a multifaceted subregional organisation with distinct institutions that helped nurture its growth. The apex institution, as provided for by Article 7 of the Treaty of ECOWAS and amended on July 24, 1993, is the Authority of Heads of State and Government, which serves as "the supreme institution of the community" and is responsible for its general direction and the control of its affairs (ECOWAS 2010). The Authority of Heads of State also elects its chairman, usually on an annual basis from the ranks of its members. The chairmanship profile of the organisation, given in Table 7.1, indicates that Nigeria and Togo, the two founders of ECOWAS, have been most favoured in the appointment, with Nigeria occupying the position ten times and Togo six times.

The second institution, after the Authority of the Heads of State and Government, is the Council of Ministers which under Article 10 of the ECOWAS Treaty of 1993 is charged with responsibility for the functioning and development of the community, making recommendations to the authority, and approving the appointment of all statutory appointees other than the executive secretary. The council comprises the minister in-charge of ECOWAS and any other minister of each member state. Two institutions that have also emerged as an integral part of the community are the Court of Justice and the Community Parliament. The latter has 115 seats, which are distributed among the fifteen ECOWAS members. Nigeria, with over half the population of the subregion, has thirty-five

Table 7.1   Annual Summits of the ECOWAS Authority, 1975–2009

Date	Venue	Chairman
November 1976	Lome	General Gnassingbe Eyadema
April 22, 1978	Lagos	General Olusegun Obasanjo
May 29, 1979	Dakar	Leopold Sedar Senghor
May 28, 1980	Lome	General Gnassingbe Eyadema
May 29, 1981	Freetown, Sierra Lone	Dr. Siaka P. Stevens
May 29, 1982	Cotonou, Benin	Mathieu Kerekou
May 29, 1983	Conakry, Guinea	Ahmed Sekou Toure
November 23, 1984	Lome	General Gnassingbe Eyadema
July 6, 1985	Lome	General Gnassingbe Eyadema
July 1, 1986	Abuja, Nigeria	General Ibrahim B. Babangida
July 9, 1987	Abuja	General Ibrahim B. Babangida
June 25, 1988	Lome	General Gnassingbe Eyadema
June 30, 1989	Ouagadougou, Burkina Faso	Captain Blaise Compaore
May 29, 1990	Banjul, Gambia	Alhaji Sir Dauda Jawara
July 6, 1991	Abuja	General Ibrahim B. Babangida
July 29, 1992	Dakar	Abdou Diouf
July 24, 1993	Cotonou	Nicephore D. Soglo
August 6, 1994	Abuja	General Sani Abacha
July 28, 1995	Accra, Ghana	Flight Lt. Jerry J. Rawlings
July 26, 1996	Abuja	General Sani Abacha
August 28, 1997	Abuja	General Sani Abacha
October 30, 1998	Abuja	General Sani Abacha
December 9, 1999	Lome	General Gnassingble Eyadema
December 15, 2000	Bamako, Mali	Alpha Oumar Konare
December 21, 2001	Dakar	Abdoulaye Wade
January 31, 2003	Dakar	Abdoulaye Wade
December 19, 2003	Accra	John A. Kufuor
January 19, 2005	Accra	John A. Kufuor
January 12, 2006	Niamey, Niger	Mamadou Tandja
January 19, 2007	Ouagadougou	Blaise Compaore
January 2008	Ouagadougou	Blaise Compaore
December 2008	Abuja	Blaise Compaore
January 2009	Abuja	Umaru Musa Yar'adua
January 2010	Abuja	Goodluck Jonathan

Source: ECOWAS Commission 2009a Appendix iii and ECOWAS 2009.

seats. The Parliament is currently being restructured with the tenure of the speaker reduced from five to four years and with plans for direct elections (ECOWAS Executive Secretariat 2009a, p. 131).

The last major institution is the Executive Secretariat, established under Article 17 of the Revised ECOWAS Treaty of 1993, which is charged with the responsibility of coordinating the day-to-day activities and programmes of the organisation. In 2007, the Executive Secretariat was transformed into a commission with a president, a vice president, and seven commissioners (Okwuosa 2009, p. 8) and with a new legal framework for enacting and implementing ECOWAS acts. In addition to the commission's seven departments, its work is also complemented by several specialised ECOWAS agencies: West African Health Organization, West African Monetary Agency, ECOWAS Youth and Sports Development Centre, ECOWAS Gender Development Centre, Water Resources Co-ordinating Unit, the West African Power Pool, and the Inter-Governmental Action Group Against Money Laundering and Terrorism Financing in West Africa. There is also the ECOWAS Bank for Investment and Development (EBID) headquartered in Lome, which replaced the ECOWAS Fund. Nigeria has approximately 32 percent equity shareholding in EBID (Okwuosa 2009, p. 12).

Nigeria's Engagement with ECOWAS

The emergence of ECOWAS as a concept in 1975 and its profound transformation into a complex organisation thirty-five years later bear testimony to the strong faith West African leaders have placed in regional integration and their perseverance in translating this faith into action, despite sharp differences in language and culture, as well as palpable disparities in human and material endowments. Nigeria's engagement with the subregional body was equally predicated on its abiding faith in regional unity and integration, a faith substantially modified by the changing fortunes of the nation's socioeconomic and political landscape and the temperament of its leaders.

The first challenge of Nigeria's foreign policy after the overthrow of General Gowon in July 1975—and it could be argued its first triumph as far as ECOWAS was concerned—was the decision to relocate the organisation's headquarters from Lome to Lagos. According to Joseph Garba, then Nigeria's commissioner of external affairs:

> [E]ven though it was common knowledge that Nigeria was the principal financier of ECOWAS, paying a third of its budget, the headquarters was being given away because Eyadema, being no fool, wanted it. The Secretary-Generalship, which Eyadema was offering in compensation, carried a four-year term, renewable only once. After at most eight years, Nigeria would have had to wait more than a century for another turn if the principle of rotation were to be rigidly followed. Murtala did not like it. My job was to let Eyadema know our feelings. (1987, pp. 4–5)

The Togolese president, of course, felt that Nigeria was acting in bad faith. He had the support of Senegal which, for its own reasons, did not want a change in the status quo. Nigeria, on its part, was able to mobilise key francophone states, including Guinea and Cote d'Ivoire, and ultimately conceded the secretary-generalship to the Ivorian technocrat, Dr. Abubakar Ouattara. Togo had to give in but not without a demand for massive financial aid. The country was apparently adequately compensated when it was agreed that the ECOWAS Fund headquarters would be in Lome.

The second aspect of Nigeria's engagement with ECOWAS pertains to the nation's effort to maintain a healthy balance between the dictates of the "national interest" and the imperatives of regional integration. This task was not an easy one, especially between 1975 and 1986. The Murtala-Obasanjo regime, coming on the heels of a liberal and open-handed General Gowon (Garba 1987) and faced with declining economic fortunes, had little room to manoeuvre. The Adedeji Panel, which was established to review the nation's foreign policy, was convinced that Nigeria could no longer afford to serve as "Father Christmas," and its external engagement, including with ECOWAS, must yield tangible benefits to the nation. These nationalistic considerations delayed the signing of key ECOWAS protocols and the take-off of ECOWAS itself.

Despite the nationalistic fervour, it was Nigeria that got its act together to oversee negotiations on the ECOWAS Protocol of 1979 relating to the free movement of persons, right of residence, and establishment of business. This development remains one of the most enduring successes of ECOWAS and laid a solid foundation for the emergence of a borderless community of people. The Protocol relating to the Free Movement of Persons, Right of Residence and Establishment was negotiated during the chairmanship of General Olusegun Obasanjo, Nigeria's military head of state, and was signed on May 29, 1979, when he handed over the mantle of ECOWAS chairmanship to President Leopold Senghor of Senegal. Although Nigeria had cause to invoke the "national interest" in the expulsion of ECOWAS citizens in 1983 and 1984 and in the closure of its national borders between 1984 and 1986, its abiding faith in the 1979 protocol and other supplementary protocols was never seriously questioned. It is indeed significant to note that it was Nigeria, under the leadership of a new democratic president, Obasanjo, that pushed for fast-tracking the implementation of many of these protocols. President Obasanjo called for a mini-summit of Heads of State and Government on March 27, 2000, on the creation of a borderless ECOWAS. The final communiqué of the Abuja meeting made far-reaching decisions on the free movement of persons in the subre- gion, including

- Granting ECOWAS citizens the maximum ninety-day period of stay at entry points by April 13, 2000
- Abolishing the residence permit requirement for each others' citi- zens in the spirit of equal treatment of ECOWAS citizens
- Issuing and the effective use of the ECOWAS travel certificate
- Adopting and the introduction of a single ECOWAS passport
- Adopting and the introduction of a multicountry, Shengen-type visa

These bold steps, spearheaded by Nigeria, put ECOWAS and West Africa in the enviable position of being the only subregion in Africa where citizens can freely travel from one country to another without a visa. Although the Shengen-type ECOWAS visa is yet to be implement- ed, the ECOWAS passport has become a reality and is used by over 70 percent of community citizens. The state of implementation of these res- olutions relating to the free movement of persons in the subregion, as at November 6, 2009, is summarised in Table 7.2.

The third aspect of Nigeria's engagement with ECOWAS is the issue of peace and security in the subregion. As Muhammad Ibn Chambas, the erstwhile president of the ECOWAS Commission, pointed out:

> ECOWAS started as an inter-governmental organization with a diplo- matic and economic development agenda. However, it did not take long before ECOWAS realized the missing link in the equation: Peace and Security. The obvious nexus between peace, security and development cannot be over-emphasized. Barely a decade after the creation of ECOWAS, conflicts emerged in Liberia and Sierra Leone as a phenom- enon not confined to the borders of individual nation-states, but with serious regional implications both in its causes and effects. (2005)

The details of Nigeria's engagement with ECOWAS to address these crises and the emergence of the Economic Community of West African States Monitoring Group (ECOMOG) are treated elsewhere in this book. In this chapter, we shall raise only three salient points. First, Nigeria was one of the first countries to realize the importance of peace and security in the ECOWAS equation and work with other member states towards its realisation. The first protocol on this issue, Protocol on Non-Aggression, was signed in Lagos in April 1978 when General

Table 7.2   State of Implementation of Protocols and Decisions Relating to the Free Movement of Persons

Country	Abolition of Entry Visa	ECOWAS Travel Journal	ECOWAS Passport	ECOWAS Brown Card
Benin				
January 4, 1981	Yes	Yes	Yes	Yes
Burkina Faso				
April 6, 1982	Yes	No	No	Yes
Cape Verde				
June 11, 1984	Yes	No	No	NA
Cote d'Ivoire				
January 19, 1981	Yes	Yes	Yes	Yes
Gambia				
October 30, 1980	Yes	Yes	No	Yes
Ghana				
April 8, 1980	Yes	No	No	Yes
Guinea				
October 17, 1979	Yes	Yes	Yes	Yes
Guinea-Bissau				
August 20, 1979	Yes	No	No	Yes
Liberia				
April 1, 1980	Yes	No	Yes	No
Mali				
June 5, 1980	Yes	No	No	Yes
Niger				
January 11, 1980	Yes	Yes	Yes	Yes
Nigeria				
September 12, 1979	Yes	Yes	Yes	Yes
Senegal				
May 12, 1980	Yes	No	Yes	Yes
Sierra Leone				
September 15, 1982	Yes	Yes	No	Yes
Togo				
December 9, 1979	Yes	Yes	Yes	Yes

Source: ECOWAS Commission 2009b.

Obasanjo was ECOWAS chairman. This spurred the subsequent adoption of related instruments, including the Protocol Relating to Mutual Assistance on Defence of 1981, which is usually cited "as the basis for the eventual establishment of ECOMOG" (Laro 2002, p. 1).

Second, and despite the involvement of other member states in the mobilisation and deployment of troops, the bulk of the troops in both Liberia and Sierra Leone, and the resources to support them eventually came from Nigeria. With the exception of General Arnold Quoinoo of Ghana, who commanded the first ECOMOG contingent in August 1990, all subsequent commanders were from Nigeria (Laro 2002, p. 5). Third, the two Nigerian military leaders who served during this period, General

Ibrahim Babangida and General Sani Abacha, were committed to the success of peacekeeping operations in the subregion. The establishment of the Standing Mediation Committee, which subsequently deployed troops to Liberia, was considered a brainchild of General Babangida (Oche 2006, p. 16), who was also made chairman of ECOWAS on July 6, 1991, during the height of the Liberia crisis. General Abacha was also closely involved in the deployment of troops to Sierra Leone and the reinstatement of President Tejan Kabbah after the coup of May 25, 1997, by Major Johnny Paul Koroma. The ECOWAS Abuja Summit of August 28–29, 1997, was decisive in placing a total embargo on the new military junta. General Abacha was made chairman of ECOWAS on August 6, 1994, and subsequently was redrafted to serve ECOWAS from 1996 to 1998, apparently to deal with the persistent subregional crises. On the whole, it could be said that Nigeria, despite the encumbrances of its military dictatorships or perhaps because of them, was able to contribute significantly to the consolidation of peace and security in the subregion. As Okwuosa pointed out, "the peace and security portfolio of ECOWAS has given that organization a pride of place on the continent," to the extent that it is regarded as a model in subregional peacekeeping (2009, pp. 4–5).

The fourth aspect of Nigeria's engagement with ECOWAS is the issue of democracy and good governance. The emerging conflicts and crises in the 1980s and 1990s in several West African countries and the resultant instability convinced ECOWAS that there could be no meaningful development without peace and security. At the beginning of the 21st century, there was a further realisation that the consolidation of peace, security, and development was equally dependent on the pursuit of good governance. This realisation was further reinforced by the changing political landscape of the subregion. Ghana had a stable democracy for several years, and Senegal had a peaceful transition, which saw the emergence of President Abdoulaye Wade. Most significantly, Nigeria had also just emerged from years of military dictatorship with the newly rebranded Chief Obasanjo as democratic president. Nigeria had sufficient moral capital to expend in order to mobilize the subregion in a convincing manner to face the challenges of good governance and development. It is therefore not surprising that at the Extraordinary Summit of ECOWAS Heads of State and Government in Abuja on April 11, 2001, the final communiqué was very emphatic on the need to strengthen democracy in the subregion, as that was generally viewed as the essential key to good governance. By December 2001, the Protocol on Democracy and Good Governance was adopted by the subregional organisation, making the issue of political governance an integral part of the West African agenda. This growing sentiment for democracy and good governance has made it less difficult for members to sanction infringement of the democratic process and to support late President Umaru Musa Yar'Adua and President Goodluck Jonathan to enforce prescribed sanctions against Guinea and Niger.

Funding of ECOWAS

Nigeria's strategic interest in the development of ECOWAS, coupled with the size of its economy, make it the principal source of funds for ECOWAS activities both before and after the introduction of the community levy. The funding formula for ECOWAS, it should be pointed out, was a contentious issue from the inception of the organisation and was one of the factors that delayed its take-off. Based on Article 2 of the Protocol Relating to the Contributions by Member States to the Budget of the Economic Community of West African States, Nigeria's assessed contribution amounted to approximately 35 percent of the community budget. After Nigeria strongly objected, it was granted a modest reduction. It was on account of this substantial financial contribution that Nigeria was able to justify the relocation of ECOWAS headquarters from Togo to Lagos. As Nwoke stated, it also argued for:

> a weighted system of voting, so that voting power would be distributed according to contribution to the Community budget, a position that would have conferred veto power status on Nigeria in ECOWAS decision-making. That proposition failed because the other member states maintained that voting must be a function of sovereign equality instead of a function of money. (2005, p. 135–136)

With the introduction of the community levy in 2003, total revenues due to ECOWAS have recorded a substantial increase, appreciating by 97 percent in 2008. It is also clear that Nigeria, with a contribution of 332,007,924 units of account (UA) between July 1, 2003, and December 31, 2008, provided 59.93 percent of ECOWAS revenues, making it by far the largest financial contributor in the subregion. In fact, it has been argued that if Nigeria were to reconcile fully its accounts with ECOWAS, the quantum of its contribution may amount to approximately 80 percent (*Field Notes* 2009–2010). The assessments, deposits, and balances relating to the community levy as at June 30, 2009, are given in Table 7.3.

Table 7.3   Summary of Member States Community Levy Deposits

Assessments and Deposits as at June 30, 2009

Member States	Currency	Assessment	Deposits	Balance	Total UA	%
Benin	CFA	1,586,334,588.00	1,156,831,084.00	429,503,504.00	1,539,678.00	1.88
Burkina Faso	CFA	1,729,261,555.00	1,818,013,025.00	−88,751,470.00	2,420,824.00	2.95
Cape Verde	ESC	0.00	0.00	0.00	0.00	0.00
Cote d'Ivoire	CFA	4,381,972,791.00	4,035,134,006.00	346,838,785.00	5,370,786.00	6.54
Gambia	GMD	15,147,830.69	13,426,207.17	1,721,623.52	339,352.00	0.41
Guinea	GNF	5,312,981,000.00	0.00	5,312,981,000.00	0.00	0.00
Guinea-Bissau	CFA	127,561,391.00	0.00	127,561,391.00	0.00	0.00
Ghana	CEDI	20,308,026.37	19,785,664.61	522,362.76	10,756,193.00	13.10
Liberia	USD	2,416,846.64	8,646,904.00	−6,230,057.36	5,787,843.00	7.05
Mali	CFA	1,878,216,172.00	1,993,288,508.00	115,072,336.00	2,652,891.00	3.23
Niger	CFA	1,024,375,876.00	741,563,809.00	282,812,067.00	987,549.00	1.20
Nigeria	NAIRA	9,224,849,221.75	8,883,010,213.69	341,839,008.06	45,153,942.00	54.99
Senegal	CFA	3,393,379,981.00	3,466,992,199.00	−73,612,218.00	4,614,019.00	5.62
Sierra Leone	LE	2,508,518,931.59	2,484,647,341.58	23,871,590.01	544,600.00	0.66
Togo	CFA	1,503,888,922.00	1,460,382,028.00	43,506,894.00	1,944,208.00	2.37
Total (UA)					82,111,884.00	100.00

Source: ECOWAS Executive Secretariat 2009a.

The problem of ECOWAS funding and related issues have begun to once again raise serious concerns among Nigeria's regional integration stakeholders about the enormity of the nation's sacrifice on behalf of ECOWAS and the lack of tangible returns from the nation's investment in the organisation (see Table 7.4). During the course of field research for this chapter, two major opinions emerged. First, that Nigeria should not remit more than 60 percent of the community levy to ECOWAS and that the outstanding 40 percent should be applied directly to supporting meaningful development projects within the subregion. Those who champion this opinion make reference to the top-heavy bureaucracies of ECOWAS institutions and the inability of the commission to engage in any tangible developmental activity in the region.

The second opinion holds that Nigeria should remain a faithful member of ECOWAS for the survival of the region and the progress of its people. This group also points out that Nigeria has worked assiduously to bring ECOWAS to where it is and any effort to scuttle these gains are not only shortsighted but counterproductive. It is therefore fundamental, according to this view, that Nigeria pay ECOWAS the requisite

Table 7.4 Breakdown of State, Population Percentage, and Financial Burden of ECOWAS

Member State	Population, %	Cumulative Financial Burden, %
Benin	3.03	1.68
Burkina Faso	5.43	2.22
Cape Verde	0.17	0.20
Cote d'Ivoire	7.15	5.93
Gambia	0.58	0.59
Guinea	3.41	0.39
Guinea–Bissau	0.55	0.14
Ghana	8.08	13.82
Liberia	1.18	0.55
Mali	4.41	2.54
Niger	5.19	1.31
Nigeria	52.48	59.93
Senegal	4.25	7.55
Sierra Leone	1.93	0.79
Togo	2.24	2.33

Source: ECOWAS Executive Secretariat 2009a.

attention it deserves and work with other member states to put in place a robust and purposeful reform agenda which would entail the following:

- Clear and unambiguous commitment to the development of the subregion such that expenditure on administration is curtailed at 40 percent of total revenues and the remaining 60 percent expended on development projects within the community. Any effort to expand the current bureaucracy must be subjected to a rigorous cost-benefit analysis before embarked upon.
- Fair formula of sharing responsibilities as well as benefits within the community and ensuring that both the weak and the strong have a real stake in the subregional organisation.
- Recognition of Nigeria's contribution to ECOWAS and ensuring that some privileges are allotted to it, including being a permanent commissioner of administration and finance (*Field Notes* 2009–2010).

Systemic Challenges

The development of ECOWAS over the last three decades was undoubtedly a challenging process, which harboured as many expectations as it did disappointments. Some of these expectations have been realised with Nigeria in partnership with member states playing a significant role. However, systemic challenges still abound, which seem to militate against the development of ECOWAS, diminish the leadership role of Nigeria, and threaten to undermine the very basis of economic integration in the subregion. The first fundamental challenge relates to problems associated with the implementation of the ECOWAS Trade Liberalization Scheme (ETLS). In an extensive evaluation of the scheme, Bappah (2007) has come to the conclusion that, despite its take-off two decades ago, its achievements have been quite modest. Although more than 807 enterprises and 2,536 products have registered under ETLS and have benefitted from it, the strong expectation that the ETLS would significantly improve trade among ECOWAS members, facilitate the flow of goods within the subregion, and encourage collective self-reliance has not been realised. A number of factors may be responsible for this failure.

First, a substantial number of nontariff barriers retard intracommunity trade within the subregion. Bappah reported that all the enterprises he surveyed "responded negatively when asked if they were satisfied with the degree of freedom with which they moved their goods within the West African market" (2007, p. 67). Second, the subregion has a low manufacturing capacity, and the few industries at hand cannot maximally benefit from the raw materials being promoted by the ETLS. The few countries that have a larger manufacturing sector, like Nigeria, have not articulated a clear vision of facilitating the participation of their enterprises in intracommunity trade. Last, protectionist tendencies still remain, which makes the implementation of a common external tariff rather difficult and arbitrary (ECOWAS Commission 2009a, pp. 73–78).

The second major challenge facing ECOWAS has been the inability of the subregion to take concrete steps required to harmonise its members' monetary policies and work towards a single currency. Progress in attaining macroeconomic convergence has been slow, and the poor performance of many of the subregional economies makes realisation of this objective a Herculean task.

It should also be pointed out that contradictory policies between the francophone Union Economique et Monetaire Ouest Africaine Zone and the anglophone West African Monetary Zone, especially as they relate to exchange rates, with the former preferring a pegged exchange regime, have not helped in the harmonisation of monetary policy. As the ECOWAS Report stated, "Any effort to develop a common strategy towards the adoption of a common currency in ECOWAS must, first of all resolve this policy difference. The choice of exchange rate regime is a critical area that must be reviewed if a single track approach is to be pursued successfully" (2008, p. 63). Nigeria has not been able to develop full confidence in the process of a West African Monetary Union nor establish effective partnerships necessary for its realisation.

The third major challenge for ECOWAS has been its inability to tackle poverty effectively and to promote human development in the subregion. According to the United Nations Development Programme Human Development Report (2009), ECOWAS member states have some of the worst indices in the world, with Niger Republic occupying the last position in the world with a Human Development Index (HDI) ranking and value of 182 and 0.340, respectively. Niger is closely followed by Sierra Leone (180th, 0.365), Mali (178th, 0.371), Burkina Faso (177th, 0.389), Guinea-Bissau (173rd, 0.396), and Guinea (170th, 0.435). The next batch of ECOWAS members in this category are Liberia (169th, 0.442), Gambia (168th, 0.456), Senegal (166th, 0.464), Cote d'Ivoire (163rd, 0.484), Benin (161st, 0.492), and Togo (159th, 0.499). Only three ECOWAS members have an HDI score of 0.5 or above: Nigeria (158th, 0.511), Ghana (152nd, 0.526), and Cape Verde (121st, 0.708). As Okwuosa lamented, "The programmes that impact on the daily lives of citizens are so absent that one encounters more EU signposts on projects in the rural villages of ECOWAS States than those of ECOWAS itself. Ordinary citizens sometimes ask what ECOWAS is all about. This is an unhappy trend" (2009, p. 5).

It is also important to take into account the fast-growing population of the region, which was just over 120 million when ECOWAS was established in 1975 and projected to increase to 430 million by 2020. Forty-five percent of this population is estimated to be under fifteen years, thereby putting West Africa in the unenviable position of having the youngest population in the world (Ibn Chambas 2005, p. 15). Urgent efforts to develop capacity must be put in place to cater to this population if peace and security is to be sustained in the subregion.

Nigeria and the Future of ECOWAS

In his lecture at the Founders Day of the Nigerian Institute of International Affairs in 2004, the immediate past president of the ECOWAS Commission, Dr. Muhammad Ibn Chambas, identified the strategic importance of Nigeria to the West Africa project and how the success of the Nigerian experience holds the key to West African integration. Ibn Chambas, however, could not hide his hopes and fears, as well as the impediments that could hamper the realisation of Nigeria's full potential in the subregion (2005, pp. 21–23). The first issue raised by the president of the ECOWAS Commission is the importance of constitutional and democratic rule to enhancing the leadership role of Nigeria:

> A democratic Nigeria in which there is respect for human rights, the rule of law, a culture of tolerance and dialogue, is morally better placed to mediate in the numerous conflicts plaguing the region and Africa. (Ibn Chambas 2005, p. 22)

Second is the creation of a socioeconomic environment,

> which is business-friendly and people-centred in which probity, transparency and accountability thrive and corruption uprooted. Such an environment will boost both domestic and foreign direct investment which, in turn, will create employment and opportunities for generating wealth. Additionally, the monetary and fiscal discipline that the reforms seek to attain will enable Nigeria to meet several ECOWAS economic policy harmonization criteria for building a West Africa—wide customs union and the circulation of a single currency. (Ibn Chambas 2005, p. 22)

Two other issues raised by Ibn Chambas pertain to the dangers of protectionism and isolationism, which strategically important countries are wont to engage in, particularly during periods of economic distress. According to Ibn Chambas,

> We must resist the temptation to protect local industries that are unwilling to make the necessary technological and managerial adjustments to compete effectively in the regional market. I dare say that producers who are unable to stand the fairly lax competition of the West African market will stand no chance of penetrating the wider African market, not to talk of the global market. (2005, p. 22)

On isolationism, Ibn Chambas believes that Nigeria must lead the way in the implementation of ECOWAS protocols on free movement of persons, goods, services, and capital:

> Our goal of achieving a borderless West Africa can only be realized if our peoples are able to freely move about in West Africa as our forefathers did before colonialism brought about the existing boundaries. Free movement will help us increase trade amongst West African States. Increased trade means that more goods and services will be produced, increased production means, in turn, increased job creation and opportunities to fight poverty and increase wealth for our people. (2005, p. 23)

The views and concerns of Ibn Chambas have also been echoed by other authors, especially those involved with economic integration policy. Oche (2006, pp. 23–25) drew attention to factors that conspired to undermine the role of Nigeria in ECOWAS, including economic stagnation and renewed French interests in the subregion as well as allegations of domination by Nigeria over its smaller neighours. Nwoke raised the issue of Nigeria's poor leadership image, which undermines the effectiveness of its role in ECOWAS (2005, p. 138). "Charity," according to Nwoke, "begins at home. Nigeria cannot provide effective sub-regional leadership when we have not done so well in the area of leadership in Nigeria" (p. 138). Despite these shortcomings, Nigeria has been able to show a number of "good leadership directions" toward facilitating subregional integration. These include its good neighbourliness policy and the establishment of a Ministry of Co-operation and Integration in Africa, as well as a Fast Track Initiative, in partnership with Ghana, to promote West African integration (pp. 140–141).

It should also be pointed out that during the course of the fieldwork for this research, several issues have been raised, especially by Nigeria's regional integration stakeholders, on the various impediments to Nigeria's leadership role in ECOWAS and what needs to be done to remove these impediments. There is a general concern that Nigeria does not have a well-articulated vision of what it wants in ECOWAS and in the West Africa project as a whole. Many Nigerian officials attend meetings without proper briefing, key issues are left unattended, and no subsisting strategy exists to realize set goals and objectives. We pay the piper but have little knowledge and appreciation of the music he plays, let alone dictate the tune. There is also a general lamentation, even among technocratic stakeholders, that the integration process has not fully incorporated important key stakeholders. The former president of the ECOWAS Commission regretted the conspicuous absence of the organized private sector from "this evolving partnership in the integration process" (Ibn Chambas 2005, p. 18). Civil society as well as community organisations are equally uninvolved at the national level. It is therefore essential to hold an ECOWAS forum that will serve the purposes of advocacy, sensitisation, and mobilisation by working with all stakeholders for the realisation of ECOWAS objectives.

Finally, many stakeholders believe that Nigeria must forge an effective partnership with key member states to ensure that ECOWAS focuses on infrastructural and socioeconomic development. The current state of human development in the subregion is seen as a great embarrassment. Plans to create an elected parliament as well as additional expenditure on ECOWAS institutions should be embarked on only when the financial resources to fund them are raised outside the budget. The future of ECOWAS lies with its ability to meaningfully and significantly address the enormous developmental challenges facing the subregion. Nigeria, as its principal financier, must guide it rightly to realize this cardinal objective.

Conclusion

Regional groupings such as ECOWAS and SADC play increasingly important roles in Africa, but the absence of effective economic integration and endemic political fragmentation are still major problems (Kingibe 2009).

This chapter has examined the role of Nigeria in the formation of ECOWAS, as well as its engagement with the regional organisation over the last three decades. Nigeria's efforts at establishing this veritable organisation and the sacrifices it has made to fund and sustain its activities demonstrate not only its status as a regional power but also its commitment to promoting mutual self-reliance and socioeconomic development in the subregion. ECOWAS has recorded many outstanding achievements, including freedom of movement of persons, residence, and establishment; innovative peacekeeping initiatives; and institution building. Nigeria's leadership and its commitment to the subregional organisation made these achievements possible. But ECOWAS is also being confronted with gargantuan problems in the areas of trade liberalisation, monetary union, infrastructure, and human development. These are equally Nigeria's problems. In the face of rising regional and developmental challenges, Nigeria must play its destined role in leading ECOWAS.

The promotion of regional integration has remained a cardinal principle of Nigeria's foreign policy since independence, giving rise to one of the major achievements of Nigeria's global engagement—the formation of ECOWAS. The fact that ECOWAS itself was formed during the terminal year of General Gowon's military regime and that key achievements, including the formation of ECOMOG and attempts to restore democracy in Liberia and Sierra Leone, were recorded under the military leadership of General Babangida and General Abacha indicate that, despite the enormity of its socioeconomic and political problems, Nigeria has endeavoured to play a crucial role in promoting regional development in West Africa.

The country's strategic leadership role will, however, depend on a number of factors. First, Nigeria will need to have a well-articulated West African agenda, with clear goals and objectives that will safeguard the development of the nation and the socioeconomic well-being of the entire subregion. Second, for Nigeria to exercise true leadership in West Africa, it must begin to shore up its moral capital in the subregion by developing a dynamic democratic culture and safeguarding the integrity of its governance and socioeconomic institutions. Third, Nigeria must realize that the exercise of leadership requires effective engagement with other countries of the subregion and develop effective partnerships to re-engineer and refocus ECOWAS activities on infrastructural and human development in order to garner a respectable place for the nation and indeed for the generality of Nigerians—a pride of place in the affairs of the subregion.

Bibliography

Adedeji, A., 1984, "Collective Self-Reliance in Developing Africa: Scope, Prospects, and Problems," in A.B Akinyemi, S.B. Falegan, and I.A. Aluko, eds., *Readings and Documents on ECOWAS*, Institute of International Affairs, Lagos, Nigeria, pp. xxi–xxxv.

Akindele, R.A., 1988, "The Domestic Structure and Natural Resources Profile of Nigeria's External Trade," in R.A. Akindele and B. Ate, eds., *Nigeria's Economic Relations with the Major Developed Market Economy Countries, 1960–1985*, Nigerian Institute of International Affairs, Lagos, Nigeria, pp. 54–83.

Akinyemi, A. B., Agbi, S. O., and Otubanjo, A.O., eds., 1989, "Nigeria Since Independence: The First 25 Years, International Relations," vol. X, in *Panel on Nigeria Since Independence History Project*, Heinemann Educational Publishers, Ibadan, Nigeria.

Akinyemi, A.B, Falegan, S.B., and Aluko, I.A., eds., 1984, *Readings and Documents on ECOWAS*, Institute of International Affairs, Lagos, Nigeria.

Bappah, H.Y., 2007, *An Assessment of ECOWAS Trade Liberalization Scheme and the Creation of a Free Trade Area in West Africa*, M.sc thesis, Ahmadu Bello University, Zaria, Nigeria.

ECOWAS, 2002–2008, *Annual Reports*, www.ecowas.int, accessed February 2010.

ECOWAS, 2010, *Institutions, Activities and Treaty*, www.ecowas.int, accessed February 2010.

ECOWAS Commission, 2008, ECOWAS Handbook on Election Observation, Abuja, Nigeria.

ECOWAS Commission, 2009a, Annual Report 2008: Forging Regional Response to Global Economic and Financial Crises, Abuja, Nigeria.

ECOWAS Commission, 2009b, *ECOWAS Common Investment Market Vision*, Abuja, Nigeria.

ECOWAS Commission, 2009c, ECOWAS Directives on the Harmonization of Guiding Principles and Policies in the Mining Sector, Abuja, Nigeria.

ECOWAS Executive Secretariat, undated, *ECOWAS Trade Regime*, Abuja, Nigeria.

ECOWAS Executive Secretariat, 2003, ECOWAS Protocol on Energy, signed at Dakar, Senegal, on January 31, 2003.

ECOWAS Executive Secretariat, 2006, *National Accounts of ECOWAS*, Abuja, Nigeria.

ECOWAS Executive Secretariat, 2009a, *ECOWAS Briefs*, Miscellaneous, Abuja, Nigeria.

ECOWAS Executive Secretariat, 2009b, Final Communique on Mini-Summit of Heads of State and Government on the Creation of a Borderless ECOWAS, Abuja, Nigeria, March 27, 2000.

Ezenwe, U., 1984, *ECOWAS and the Economic Integration of West Africa*, Books Publishers Ltd., Ibadan, Nigeria.

Field Notes (obtained in interviews by the author), October 2009–January 2010, "Interviews with Officials of Ministry of Foreign Affairs, ECOWAS, NEPAD and Retired Officials and Diplomats."

Gambari, I., 1989, *Theory and Reality in Foreign Policy Making: Nigeria after the Second Republic*, Humanities Press International, New Jersey, US.

Garba, J., 1987, *Diplomatic Soldiering: The Conduct of Nigerian Foreign Policy, 1975–1979*, Spectrum Books Ltd., Ibadan, Nigeria.

Gana, A.T., 1989, "Nigeria, West Africa and the Economic Community of West African States," in A.B. Akinyemi, S.O. Agbi, and A.O. Otubanjo, eds., *Panel on Nigeria Since Independence History Project*, Heinemann Educational Publishers, Ibadan, Nigeria, pp. 117–137.

Ibn Chambas, M., 2005, *The ECOWAS Agenda: Promoting Good Governance, Peace, Stability and Sustainable Development*, Nigerian Institute of International Affairs, Lagos, Nigeria.

Irele, M., 1990, *The Economic Community of West African States [ECOWAS]: A Bibliography and Source*, Nigerian Institute of International Affairs, Lagos, Nigeria.

Kingibe, B., 2008, "Safeguarding Nigeria's Global Strategic Interests," presented at the Induction Programme for Newly Appointed Ambassadors, Ministry of Foreign Affairs, Obudu Ranch Resort, Cross River, February 7.

Laro, K., 2002, *Regional Initiatives in Peace-Keeping: The Case of ECOMOG in Liberia and Sierra Leone*, Nigerian Foreign Service Club Lecture Series.

NEPAD (New Partnership for Africa's Development), 2001, *The New Partnership for African Development Document*, Abuja, Nigeria, October.

NEPAD, 2003, *African Peer Review Mechanism [APRM] Guidelines*, Abuja, Nigeria, March 9.

Nwoke, C.N., 2005, "Nigeria and ECOWAS," in U.J. Ogwu, ed., *New Horizons for Nigeria in World Affairs*, Nigerian Institute of International Affairs, Lagos, Nigeria.

Nwolise, O.B.C., 1989, "The Civil War and Nigerian Foreign Policy," in A.B. Akinyemi, S.O. Agbi, and A.O. Otubanjo, eds., *Panel on Nigeria Since Independence History Project*, Heinemann Educational Publishers, Ibadan, Nigeria, pp. 192–225.

Oche, O., 2006, "Nigeria's Role in ECOWAS," presented at a Workshop on International Relations, Abuja, Nigeria, October 16–20.

Okwuosa, A.C., 2009, "Nigeria and ECOWAS: Successes and Challenges in Regional Balance and Regional Integration," presented at the Induction Programme for Newly Appointed Ambassadors, Ministry of Foreign Affairs, Obudu Ranch Resort, Cross River, February 7.

Otubanjo, F., 1989, "Phases and Changes in Nigerian Foreign Policy," in A.B. Akinyemi, S.O. Agbi, and A.O. Otubanjo, eds., *Panel on Nigeria Since Independence History Project*, Heinemann Educational Publishers, Ibadan, Nigeria, pp. 1–11.

Rukato, H., 2010, *Future Africa: Prospects for Democracy and Development under NEPAD*, Africa World Press, Lawrenceville, NJ, US.

United Nations Development Programme, Human Development Report 2009, www.hdrstats.undp.org, accessed February 2010.

8

Nigeria, OPEC, and the Middle East

Abubakar Siddique Mohammed

The history of oil is the history of a struggle for power. Marked by conflicting relations between actors whose motivations are not strictly economic, oil has been used as a weapon in international relations by both producers and buyers. This is the context for any attempt to understand the relationship between Nigeria, the Organization of Petroleum Exporting Countries (OPEC), and the Middle East. While the early phase of the development of Nigeria's oil industry owed a great deal to the geopolitics of Arab North Africa and the Middle East, the country's membership in OPEC has had a far-reaching impact on both the international political economy of oil and Nigeria's development efforts.

From the onset, many factors combined to destine Nigeria to play a major role in the international oil industry and to ensure that major oil-consuming and -producing countries would directly and indirectly influence the country's internal politics and its international relations. Nigeria is situated in the Atlantic Basin, closer to the United States and Europe than is the Middle East, which features most of the major global crude oil–producing countries, such as Saudi Arabia, Kuwait, and Iraq. Though Nigeria has a large Muslim population and long contact with the Middle East, especially Saudi Arabia, it has nevertheless been removed from the many conflicts of the region with their attendant disruptions in oil production.

An important advantage for the Nigerian oil industry is the quality of its sulphur-free crude. Its flagship, Bonny Light, compares favourably with the Arabian Light of Saudi Arabia. These factors explain why Nigeria has on several occasions played a major if not critical role in the global oil market. The development of the Nigerian oil industry, however, has gone through phases, each of which has been influenced by the country's internal political dynamics, the role of major actors in OPEC, and the general global political and economic situations.

The Early Phase

In 1914 the British colonial administration enacted the Colonial Mineral Ordinance to regulate the oil industry, which vested complete ownership rights of Nigeria's oil in the British Crown. The ordinance also restricted issuance of mining leases to her majesty's subjects and/or British companies, which ensured that the industry remained for some years the exclusive preserve of British companies. Prior to this legislation, in 1908, a German company, the Nigerian Bitumen Corporation, had been given a licence by the colonial administration to explore for oil in Nigeria. It drilled fourteen wells in the Lagos area but the outbreak of World War I terminated operations.

In 1937, Shell-D'Arcy, an Anglo-Dutch consortium of Royal Dutch Shell and British Petroleum, was formed, signalling renewed interest in exploration activities in Nigeria. In 1938, the company was awarded an oil exploration licence, which covered the whole of the country and gave the company the right to choose where and when to explore for oil. The outbreak of the Second World War halted its activities, but exploration resumed in 1946. In 1956, Shell D'Arcy, which had then become Shell-BP, discovered oil in commercial quantity at Oloibiri. Two years later, in 1958, oil tanker Hemifusus lifted Nigerian crude oil for the world market, with a daily production of 5,000 barrels. Before 1955, Shell-BP enjoyed a monopoly status over the Nigerian oil industry, determining where and when to produce. According to Pearson, by 1957, "Shell-BP had reduced its acreage to 40,000 square miles of Oil Prospecting Licenses. Of this acreage Shell-BP converted nearly 15,000 square miles into Oil Mining Leases (OML's) in 1960 and 1962 and returned the residual to the Nigerian government" (1970, p. 15). The remaining acreage was then allocated to the new entrants Tenneco, Gulf, Agip, Safrap, and Philips as onshore oil exploration licences. Later, Esso, Safrap, and Great Basins were allocated additional onshore licences.

The offers continued when, in 1960, Nigeria divided its offshore continental shelf into twelve blocks of approximately 1,000 square miles each. Four of these went to Shell-BP, two were secured by Gulf, two by Mobil, and two by Texas Overseas (Pearson 1970, p. 18). It took Shell-BP twenty years (1938–1958) to start producing, although, "as far back as 1946, they were sure that oil was available" (Usman 1979, p. 22). That the company determined the "pace of development of the petroleum economy in Nigeria" was partly explained by the monopoly it enjoyed, as well as the international context at the time when Anglo-American oil companies controlled the industry in the capitalist world and coordinated global production and sale (Usman 1979). Shell-BP not only chose the best fields but it also underpaid Nigeria, taking advantage of the country's weak legislation. For example, on the average, Shell-BP paid £190 per 1,000 barrels in 1957–1958 to 1965–1966 in contrast to between £270 and £340 paid in other countries (Schatzl 1969, p. 11).

Despite the fact that colonial oil policy determined the production and export of Nigerian crude oil, as Frynas (2000, p. 11) noted, the quantity produced was small in comparative terms. Indeed, at the time of independence in 1960, Canada, Qatar, Brunei, and Trinidad, all members of the British Commonwealth, produced more oil than Nigeria, whose share was only 1.8 percent of total British Commonwealth crude production. While Nigeria's oil industry at the time of independence was insignificant, it had potential for future expansion, though foreign oil companies had no serious plan for active Nigerian participation in the industry.

Post-Independence Phase

The post-independence administration of Prime Minister Tafawa Balewa continued with the policy inherited from the colonial administration. The Report of the Crude Oil Sales Tribunal notes that the Balewa administration "during the period 1960 to January 15, 1966 did not include oil within their scheme of things and consequently did not evolve an oil policy" (Federal Government of Nigeria [FGN] 1980, p. 14). Apart from allocation of acreage to the transnational oil companies, the government's only obvious practical link with the oil industry was through the petroleum section of the Ministry of Finance, which collected petroleum profit tax. A dearth of indigenous technical expertise resulted in Nigerian authorities remaining in the dark about industry operations. The Balewa administration did not know the "true extent of the country's reserves [and was unfamiliar] with the ramifications that oil production might have" (Pearson 1970, p. 136). The post-independence administration's lack of capacity regarding developments in the oil industry were illustrated by the fact that "discussion of this important sector has always been in generalities. . . . Any meaningful policy regarding the petroleum industry has therefore not been possible beyond broad guidelines" (FGN 1970, p. 162).

In 1965, the Port Harcourt Oil Refinery was "established primarily to meet domestic requirement for refined petroleum products" (FGN 1970, p. 162) after persistent demand by the government. It was built to refine only 38,000 barrels per day (b/d) and refined crude for the transnational oil companies which effectively "screened" it from the market by controlling marketing and distribution. However, developments on the global petroleum scene, which ultimately culminated in the formation of OPEC, had a profound effect on the Nigerian energy scene, especially in shaping its petroleum policy.

Formation of OPEC

Before the mid-1960s, the crude oil market was dominated by the United States. The emergence of former Soviet bloc countries in North Africa and the Middle East, as well as Venezuela and Iran, as major players resulted in multiple markets and declining US dominance of the global oil industry. This development brought into question the international price fixing method, which was anchored on factors determined by the US oil industry, its organisational system, its production costs, and the productivity of its oil industry. Potentially, the United States and the former Soviet bloc were self-sufficient, but while the United States was becoming a net importer, the Soviet bloc was a net exporter, which introduced new dynamics in global energy politics.

Broadly speaking, a polarisation of supply and demand existed. Venezuela (which was later to become the initiator of OPEC), the Middle East, and North Africa had minimal demand in relative terms given their low level of industrialisation. The larger consumers, especially Western Europe and Japan, had little or no crude oil production. Japan, in particular, was rebuilding and modernising its war-torn economy and was making enormous demand for raw materials in the world market.

The Middle East was in a vantage position to benefit from these developments due to its favourable geographical location, low production costs, and considerable reserves (more than the United States). The region produced a third of the non-Communist bloc oil and held 60 percent of world reserves, making it the major centre of oil geopolitics. This called into question the Achnacarry Agreement of 1928 among the "Seven Sisters," the major oil companies in control of the industry globally, which stated that wherever oil comes from, its prices should be the same in every export centre of the world, as in US ports along the Gulf of Mexico (Madelin 1975, p. 10). Consequently, the relationship between the transnational oil companies and their host governments began to come under serious scrutiny and strain as companies' activities were increasingly at variance with the national aspirations of their hosts. In reaction, the Arab League met in Cairo in April 1959 with the participation of two non-Arab countries: Venezuela, which had been in the forefront of the struggle for oil-producing states to control their oil resources, and Iran, which had been at the receiving end of the exploitation by the oil companies, backed by their home governments. The Cairo meeting considered oil, like all other natural resources, as national assets over which producing countries should exercise permanent sovereignty.

As Ayoub (1993, p. 5) notes, the dominant idea at the time was that political independence would be empty if it were not accompanied by the transfer of property and resources controlled by foreign companies to the public sector. It was the era of resource nationalism, and at the Cairo meeting the principle of creating OPEC was agreed upon. On September 15, 1960, the organisation officially came into existence with five members: Saudi Arabia, Kuwait, Iraq, Venezuela, and Iran. Together, these countries controlled 90 percent of global oil exports: 40 percent for Saudi Arabia, Kuwait, and Iraq combined; and 50 percent for Venezuela and Iran. Eight other countries later joined OPEC: Qatar (1961), Indonesia (1962), Libya (1962), United Arab Emirates (1967), Algeria (1969), Nigeria (1971), Ecuador (1973), and Gabon (1975). After its formation, OPEC moved rapidly to put in place a common fiscal system, and the move towards effective state intervention had begun. UN Resolutions No. 1803 (XVII) in 1960 and No. 2518 in 1966 were interpreted by the oil-producing countries as a reaffirmation of their right to exercise control over their natural resources. In 1968, OPEC, in line with these resolutions, adopted Resolution XVI-90, which called on its member countries to acquire, by 1982, at least 51 percent state participation in the capital of transnational petroleum companies. These developments posed serious challenges to the transnational oil companies of the West, which were gradually losing control of crude oil reserves, not only in OPEC countries but also in non-OPEC states.

Impact on Nigeria

The seeming disinterest by Nigerians in the oil industry began to change in 1965 when Prime Minister Balewa (in a speech to the Chamber of

Commerce) and Minister of Finance Okotie Eboh (in his annual budget address to Parliament) revealed the potential impact of oil revenue on the balance of payments. Not only did these speeches change the general political feeling from apathy to euphoria, they also laid the foundation for later developments in the Nigerian oil industry and set the context of its relationship with the oil companies, OPEC, and the Middle East. The Balewa administration was overthrown in January 1966 before evolving a policy that could have profoundly impacted the Nigerian oil industry, its relationship with the transnational oil companies, or oil-producing countries that had regrouped in OPEC. Subsequent military regimes, however, would focus on the challenges.

In 1964, Nigeria sent an observer delegation to the OPEC Conference and adopted the organisation's terms for tax assessment, resulting in the promulgation of the Petroleum Profit Tax (Amendment) Decree in 1967. Under this decree, tax was to be assessed on posted prices, and royalty was to be assessed as current operational expenditure, thereby excluding it from the state's 50 percent share of profits as was the case before promulgation of the decree.

Similarly, the Declaratory Statement of Petroleum Policy in Member Countries, issued in 1968 by OPEC, made reference to the inalienable right expressed by the United Nations of all countries to exercise permanent sovereignty over their natural resources in the interest of their national development and demanded that the exploitation of the exhaustible petroleum resources of OPEC member countries should be geared towards securing the greatest possible benefit for its member countries. The statement had a profound effect on Nigerian policymakers. For example, the declaration urged members to acquire "participation in concession" and to speed up the process of taking over acreages to be determined by them. Although Nigeria was not a member of OPEC at that time, it nevertheless took a major step towards realising the organisation's directives. In 1969, the government promulgated Petroleum Decree No. 51 that vested in the Nigerian state "the entire ownership and control of all petroleum; under or upon any lands to which" the section applies; that is, all land covered by water which

- was in Nigeria,
- was under the territorial waters of Nigeria, or
- formed part of the continental shelf.

The decree also empowered the commissioner for mines and power to grant

- a licence to be known as an oil exploration licence,
- a licence to be known as an oil prospecting licence, or
- a lease to be known as an oil mining lease (Law of the Federation, vol. 13, Chapter P10, Petroleum Act).

Furthermore, the decree imposed a mandatory requirement on all oil companies to be incorporated in Nigeria under the Companies Decree 1968 and established a Nigerian Petroleum Advisory Board to advise the government on the formulation of oil policy.

The Gowon regime, in line with OPEC member countries, moved to restrict favourable tax conditions that the oil companies had enjoyed since the colonial era. The Petroleum Decree also provided for compulsory 51 percent Nigerian state participation in all new concessions.

An important factor that combined to push the nationalistic drive exhibited by the Gowon regime was the Biafran war of secession, which began in 1967. Support for Biafra, the territory which contained some two-thirds of Nigeria's then-known oil reserves by French oil company Safrap, led the federal government to question the participation of foreign oil companies in the country's development. Added to this were the oil companies' lackadaisical attitudes towards technology transfer, which would have contributed to social development and the employment of indigenous staff. Nigeria called upon countries of the East, particularly Romania and the USSR, to train Nigerians in the petroleum sector. Indeed, the first petroleum institute in Nigeria was established with the assistance of the Soviet Union.

In 1971, the Gowon administration joined OPEC, and in line with the organisation's decision that host government participation in the oil industry should be enhanced, the administration established the Nigerian National Oil Corporation (NNOC) by Decree No. 18 of April 1, 1971, which paved the way for the country's direct participation in all aspects of the petroleum industry. The corporation was given the task of training indigenous workers; managing oil leases over large areas of the country; encouraging indigenous participation in infrastructure development for the industry; managing refineries; participating in marketing and ensuring price uniformity across the domestic market; developing a national tanker fleet; constructing pipelines; and investing in allied industries, such as fertilizers. Given the highly complex nature of the oil industry and the dearth of highly competent Nigerians, the objectives that the NNOC was tasked to achieve were far too ambitious (Field 2001, p. 1).

Participation began with the NNOC's acquisition of a 33.33 percent stake in the Nigerian Agip Oil Company and 35 percent in Safrap, the

Nigerian arm of the French company Elf. The acquisition continued after Nigeria joined OPEC, with the NNOC acquiring 35 percent stakes in Shell-BP, Gulf, and Mobil on April 1, 1973, and that year entering into a production-sharing agreement with Ashland Oil. On April 1, 1974, stakes in Elf, Agip/Phillips, Shell-BP, Gulf, and Mobil were increased to 55 percent, and on May 1, 1975, the NNOC acquired 55 percent of Texaco's operations in Nigeria.

Despite limited powers, the NNOC made its mark in the export of Nigerian crude oil. Boosted by the sharp price rises that followed the first oil shock of 1973, Nigeria saw its oil export earnings rise from 219 million naira in 1970 to 10.6 billion naira in 1979, thereby achieving an enviable status as the first sub-Saharan African country to successfully exploit its oil reserves. NNOC's weaknesses were soon to become obvious, however, as it attempted to implement objectives set for it. Following reorganisation of the Nigerian oil industry in 1977, the NNOC was transformed into the Nigerian National Petroleum Corporation.

1973 Arab-Israel War and
Its Impact on Nigeria's Foreign Policy

Two years after Nigeria joined OPEC, political tension in the Middle East led to war on October 6, 1973, between Syria and Egypt on one hand and the State of Israel on the other. The war and developments in the global oil industry were to impact the Nigerian oil industry and the country's relations with Israel.

Rising demand for oil coincided with the high political tension in the Middle East. For the first time, the spot market price—the day-to-day market—was higher than the posted price. On the East Coast of the United States the combined effect of low gas price, refining capacity shortage, and environmentalists' success led to serious shortages in petroleum products and gas. The Shah of Iran, whose country was then the world's second-largest exporter of oil, argued that oil prices must rise, as the price the West was paying for crude oil was too low compared to costs of goods imported from the West.

On the political scene, tension was further heightened when Kuwait called on the Arab countries to use their oil as a political arm should there be war between Arab countries and Israel. A series of campaigns mounted by Saudi Arabia and the oil companies operating in the United States to dissuade the Nixon administration from supporting Israel fell on deaf ears. In September 1973, President Richard Nixon publicly and officially refused to link US policy in the region to Arab oil. Two days after the commencement of the Arab-Israeli war, OPEC and representatives of the oil companies met to negotiate a review of crude prices, which took into consideration the consecutive devaluation of the US dollar, the jettisoning by Nixon in August 1971 of gold convertibility, and the high inflation prevalent at the time. OPEC demanded a substantial increase in crude oil prices, while oil companies insisted on a 15 percent increase. Thus on October 16, ten days after the Shah of Iran had warned that the price of oil would be increased and a few days after US reaffirmation of its support for Israel, Gulf producers seized the initiative by raising the posted price of oil by 70 percent—from $2.989 to $4.119 a barrel for Arabian Light from Saudi Arabia (Martin 1990, p. 56). This marked the first time OPEC had unilaterally fixed the price of its crude oil.

The following day, member countries of the Organisation of Arab Petroleum Exporting Countries (OAPEC), at their meeting in Kuwait, placed an embargo on oil supply to the United States, which they designated as a "principal hostile country," in response to US support for Israel of $2 billion in emergency aid, including an outright grant of $1.5 billion. The embargo was later extended to Western Europe and Japan. Arab countries also agreed to cut oil production by 5 percent from September's output and to continue until their economic and political objectives were met. The reduction, which was on the order of 2 million b/d, had in just three months pushed the spot market price substantially higher than the posted price. By December, the official price of Arabian Light of Saudi Arabia, fixed at $11.651, sold for $19.35 in the open market (Chevallier 1986, p. 7). The Arab-Israeli war gave a push to the inevitable price rises, which continued not as a result of collective action by OPEC as a group but by some of its Arab members who together with Egypt, Syria, and Tunisia teamed up in OAPEC.

The Arab-Israeli conflict was to have both an economic and political impact on Nigeria. Economically, the Nigerian oil industry was given a boost as the United States turned to it and other non-Arab members of the organisation—Iran and Indonesia—to offset the production cuts by modest increases in their own production. Revenues from oil rose from 1,176.2 million naira in 1972 to 1,893.5 million naira in 1974 to 5,365.7 million naira in 1985, consolidating the dominance of oil in the total export earnings of Nigeria (Kwanashie 1991). Although the decision by members of OPEC to cut production was political, other members came under heavy pressure to create a permanent mechanism through which OPEC members could maintain high prices at the end of the boycott.

The political impact of the Arab-Israeli conflict on Nigeria has to be understood against the background of the composition of OPEC itself and the relationship between Nigeria, the Arab countries of the Middle East, and Israel. At the time of the conflict, OPEC consisted of eleven countries, seven of which were Arab states either in conflict among themselves or with others. Nigeria's membership in the organisation meant that it could not completely insulate itself from these conflicts. For centuries, Nigeria had maintained contact with Arab countries of North Africa and the Middle East through trade and pilgrimage to Saudi Arabia. In the 1960s and 1970s, many Muslim organisations benefitted from financial assistance from Saudi Arabia—one of its objectives being to contain the spread of Sufism in the country and to spread Wahabism, the Saudi form of Sunni Islam, which "sought to regenerate Islam through a return to original purity of the religion" (Corbin 2002, p. 4).

Saudi support also helped anti-Sufi reformists to build mass movements, especially in the northern states, challenging religious, political, and social hierarchies. The chief Imam of Medina, Saudi Arabia, Sheikh Abdul Azeez, visited Nigeria in June–July 1963 and opened the £100,000 Sultan Bello Mosque in Sokoto. In June 1964, Prince Faisal of Saudi Arabia donated £60,000 to the Sarduana of Sokoto, the premier of Northern Nigeria and at one time the vice president of the Muslim League, "to continue the work of promoting Islam" and also donated £40,000 for the construction of Lagos Central Mosque. There were also unofficial donations, "probably amounting to millions of pounds" (Paden 1986, p. 543). Many Nigerian Muslims have since the 1960s secured scholarships to study in the Middle East. The 1940s witnessed the influx of Lebanese immigrants from all faiths, with estimates putting the population in Nigeria at 40,000. It is understandable therefore that before the creation of states in Nigeria, the Northern regional government was not friendly to the State of Israel, and the region rejected aid advanced to it by Israel. In an address to the league, the Sardauna justified the rejection of the aid thus:

> It is also fitting at this juncture for me to mention the numerous attempts made by the Jews to entice underdeveloped countries to their side. Barely two years ago, they offered a sizable amount of loan to the Federation of Nigeria. The offer was accepted by all the governments except we in the North who rejected it outright. I made it vividly clear at the time that Northern Nigeria would prefer to go without development rather than receiving an Israeli loan to aid. We took this step only in good faith as Muslims. (Paden 1986, p. 541)

Although the Balewa administration at the federal level established diplomatic relations with Israel, this came under serious strain in 1966 during the military regime of General Yakubu Gowon due to the support Israel gave Biafran secessionists. Diplomatic relations were not broken, but a strongly worded protest letter was sent to Israel when its foreign minister, Abba Eban, revealed that Israel had indeed aided Biafra, further arguing that had other countries done so the result of the war would have been different (Ambe-Uva and Adegboyega 2007). Quite predictably, the Arab countries, particularly Egypt, supported Nigeria.

Upon the outbreak of the Arab-Israeli war, Nigeria repaid its political debt to the Arab countries by supporting their cause. The federal government's position was that had Israel withdrawn its forces from the occupied Arab territories in accordance with the 1967 UN resolution, there would not have been war. Nigeria also supported the Organization of African Unity resolution sponsored by Arab countries urging members to sever diplomatic relations with Israel.

Fall of the Shah of Iran and Its Aftermath

In 1979, six years after the first oil shock, the world economy was plunged into another spiral of oil price hikes caused by political and technical factors. Events leading to the Iranian revolution contributed to destabilising the market when, in October 1978, workers in the Iranian oil industry went on strike, heralding the death knell of the Pahlavi dynasty. By December of the same year the strike had deprived the world market of the total production of Iranian oil of approximately 6 million b/d. Although Saudi Arabia, Nigeria, Venezuela, and Libya increased their production to meet the shortfall, they could not stem the tide of price hikes. This was aggravated by the failure of Saudi Arabia to produce to capacity. Exactly four days after the fall of the Shah of Iran in January 1979, Saudi Arabia announced that for technical reasons it could produce only 9.5 million b/d, a reduction of 1 million b/d below its December 1978 production. Oil companies' stocks were running low, which led to massive restocking by the oil companies. The frantic demand considerably impacted the spot market trading in limited stocks because transnational oil companies, with preferential crude, had reduced supplies to third parties. Oil-exporting countries were increasingly selling only a part of their production on the spot market. The growing gap between the spot market price and the official price for short-term contracts led Saudi Arabia, an advocate of price stability, to accept higher price increases. By the fourth quarter of 1979, the price of oil had risen to $35 per barrel (Martin 1990, p. 56).

As was the case during the first oil price shock, Nigeria witnessed increasing demand for its crude oil. Total export of crude oil rose from 667.4 million barrels in 1978 to 818.7 million in 1980. On the average, production rose from 1.8 million b/d in 1978 to 2 million b/d in 1979.

Iran–Iraq War

In August 1980, Iraq launched an attack on Iran and advanced rapidly into the country. Iraq began preparing for the war after the Shah's fall and had been "building up substantial stocks of arms and spare parts, as well as monetary reserves amounting to $35,000 million" (Terzian 1985, p. 282). It also increased its oil production in 1979 and 1980. The attack reversed the seemingly cordial relations established between leaders of the two countries, Mohammed Reza Pahlavi, the Shah of Iran, and Saddam Hussein, the vice president of Iraq, who had signed the Algiers Accord of 1975.

Various reasons have been advanced for Saddam Hussein's actions and the support he received from Arab countries of the Gulf. One was that the Iranian revolution's overthrow of the monarchy implicitly "threatened all the regimes in the Muslim world, just as the French revolution threatened all the crowned heads of Europe." And, whereas the initial threat of the popular revolution was not an Islamic jihad, nevertheless it showed that repressive dictatorial regimes can be overthrown by the oppressed through mass action (Muhsin et al. 1990, p. 229). Neither Saddam Hussein, whose regime was as brutal as the Shah's, nor the autocratic monarchies of the Gulf welcomed the new order in Iran. To these countries, war would pave the way for the formulation of a pact guaranteeing their security and eliminate Iran's influence as well as Iraq's opposition to them. Saudi Arabia, Kuwait, Qatar, United Arab Emirates (UAE), Bahrain, and Oman signed a mutual security pact in November 1980, two months after the outbreak of the war, and in February met in the Kuwaiti capital to formalize the creation of the Gulf Cooperation Council.

These developments had serious consequences on OPEC and relationships among its member countries. First, it paralysed to some extent the operations of the organisation. Two of its powerful members, with the largest reserves after Saudi Arabia, were locked in war. OPEC as a body was rendered powerless. In its place, Saudi Arabia, Kuwait, Qatar, and the UAE—Gulf countries not directly involved in the war—met to formulate a regional coordination of oil policy. In reaction, Nigeria, Gabon, Libya, and Algeria—all four African countries— met in Algiers, the capital of Algeria, to consider their response should there be a shortage in the world market. Contrary to expectations, rather than a shortage, there was a glut. The situation was compounded by Saudi Arabia's decision to maintain its oil production, rejecting all appeals to do the contrary. Its objective was to bring prices down to levels acceptable to it. As if to drive producers like Nigeria from the market, Sheikh Ahmed Zaki Yamani, minister of petroleum and mineral resources of Saudi Arabia from 1962–1986,

> even went so far to appeal solemnly to the consumer countries to help Saudi Arabia in its trial of strength against its own OPEC partners. He asked the Americans momentarily to suspend their programme of building up "strategic stock" so as not to increase demand and maintain the pressure on prices. When prices have fallen, you can start buying again, at lower cost, he advised them. (Terzian 1985, p. 287)

Saudi Arabia did so because at that time it accounted for 40 percent of total OPEC production and approximately half of its exports. An effective 10 percent cut by the other twelve members of the organisation and even higher cuts by Nigeria, Venezuela, Kuwait, and Qatar withdrawing over 1.3 million b/d could not reverse the trend, as supply far exceeded demand. It was a turbulent period for OPEC as member countries engaged in an acrimonious attempt to grapple with the glut.

Since 1973, when OPEC initiated exercising its influence on the price of crude oil, far-reaching adjustments have been made in its supply and demand. The role played by countries of the Organisation for Economic Co-Operation and Development (OECD) is significant in this respect. They reacted resolutely to the rise in prices and modification of the power relations between the oil-producing countries and the transnational oil companies by evolving strategies to deal with their vulnerabilities linked to their dependence on OPEC oil. They diversified their sources of import, promoted where possible national production, and rationalised the utilisation of energy—the elimination of wastages, development of new technologies, and restructuring of national energy systems—replacing oil where possible with other sources. In addition, the rise in crude oil price transformed hitherto unprofitable reserves into profitability. Having lost control over Middle East reserves, the transnational oil companies intensified their search in other regions of the world, particularly Asia, Africa, and Latin America. Some forty countries gave out new concessions for the first time. Thirteen of these were given to the transnationals, while seventeen were given to independents. The heavy burden on oil-importing countries imposed by the rise in crude oil encouraged them to develop, where possible, their own national resources. This was the route taken by the UK, as well as Norway, Brazil, Egypt, India, Malaysia, and China. Added to this was the rising significance of oil production by other non-OPEC countries, such as Russia, Mexico, and the United States, which increased from 17 million b/d in 1965 to 33.5 million b/d in 1985, making them direct competitors with OPEC.

Towards 1980, measures taken in response to the first oil shock were reinforced during the second shock, leading to a series of outcomes. Between 1978 and 1980, consumption in the United States, the world's major consumer, fell by 10 percent, while the volume of its importation also fell by 20 percent. These two factors, in addition to a third, the rise of new oil supplies by non-OPEC producing countries, led to excess inventory on the international market. But if we consider the fact that since 1970 the importance of OPEC had depended partly on the reality that world demand for oil supplies was higher than supply, it could easily be concluded that the emergence of the new sources of supply would lead to some erosion of OPEC's significance in the world energy market. Thus, although between 1969 and 1973 demand for OPEC oil increased by 15 million b/d and its share in world production rose from 46 to approximately 55 percent, this share fell to 50 percent in 1979 and then to 30 percent in 1985, and capacity utilisation also fell from 82 to 56 percent over the same periods (Criqui and Kounetzoff 1987, p. 35).

OPEC's strategy of defending its price also contributed to the fall. Its situation, particularly the coming on-stream of reserves in the non-OPEC countries, placed OPEC in a dilemma. As a cartel with dominant market share, it was capable of either defending the prices of its crude or the total output produced but not both (Chatelus 1987, p. 130). OPEC elected to defend its prices. As a result, its members reduced their production. By October 1980, OPEC's daily production was as low as 23 million b/d, which represented 8 million b/d less than the year before—the lowest level since 1970. The glut continued when Iraq reentered the market after repairing its war-damaged oil facilities (Criqui and Kounetzoff 1987).

As for Saudi Arabia, with reserves estimated at the time to last for 100 years and with considerable foreign reserves, its preoccupation was with price stability and ensuring that prices were kept higher than if determined by the free market but low enough to make alternative fuels and technologies uncompetitive, especially in its primary market—the transport sector

(Bourdaire and Noreng 1991). This position was advanced by Zaki Yamani in a speech at a Saudi petroleum university when he said, "If we force Western countries to invest heavily in finding alternative sources of energy, they will. . . . This will take them no more than seven to 10 years and will result in their reduced dependence on oil as a source of energy to a point which will jeopardize Saudi Arabia's interests" (*Alexander Gas* 2003, p. 1). Apart from its excess capacity, Saudi Arabia was able to use "the oil weapon" to push its strategy through because of its "adequate foreign financial reserves cushioning the blow of lower oil revenues."

Nigeria, Libya, Algeria, and Gabon opposed the Saudi policy. They refused to yield to Saudi pressure to cut the price of their crude oil by $5 (from $40 to $35) and unanimously affirmed, at the end of a meeting held in Algeria on June 22, 1981, their determination to maintain the official selling price of their oil. But the *rapport de force* between them and the oil companies had changed. To pile on pressure, the oil companies began cancelling contracts they had entered into with these countries. Nigeria was hit hard. By July, its oil production had fallen to less than 900,000 b/d, which represented 60 percent less than what it produced in the same period in 1980, forcing it to break ranks with its co-African producers. Attempts by the two African Arab countries to convince it to adhere to their strategy fell on deaf ears as combined pressure from the Saudis and the oil companies had resulted in both political and economic tensions in the country. As a result, the government decided to lower the prices of Nigerian crude and by so doing broke ranks with the African bloc, a triumph for the Saudis.

With its large population, failed economic transformation, and near total dependence on crude oil for revenues, Nigeria had become one of the weak links in OPEC. As Terzian notes, "The oil companies put every ounce of pressure they could muster on Nigeria" (1985, p. 297). Thus three days after the end of OPEC's Geneva conference on March 20, 1982, Nigeria's production fell by 50 percent, from 1.2 million b/d to only 600,000 b/d. The companies refused to buy Nigeria's oil, arguing that it was costing them $5.50 a barrel more than North Sea crude, which competed favourably with Bonny Light in terms of quality. Indeed, increasingly sophisticated refining and catalytic conversion made heavier crude more competitive with light Nigerian oil (Ahmad Khan 1994, p. 52).

This left the Shagari administration and the national economy dependent on oil in a precarious situation. However, the collapse of oil prices had by then hit the kingdom of Saudi Arabia hard and forced Zaki Yamani to make an about face. President Shagari's special adviser on energy, Yahaya Dikko, called on Yamani to intervene. Failure to do so would mean that Nigeria could no longer respect the OPEC price structure, further muddling the market. Yamani quickly offered Riyadh's financial support to Nigeria and threatened several major US oil companies with lack of access to Saudi oil if they did not start lifting oil in Nigeria. On his advice, the Kuwaiti minister, Ali Khalifah Al Sabah, did likewise, though the companies prevaricated for a week, capitulating only after Yamani threatened, in a speech in London, to call for an extraordinary conference and impose sanctions should they fail to honour their commitments to Nigeria (Terzian 1985, p. 299).

For Nigeria and its government the damage had already been done. Nigeria's external debt had risen from 2,331.2 million naira to 8,819.4 million naira (Bullion 1987, p. 13). On Monday, April 19, 1982, President Shehu Shagari took the dramatic step of tabling before the National Assembly the Economic Stabilisation (Temporary Provisions) Act of 1982 to deal with the situation. He informed the National Assembly:

> Our economic situation is serious and calls for urgent solutions. I have therefore found it necessary to introduce some measures which will help to contain the situation. These measures taken by themselves are not adequate response to our present economic situation. . . . I am therefore placing before you an Enabling Bill, the passing of which will enable me to deal promptly and decisively with the situation. (Mohammed 2007, p. 217)

The bill was passed without debate. The entire process took only fifteen minutes, and within a few hours President Shagari signed it into law. Although the package of measures unveiled and implemented was very much along the lines of the austerity packages of the International Monetary Fund and the World Bank, the economy continued its downward slide until his administration was overthrown in 1985.

By the time General Muhammadu Buhari assumed the reins of power, opinion against OPEC had started hardening. Anti-OPEC sentiments were being expressed by some Nigerian leaders and scholars. Indeed the Nigerian house of representatives had in one of its sessions in 1983 passed a resolution urging the government to quit OPEC unless Nigeria's quota was raised.

General Buhari, who served as federal commissioner for petroleum in 1976–1978 and chaired the Nigerian National Petroleum Corporation, came to power with considerable experience in the oil industry. He opposed the position canvassed by the small, vocal, but influential group pushing for Nigeria's withdrawal from OPEC. Such an action would have created a free-for-all in the oil market, which could have been detrimental to not only members of OPEC but also to other non-OPEC members such as Britain and Norway. He instead demanded and obtained an increase of "a quota of 150,000 barrels a day" for Nigeria and also Nigeria's right to fix prices of its crude oil to be competitive with North Sea oil. It was a turbulent moment. According to minister of petroleum resources, Professor Tam David West,

> When we cut our oil price, we shook the world. They wanted to price us out of the market. For the first time, a despatch rider had to take me to Dodan Barracks. Buhari was once Oil Minister, so he knew the intrigues. I told the Commander-in Chief: "We have three moves. First, don't move. Second, shave off exactly the same price as the competitors. Third, shock the world!" He laughed and said: "Shock the world to show them we can survive; shave off two dollars!"
>
> We shaved off double the amount that the rest did, and consequently they panicked. Britain never expected this nor Norway. . . . Sheikh Yamani had to fly in here to Lagos. We had to meet later in a secret place on the outskirts of Geneva—the world press was focusing so much on me. I had to change cars three times for camouflage. Then we sat down to negotiate whether Nigeria would get in line. I said we would not do so. I asked the British Oil Minister: "Mr. Walker is it true that the Americans gave you two billion dollars or one billion dollars to undercut us?" He laughed it off with an: "I hope it is true . . ." But I noted that he never said an outright, "No." (Interview with Chidi Chike Achebe in "NigeriaWorld: The Chinua Achebe Foundation Interview Series." *A Meeting of Minds*, June 14, 2000, p. 4)

At the end of this meeting with General Buhari, Sheikh Zaki Yamani was reported as saying, "I personally believe that Nigeria should have special treatment, for obvious reasons."

Apart from the difficulties Nigeria encountered in selling its crude oil, the changed context in the international energy scene also had the effect of changing the *rapport de force* between Nigeria and the transnational oil companies. In line with OPEC resolutions, the federal government began acquiring equity through the NNOC, and later the Nigerian National Petroleum Corporation (NNPC), in the transnational oil companies operating in Nigeria in 1971 and by 1973 had acquired 35 percent equity in all of the companies. In 1975, the government increased its equity stake in the companies to 55 percent and by 1979 had raised it to 60 percent. When the government nationalised British Petroleum's equity in Shell-BP, it raised its stake in the company to 80 percent, leaving Shell with only 20 percent. Participation was in the form of joint ventures where costs and revenues were split between the partners based on their equity holdings.

By the 1980s, no new investment was forthcoming in the industry. This resulted in a lull in exploration activities at a time when Nigeria needed to increase its reserves. The fall in revenue as a result of the glut also coincided with falling oil reserves. It was estimated that reserves fell from 18.2 billion barrels in 1978 to 16.2 billion in 1983 and then to 16 billion in 1984 (NNPC 1992, p. 83). In addition, the transnational oil companies were lifting less oil than was desired by the government, arguing that the posted price of Nigerian oil was $40 for Bonny Light, which was facing stiff competition from North Sea oil, and that since buyers of Nigerian oil were not given any discount in a period of general recession, they had no option but to invoke the clause in their contracts allowing them to reduce their lifting by 10 percent. They also argued that the profit margin of $0.79/barrel allocated to them in 1975 was insufficient.

Nigeria responded by increasing the margin to $1.6 in a memorandum of understanding signed in 1982. As this did not improve the situation, the government authorised the NNPC to sell part of its equity oil directly to buyers instead of relying on its traditional partners—with disastrous result. Between 1979 and 1983, seventy-two Nigerian companies were authorised to sell Nigerian crude, but, according to Professor David West, only twenty-seven of them were found to be active in the oil industry. Because of the chaotic situation, it was estimated that Nigeria's loss was a million US dollars per day due to fraudulent exports of between 50,000 and 70,000 b/d sold on the Rotterdam spot market without authorisation of the federal government. The government then changed strategy by selling oil directly to refiners and independents. This also failed because of corruption by foreign companies, NNPC officials, or intermediaries and the nonpayment for oil delivered. A typical example is the case of an oil company that lifted US$200 million without payment but still requested contract renewal. Experiments with countertrade in response to foreign exchange shortages, current account deficits, and heavy debt-servicing burdens also proved disastrous. OPEC saw the device as a means of producing more than Nigeria's OPEC quota. Countertrade oil inevitably ended up on the spot market, depressing prices even further. There was no serious reaction from OPEC member countries, however, because "the long term benefits of co-operation among OPEC members must have outweighed the short-term sacrifices required to hold the cartel together" (Blaydes 2003, p. 2).

Given these developments, the government beat a retreat and encouraged the oil companies with yet another memorandum of understanding in 1986, which guaranteed them a minimum fiscal margin of $2 per barrel after tax and royalty. This was raised to $2.50 in 1991. Results have been encouraging. According to Kupolokun, "proven crude oil reserves have grown steadily over the years and are now estimated at 35bbls [billion barrels]" (2009, p. 22).

New Challenges in Nigeria-OPEC Relations

Any discussion on the outlook for the Nigerian oil industry and the country's future relations with OPEC will benefit from an examination of the global dynamics driving the industry today. With the industrialisation of developing countries such as China, India, and Brazil, the growth in energy demand in hitherto low-consuming countries has been unprecedented. The industry has also witnessed shifting trends in global energy demand from West to East and the concentration of reserves in fewer countries. Nigeria also has the imperative for rapid growth and development, as well as the need to resolve the crisis in the Niger Delta, which has disrupted oil production and the supply of gas, especially to the Nigerian electricity industry. Imobighe argues quite correctly that the conflict in the Niger Delta region

> is basically an oil related conflict, which is being played out at different levels of relationship. At one level is the confrontation between the local communities and the oil companies. At a corresponding level you have the confrontation between the local communities, especially militant youths, and the Nigerian authorities. And ironically, at the third level, there are widespread hostilities between some of the local communities themselves. (2004, p. 103)

Demography and economic growth are two other factors that have to be taken into consideration. The world's population is expected to grow by an average of 1 percent per annum over the years from 2006 to 2030, reaching some 8.2 billion, an increase of 1.7 billion. More than 94 percent of this growth will occur in developing countries. The rate of expansion, however, will gradually slow in all regions. On the other hand, world economic growth is assumed to be at an average of 3.5 percent per annum to 2030, with the highest growth coming from South Asia, predominately India, Pakistan, and China at an average of 5 percent. According to Economist Intelligence Unit (Economist Intelligence Unit 2006, p. 8), rapid growth in China and India will increase Asia's slice of world GDP from 35 percent in 2005 to 43 percent in 2020.

These factors have implications for global energy demand, the growth of which has been steady. Forecast growth in Asia is almost double the world average. According to the International Energy Agency, in 2003, the world experienced growth in oil consumption of 2.0 percent. It was even stronger in 2004, with a growth rate of 3.6 percent—from 79.8 million b/d to 82.6 million b/d. China accounted for 30 percent of this increase, driven largely by the country's almost 10 percent economic growth rate that year. Energy Information Administration projects that the Chinese economy will continue to grow (GAO 2007, p. 8). Judging by the current per capita consumption in China, India, and Pakistan, there is significant scope for further sustained demand. In 2006, "India's oil consumption was less than 40 per cent of China's, but because it has embarked on . . . [a] growth turnpike its demand for oil will accelerate" (Yergin 2006, p. 72). Global capacity additions will be inevitable in order to keep prices manageable.

Figure 8.1 indicates that on a global scale approximately 900 billion barrels (78 percent) of the world's reserves are in OPEC member countries. With advancing technologies, reserve availability is not the critical challenge to meeting global capacity additions, as sufficient reserves exist to meet demand for decades to come. The main challenge is timely development of reserves and security of supply deliveries (Kupolokun 2009, p. 10).

Furthermore, a significant portion of the world's remaining reserves are held and managed by national oil companies, particularly in OPEC countries. There is therefore increasing dependence on both OPEC and its national oil companies to ensure global availability. Between 2012 and 2020, an additional 4.6 million b/d of OPEC crude will be required

Figure 8.1   OPEC Share of World Crude Oil Reserves (2004)

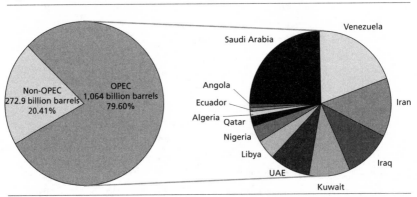

Source: Kupolokun 2009, p.10.

when output level reaches 35.5 million b/d, while demand addressed to OPEC is not forecast to grow beyond 34 percent by 2020.

In terms of upstream investment, approximately $1.6 trillion will be required from 2007 to 2020 with OECD countries accounting for 42 percent. On their part, OPEC countries are embarking on significant upstream investment such that cumulative investments from 2007 are estimated at $248 billion by 2015, escalating to $400 billion by 2020.

It was estimated that the demand addressed to OPEC is expected to grow at 2 percent annually between 2005 and 2010. However, the organisation's capacity growth rate is almost the same—about 3 percent annually. Nigeria's planned capacity growth is at an average of 6 percent annually, higher than OPEC's. Given this distortion, the adaptation of quotas to the principle of proportionate spare capacity will be necessary in the long run. In other words, the adaptation of an OPEC quota mechanism, which takes into consideration installed capacity, is imperative if Nigeria is to monetise its capacity increases.

Moreover, the current OPEC quota mechanism has implications for Nigerian oil production. If the country adheres to its productive capacity, it will grow only modestly to 2.9 milliion b/d by 2010 against the unconstrained planned capacity projection to attain 4.2 million b/d. However, if an OPEC quota mechanism reflective of Nigeria's capacity is adopted by the organisation, the country's capacity will rise to 3.7 million b/d. Therefore, current quota allocation will result in virtually no growth, while a capacity-based allocation mechanism will result in modest growth to 3.7 million b/d as opposed to the possible 4.3 million b/d by 2010. These scenarios have varying impact on net revenue to Nigeria (Kupolokun 2009, p. 39), and the issue of quota allocated to Nigeria has been a bone of contention in the country. Some commentators have even called on the federal government to pull Nigeria out of the organisation as was done by Indonesia and Gabon.

Conclusion

Nigeria's membership in OPEC in the 1970s was partly influenced by the resource nationalism of the founding members of the organisation—the drive for the control of their hydrocarbon resources and the need to channel those resources towards national economic development. While oil policies—fiscal and participation regulations—were generally fashioned in line with decisions and resolutions of OPEC, Nigeria opted for a gradualist approach. The early phase of the development of Nigeria's oil industry owed a great deal to the geopolitics of Arab North Africa and the Middle East and helped to modify the *rapport de force* between Nigeria and the oil companies operating in the country.

Although Nigeria was never directly involved in the major conflicts in the Middle East, which in most cases involved other OPEC member countries, it was not insulated from their outcomes. Conflicts involving member countries of OPEC, such as the Iran-Iraq war of the 1980s and the Iraqi invasion of Kuwait on August 2, 1990, had the effect of paralysing the organisation, inducing mutual destruction of belligerents' oil facilities and distorting oil prices in the international market as operators reacted or scrambled for oil to guard against shortages. Nigeria, like other non–Middle East OPEC member countries, has always been expected, especially by the United States, to meet the shortfall in supply. The instability in the Middle East and the need for uninterrupted supply of oil partly explains the intense pressure put on successive Nigerian administrations to quit OPEC.

One conflict in the Middle East that continues to have political significance in Nigeria is the Arab–Israeli conflict. Nigeria has a large Muslim population and lengthy relationships with Middle East countries, especially Saudi Arabia. During the Nigerian civil war (1967–1970), the federal government was supported by virtually all countries of the region in contrast with Israel, which gave subterranean support to Biafra. Nigeria did not break diplomatic relations with Israel as some domestic political forces had wanted, especially after Abba Eban, the Israeli foreign minister, had gone public with his country's support for Biafra. Nigeria did, however, severe diplomatic relations with Israel in support of the Arabs in the 1967 war. It also supported all resolutions passed in the General Assembly of the United Nations calling on Israel to withdraw from the occupied territories.

Although Nigeria has cordial relations with OPEC member countries of the Middle East, and all subscribe to OPEC's objective of coordinating and unifying its members' petroleum policies in order to secure fair and stable policies for petroleum producers, they have tended to act unilaterally in pursuit of their national interests. This could partly be explained by revenue needs determined by development strategies.

With limited reserves and a large population, in contrast with Saudi Arabia and Kuwait, which have small populations and reserves that could last for over 100 years, coupled with its failure to significantly transform its oil-dependent economy, Nigeria is considered one of the weak links in OPEC, despite its active role in the organisation, particularly in times of crisis. This perception of Nigeria's weakness may explain the tolerance exhibited by some OPEC members, especially Saudi Arabia, when Nigeria broke ranks twice in the 1980s in the face of declining foreign exchange by first reducing the price of its oil and second by adopting countertrade arrangements, which further depressed prices in the world oil market.

Nigeria, however, has remained a loyal member of OPEC, despite the enormous domestic pressure its leaders have periodically come

Appendix: Nigeria's Crude Oil Production and Export

Year	Crude Oil Production (million barrels)	Crude Oil Exports (million barrels)
1970	395.689	383.455
1971	558.689	542.545
1972	665.295	650.64
1973	719.379	695.627
1974	823.32	795.71
1975	660.148	627.638
1976	758.058	736.822
1977	766.055	715.24
1978	696.324	674.125
1979	845.463	807.685
1980	760.117	656.26
1981	525.291	469.095
1982	470.638	401.658
1983	450.961	392.031
1984	507.487	450.58
1985	547.088	486.58
1986	535.929	486.584
1987	483.269	390.514
1988	529.602	435.797
1989	625.908	522.481
1990	660.559	548.249
1991	689.85	585.838
1992	711.34	604.3
1993	691.4	563.614
1994	696.19	578.044
1995	715.4	616.9
1996	740.19	648.69
1997	759.71	673.34
1998	776.01	687.39
1999	778.9	666.49
2000	797.88	688.08
2001	817.15	674.93
2002	655.06	490.81
2003	655.06	490.81
2004	900.6	736.4
2005	919.2856	846.1797
2006	813.95	656.09

Source: Central Bank of Nigeria, *Statistical Bulletin,* Vol. 18, December 2007.

under to quit the organisation, particularly because of the export quota allowed the country since the mid-1980s. Gabon left in 1994, and Ecuador and Indonesia suspended their memberships in 1992 and 1999, respectively. To ease the periodic domestic pressure on Nigerian governments and keep it within the organisation, some compromises will have to be arrived at, more so given the country's planned capacity upgrade and its ongoing attempt at economic transformation requiring substantial public investment.

Bibliography

Ahmad Khan, S., 1994, *Nigeria: The Political Economy of Oil*, Oxford University Press, Oxford, UK.

Alexander Gas and Oil Connections, 2003, "How OPEC Keeps America Hooked on Oil Imports," vol. 8, no. 8 (April 17).

Ambe-Uva, N., and Adegboyega, K.M, 2007, "The Impact of Domestic Factors on Foreign Policy: Nigerian/Israeli Relations," *Alternatives*, vol. 6, no. 3 and 4 (Fall & Winter), pp. 44–59.

Ayoub, A., 1993. *Le Petrole, Economie et Politique*, mimeo, College de France, Paris, *Cahier de Recherche*, no. 93–11.

Blaydes, L., 2003, *Rewarding Impatience: A Bargaining and Enforcement Model of OPEC*, Department of Political Science, University of California, Los Angeles, CA, US.

Bourdaire, J.M, and Noreng O., 1991, "The OPEC Strategy Dilemma, Middle East Politics, and the Figures That Don't Match: The Rising Need for the Middle Eastern Oil—Kuwaiti, Saudi, and Iraqi Strategies." In *Phoenix-Like OPEC: Changing Structures, Markets, and Future Stability and the Oil Gas Relationship*, International Research Centre for Energy and Economic Development, Boulder, CO, US, pp. 7–14.

Bullion, 1987, "Central Bank of Nigeria," vol. II, October–December, p. 13.

Chatelus, Michel, 1987, "Policies for Development: Attitudes Toward Industry and Services." In *The Rentier State,* H. Beblawi and G. Luciani, eds., Croom Helm, London.

Chevallier, A., 1986, *Le Petrole*. La Decourvete, Paris.

Corbin, J., 2002. *Al-Qaeda. The Terror Network That Threatens the World*, Thunder Mouth Press/Nation Books, New York, US.

Criqui, P., and Kounetzoff, N., 1987, *Energie 1995: Après Les Chocs*, Economica, Paris.

Economist Intelligence Unit, 2006, "Foresight 2020: Economic, Industry and Corporate Trends," a report from the Economist Intelligence Unit sponsored by Cisco Systems, March.

Federal Government of Nigeria, 1970, Second National Development Plan: 1970–1974, Federal Ministry of Information, Printing Division, Lagos, Nigeria.

Federal Government of Nigeria, 1980, Report of Crude Oil Sales Tribunal of Inquiry, Federal Government of Nigeria, unpublished federal document, April–June.

Field, G., 2001, "Nigeria National Petroleum Corporation," in *International Directory of Company History*, vol. 72, pp. 1–4.

Frynas, J.G.G, 2000, *Oil in Nigerian Politics: Conflict and Litigation Between Oil Companies and the Village*, Transaction, Edison, NJ, US.

GAO (United States Government Accountability Office), 2007, "Crude Oil (GAO): Uncertainty About Future Oil Supply Makes It Important to Develop a Strategy for Addressing a Peak and Decline in Oil Production." Report to Congressional Requesters. Washington, DC, US.

Imobighe, T.A., 2004, "Conflict in Niger Delta: A Unique Case, or a 'Model' for Future Conflicts in Other Oil Producing Countries," in R. Traub-Merz and D. Yates, eds., *Oil Policy in the Gulf of Guinea. Security & Conflict, Economic Growth, Social Development*, Friedrich-Ebert-Stiftung, Bonn, Germany.

Kostiner, J., 2009, *Conflict and Co-operation in the Gulf*, VS Verlag fur Sozia Wissenschaften, GWV fachverlage GmH, Wiesbaden, Germany.

Kupolokun, F., 2009, "The Nigerian Oil and Gas Industry," unpublished.

Kwanashie, M., 1991, *The Nigerian Economy: Structure, Organization and Management in Basic Framework for Industrial Policy in Nigeria*, Federal Ministry of Industries, Policy Analysis Department, Abuja, Nigeria.

Lax, H.L., 1983, *Political Risk in International Oil and Gas Industry*, International Human Resources Development Corp., Boston, MA, US.

Madelin, H., 1975. *Oil and Politics*. Saxon House, D.C. Heath Ltd., Westmead, England.

Martin, J.M., 1990, *L'Economie Mondiale de l'Energie*, La Decourvete, Paris.

Mohammed, A.S., 2007, *Impressions and Facts: Nigeria Under General Ibrahim Babangida, 1985–1993*, Centre for Democratic Research, Development and Training, Zaria, Nigeria.

Muhsin, J., Harding, G., and Hazelton, F., 1990, "Iraq in the Gulf War," in *Saddam's Iraq: Revolution or Reaction*, Zed Books, London.

NNPC (Nigerian National Petroleum Corporation), 1992, *The Nigerian Oil Industry: The Babangida Era*, NNPC, Lagos, Nigeria.

Paden J., 1986, *Ahmadu Bello, Sardauna of Sokoto, Values and Leadership in Nigeria*, Hudahuda Publishing Co., Zaria, Nigeria.

Pearson, S., 1970, *Petroleum and the Nigerian Economy*. Stanford University Press, Palo Alto, CA, US.

Perry, G., Ogunkola, O., and Olivera, M., 2009, *Oil Institutions, "Tale of Two Cities": Nigeria and Colombia*, unpublished.

Schatzl, L.H., 1969, *Petroleum in Nigeria*. Oxford University Press, Oxford, UK.

Terzian, P., 1985, *OPEC: The Inside Story*. Zed Books, London.

Usman, Y.B., 1979, *For the Liberation of Nigeria*. New Beacons, London.

Yergin, D., 2006, "Enduring Energy Security," *Foreign Affairs*, March/April, pp. 69–82.

9

Prometheus as Good Samaritan: Nigeria's Bilateral and Multilateral Assistance Since Independence

Obadiah Mailafia

This chapter examines Nigerian economic diplomacy from the viewpoint of its bilateral and multilateral assistance to other African countries. Prometheus, according to Greek legend, stole the fire of the gods, for which he was punished by being permanently manacled, never to grow and never to make progress. The dissonance between Nigeria's promise of greatness and its mediocrity on most indices of economic development is reminiscent of the legend of the chained Prometheus. The chapter is divided into the following: (1) theoretical considerations, (2) the changing economic and policy context, (3) bilateral and multilateral assistance, and (4) conclusions and recommendations.

While much has been written on the country's foreign policy since independence, much less is known about its foreign aid programmes and its international economic diplomacy in general (Ogwu and Olukoshi 1991 and 2001). Part of the problem of researching this topic is the simple fact that a good many grants given by succeeding regimes have not been properly documented. This is particularly true of the military era, when several extra-budgetary payments were made to foreign governments and leaders without recourse to formal financial appropriation and accountability procedures.

Theoretical Considerations

In a universe characterised by Hedley Bull (1977) as an "anarchical society," a gesture of abiding curiosity is why countries extend altruistic behaviour to their neighbours. Today, the volume of official development assistance from rich to poor countries runs at over US$100 billion annually. The African continent alone accounts for over a quarter of these funds, which go into a range of sectors from humanitarian assistance to budgetary support, infrastructure, agriculture, poverty alleviation, and social development. Several countries, among them Tanzania, Uganda, and Mozambique, have become aid dependent, given that aid accounts for nearly 50 percent of their annual budgets.

Although aid from rich to poor countries is the norm, much less well-known is the phenomenon of development assistance from developing countries to other low-income countries. China is still classified as a developing country, yet it is evident that Chinese aid is so significant in Africa that it is virtually overtaking aid from Organisation for Economic Co-Operation and Development countries. With external reserves currently estimated at over US$2.3 trillion, China is awash with funds for investments as well as aid giving. Much Chinese official development assistance to Africa is linked to the country's commercial and investment interests, particularly in oil and mining.

In the 1980s, under the aegis of the United Nations General Assembly, the international community committed itself to encouraging technical assistance among developing countries. The idea was to encourage developing countries to share experiences with one another and to exchange best practices for the promotion of mutual economic development. The establishment of the Organization of Petroleum Exporting Countries (OPEC) Fund in the late 1970s was a major turning point. It provided a framework by which oil-rich developing nations could provide much-needed assistance to their less-endowed counterparts. Countries such as Saudi Arabia, Kuwait, Libya, and Nigeria have been active contributors to the fund.

Historically, Nigeria has been a major contributor to the United Nations and to multilateral institutions such as the Commonwealth of Nations; the African, Caribbean and Pacific Group of States (ACP); and African regional institutions, among them the African Union and the Economic Community of West African States (ECOWAS). However, in this paper, we shall limit our focus to cases where Nigeria is a major singular player rather than where it is one among a number of multidonor countries.

The question remains: In a world where loyalties do not extend beyond sovereign borders, why do countries extend the hand of generosity to others? In international relations theory, the phenomenon of aid giving has several explanations (Holsti 1994). The first explanation relates to the theory of realism.

In the epistemology of international relations, Hollis and Smith (1991) insist there is a difference between "explaining" and "understanding" what happens in international affairs. While realist theory provides ample explanation for the games nations play, the moral or idealist approach is also valid for understanding why nations behave the way they do. Simply put, countries extend help to others on the basis of calculated self-interest. Such interests may be concealed, barely veiled, explicit, medium term, or long term. From this perspective, aid is one of the instruments in the kitty of economic statecraft to be deployed in the pursuit of national ambitions. Related to this is the notion of aid as a form of imperialism.

Several writers, notable among them Teresa Hayter (1971), popularised the notion of "aid as imperialism" during the heyday of the Cold War when aid was used as part of the instrumentalities of *informal empire*, a mechanism for wooing friends and influencing allies as well as cajoling satellite nations in the periphery of world capitalism. Second, states can and do give aid for altruistic purposes. Richer countries come to the aid of their lesser-endowed neighbours for reasons of charity and generosity. Sometimes this help is a blend of altruism and self-interest. However, during humanitarian emergencies, conflict, or natural disasters, much of this assistance comes largely as altruistic aid.

Yet another explanation for aid is its use as a vehicle of economic statecraft. Aid can be used to facilitate trade and investments. For example, trade finance facilities are often used by industrialised countries to facilitate imports into developing countries. China provides assistance for infrastructure projects in many African countries as part of a package of its investment activities in oil and mining.

Whatever the motivations for aid giving, there is an emerging consensus that developing nations will continue to need one form of assistance or the other into the foreseeable future. From the 1960s to the present, much of the economic rationale for aid was anchored on neo-Keynesian growth models which emphasised the gaps in savings and capital that needed to be sourced from outside the developing countries. According to Roger Riddell:

> It was in increasing the investment rate to accelerate the process of economic growth and achieve . . . takeoff that Rostow gives a critical role to economic aid. Within the Harrod-Domar paradigm, the investment rate of the developing countries is raised by injections of foreign capital, so augmenting the domestic savings rate without reducing the level of domestic consumption. While aid is not absolutely necessary to raise the level of investment, it speeds up the historical process of reaching the

state of self-sustaining growth, particularly by providing the means to expand and deepen social overhead capital. (1987, p. 88)

There is by no means universal unanimity regarding the economic as well as moral justification for aid. For some neoclassical economists, notable among them Peter Bauer (1972), aid has the effect of "crowding out" private initiative and creating misguided feelings of entitlement.

Domestic Economic Policy Context

This section reviews the evolving policy context that has continued to shape opportunities as well as constraints for Nigeria's external assistance programmes and activities. As is well known, the country has an oil-dependent economy. Foreign earnings from the petroleum sector have largely provided the resources with which the government has been able to provide assistance. Dwindling oil revenues mean less opportunity for charity.

Nigeria has vast natural and human resource endowments, with an estimated population of 150 million people in 2009 and an annual demographic growth rate of about 2.2 percent (US Department of State 2009). The country is potentially the largest consumer market on the continent. In spite of a substantial petrochemical sector, the economy is still predominantly agrarian. Its other potentials include a vibrant private sector, highly motivated entrepreneurs, vast and fertile agricultural lands, and an educated workforce. Nigeria produces and exports crude oil—the sixth-largest exporter in OPEC—and is richly endowed with gas and solid minerals. Notwithstanding the potential, the country's economic and social conditions have remained far below the minimum expectations of ordinary citizens. Some of the socio-economic indices, though much improved, still remain a long shot from the internationally agreed UN Millennium Development Goals targets. It is estimated that half of the population lives in absolute poverty, and life expectancy is 52 years (National Bureau of Statistics 2009). Nigeria has one of the highest infant and maternal mortality rates in the world, with an infant mortality rate of 84 deaths per 1,000 live births. It also ranks 158 out of 177 on the UN Development Programme's Human Development Index. A large proportion of Nigerians have limited or no access to the most basic amenities, such as clean drinking water, basic health and protection against communicable diseases, decent housing and sanitation, reliable transportation networks, physical security, and sustainable sources of livelihood.

Nigeria's mineral endowments provide the potential for a wide range of industries from steel to petrochemicals, glass, ceramics, and other manufacturing sectors and related services. In spite of these potentials, the country's industrial development remains weak. According to Table 9.1, most of the country's population is engaged in agriculture and retail trading (65 percent), with manufacturing occupying only 10 percent of the adult working population. To further buttress the weakness of the manufacturing sector, a comparative overview of manufacturing value added as a percentage of GDP in a few selected emerging markets (Table 9.2) puts the country at an unimpressive 4 percent in 2005, in comparison to 19 percent for South Africa, 17.7 percent for Mexico, and 8 percent for Ghana.

Before the discovery of oil in 1958, agriculture was the predominant engine of growth, with the country well noted as an exporter of agricultural products such as cocoa, groundnuts, cotton, rubber, and palm produce. The oil bonanza of the 1970s diverted government attention to an unhealthy dependence on crude oil as a major source of export earnings and government revenues. Nigeria is the world's eighth-largest oil producer and has the seventh-largest reserves of natural gas. Activities in the petroleum sector represent nearly 95 percent of export earnings and over 80 percent of government revenues in Nigeria (CIA *World Fact Book,* 2009). In 2007, the share of industry to GDP was 39 percent, attributed to heavy production in oil and gas. Table 9.1 shows that during the years 1999–2008 the oil sector accounted for 23.15 percent of GDP, although its contribution to overall output growth has been in decline. Proven oil reserves are estimated to be 36 billion barrels while natural gas reserves are well over 100 trillion cubic feet. Nevertheless, the country lacks functional refineries and has to import most of its refined petroleum products. Perhaps nothing better illustrates the country's weak economic position than this paradox of the sixth-largest exporter in OPEC having to import most of its refined petroleum needs. Many of the oil importers, in connivance with government functionaries, have behaved in the manner of cartels with a vested interest in ensuring that refineries do not actually function.

The Nigerian economy continues to exhibit all the classic symptoms of the *rentier state,* defined by Douglas Yates (1996, p. 11) as one in which the government receives on a regular basis substantial amounts of external economic rent. The four principal characteristics of the rentier state are said to be one in which (1) rent situations predominate, (2) the origin of the rent is largely external to the economy, (3) only a few are engaged in the generation of the rent, and (4) the government is the

Table 9.1   Average Sectoral Performance, 1999–2008

Activity	Percentage of GDP	Percentage of Growth	Percentage of Contribution to GDP Growth
GDP	**100**	**7.76**	**100**
Oil GDP	23.15	2.23	–4.49
Non-oil GDP	76.85	9.48	104.45
Agriculture	**41.53**	**7.48**	**45.85**
Crops	36.92	7.70	40.88
Livestock	2.67	6.19	2.62
Fishery	1.38	6.51	1.92
Forestry	0.55	5.14	0.43
Industry			
Crude petroleum	23.15	2.23	–4.49
Solid minerals	0.28	11.06	0.44
Coal	0.00	7.33	0.00
Metal ores	0.00	8.51	0.00
Quarrying	0.28	11.08	0.44
Manufacturing	3.88	9.05	5.20
Oil refining	0.12	12.04	0.19
Cement	0.07	9.73	0.10
Other manufacturing	3.68	8.99	4.92
Building and construction	**1.66**	**8.70**	**2.38**
Wholesale and retail trade	**14.16**	**15.96**	**28.78**
Services	**29.51**	**12.78**	**50.58**
Transport	2.53	12.72	3.67
Road	2.26	13.9	3.35
Air	0.06	6.98	0.06
Water	0.06	4.61	0.04
Rail and pipelines	0.00	5.92	0.00
Transport services	0.15	5.58	0.22
Communication			
Telecommunications	1.62	50.90	6.62
Post	0.06	8.49	0.08
Broadcasting	0.08	8.39	0.11
Utilities	3.41	19.35	4.10
Electricity	3.28	24.46	3.91
Water	0.13	10.03	0.19
Hotel and restaurants	0.36	31.39	0.89
Finance and insurance			
Financial institutions	3.93	2.16	1.79
Insurance	0.13	6.33	0.14
Real estate and business services			
Real estate	1.47	9.67	2.20
Business services	0.12	5.51	0.12
Public administration	0.73	4.77	0.50
Social services	0.22	9.50	0.30
Education	0.18	9.70	0.25
Health	0.04	8.56	0.05
Private and nonprofit			
Organisations	0.00	10.28	0.01

Source: National Planning Commission 2009.

Table 9.2   Manufacturing Value Added, 1980–2005 (as percentage of GDP)

	1980	1990	2000	2005
Brazil	33.5	na	17.1	na
Ghana	7.8	9.8	9.0	8.6
Indonesia	13.0	20.7	27.7	na
Mexico	22.3	20.8	20.3	17.7
Nigeria	8.4	5.5	4.5	4.6
South Africa	21.6	23.6	19.0	19.1

Source: World Bank database, 2007.

chief recipient of the external rent. Central to all this is the so-called *Dutch disease*, manifested in historically high exchange rates, enclave economies, and high inflation. Evidence of collapsed basic infrastructure and services and increased widespread poverty among Nigerians accentuates resource mismanagement in governance, which has become the bane of the nation's growth efforts.

The trajectory of Nigerian manufacturing capacity utilisation from 1980 to 2002 indicates a dismal performance, with only marginal improvements in the years after 1999. The sharp fall in 1982 was due to the oil price shock and the ensuing austerity measures by the Shehu Shagari administration. The downward trend continued into 1985. The years 1986–1989 showed some marginal improvements, but poor implementation of the Structural Adjustment Programme (SAP) resulted in capacity utilisation slipping back by 1990.

In a pathbreaking study, Peter Lewis (2007) undertook a comparative analysis of national development policy choices in Indonesia and Nigeria, demonstrating how ruling elites in the Asian country adopted approaches that enhanced structural transformation while those of Nigeria settled for a "prebendal" approach that foreclosed long-term growth. As a consequence, Nigeria's industrial base remains relatively underdeveloped (Table 9.2). The sector has yet to take advantage of available resources and the relative abundance of cheap labour due to high production costs, low levels of productivity that translate into low value added, and low capacity utilisation. The poor business climate and low levels of infrastructure also discourage foreign direct investment in the manufacturing sector. Several foreign-owned manufacturing firms have relocated to the neighbouring country of Ghana where electric power is in constant supply, infrastructure is better developed, and the policy environment more predictable. The Nigerian business environment does not support wealth creation, while the mindset of the ruling elites seems more oriented to consumption rather than productivity and genuine development (Joseph 1987). The competitive structure of the economy is also weak, with numerous cartels and monopolies in diesel and refined petroleum distribution, cement production and market, rice and sugar importation, automobile spare parts, pharmaceuticals, and truck haulage and luxury bus transportation.

Evolution of Economic Policy

When Nigeria was under the tutelage of the British, colonial authorities did not pursue an explicit policy of industrialisation. Much of what went by way of trade and industrial policy was largely a series of ad hoc measures relating to customs duties, tariffs, and import waivers to industrialists under the Aid to Pioneer Industries Ordinance 1952. There also existed infrastructure support by way of the provision of utilities services such as water, power, and industrial estates; some modicum of credit facilities; and some level of protection from foreign competitors. Promotion of industrial development was anchored on two institutions: Nigeria Local Development Board and the Department of Commerce and Industry. The board was entrusted with the responsibility of promoting development of village crafts and local artisanal industries. It was also expected to explore development of suitable industrial processes for processing of local products and was responsible for evaluating the technical suitability of projects approved by the Governor-in-Council while also seeking ways to boost local trade and development of local industries.

Import-Substitution Industrialisation

When independence arrived in October 1960, the country was confronted with the twin challenges of a highly rudimentary level of industrial development on the one hand and a deteriorating balance of payments position owing to the country's import dependence on the other. To address these challenges, the authorities anchored their industrial policy on an import-substitution industrialisation strategy, on the assumption that it would lessen dependence on imported manufactures, thereby helping to conserve much-needed foreign exchange.

During the First National Development Plan 1962–1968, a strong commitment was made towards diversifying the economy and pursuing a more rigorous industrialisation policy, including introduction of heavy industries (Okigbo 1989). It was during this period that money was earmarked for the building of three multipurpose dams at Kainji, Jebba, and Shiroro, and other important capital items such as iron and steel and oil refining. The regional governments in the three regions—East, West, and North, and later, in 1964, Mid-West—deliberately promoted industrialisation even without any formal industrial policy. In the first three years of independence, value added in manufacturing grew by an average of 11.4 percent per annum. Rapid growth of manufacturing and diversification of industrial activity were major objectives of industrial sector development as articulated in the various national development plans (1962–1968, 1970–1974, and 1975–1980).

Despite the tragic civil war of 1967–1970, the first decade of independence was marked by significant achievements in industrial development. The number of local firms proliferated, and domestic manufacturing increased in such areas as domestic consumables, engineering, metal products, household apparatus, and agricultural machinery. The Second National Development Plan 1970–1974, emphasising the three "Rs" of reconciliation, rehabilitation, and reconstruction, was probably one of the most successful ante-bellum recovery efforts in the developing world (Okigbo 1989, pp. 79–102). Its targets of building "a united, strong and self-reliant nation, a great and dynamic society, a just and egalitarian society, a land of bright and full employment for all citizens, and a free and democratic society" provided a strong rallying point for the post-war reconstruction effort.

In the 1970s, a policy of industrialisation and backward integration resulted in a boom in Nigeria's industrial sector. Reconstruction efforts made after the civil war under the Second National Development Plan achieved remarkable results. Measures were taken to rehabilitate damaged industrial capacities and to promote expansion of intermediate and capital goods industries in order to raise the contribution of value added in the manufacturing sector. With favourable economic and production indices in place, Nigeria's manufacturing industry produced many goods—textiles, tyres, cars, food, plywood, and newsprint for domestic as well as external markets. Through the various industrial estates scattered across the country, a large population of workers were engaged in productive employment. This upward trend in the tertiary sector continued well into the early 1980s.

Following the collapse of oil prices in 1982 and the ensuing austerity measures imposed by the civilian administration of Shehu Shagari, the manufacturing sector went into a massive slump, as indeed did the rest of the economy. With the reduction in export earnings, the hard currency with which to import industrial inputs was no longer easily available. As a consequence, there was a spate of factory closures, with capacity utilisation continuing in its downward swing and massive lay-offs in the manufacturing sector.

Manufacturing output fell drastically to an annual average of about 2.6 percent during the period 1986–1998. In fact, for the period 1993–1998, growth in the subsector was negative. It is clear from the foregoing that Nigeria has not succeeded in appreciably raising its level of manufacturing and industrial performance over the last twenty-five years. On the contrary, the economy has experienced some level of de-industrialisation and declining manufacturing performance, reflecting the weak competitiveness of the sector. Nigeria is ranked 83 out of 117 countries on the United Nations Industrial Development Organization Competitive Performance Index and lower than its comparators, including other major oil-producing countries. The economy's weak industrial com-petitiveness is evidenced in several other indicators of sector performance. The share of manufacturing in GDP fell from 8.4 percent in 1980 to 5.5 percent in 1999 and 4.2 percent in 2007 (World Bank 2008).

The introduction of SAP in July 1986 marked a major paradigm shift in economic policy. The reform programme provided various incentives, which were granted to the manufacturing sector as a means of lifting the sector from the prevalent low performance level and increasing its contribution to the GDP. The government rationale behind SAP was to arrest the prolonged economic recession occasioned by the collapse of the world oil market from the early 1980s and the attendant sharp fall in foreign exchange earnings, which adversely affected eco-nomic growth and development in Nigeria. SAP provided an opportuni-ty to revamp the industrial sector. However, the Nigerian experience with SAP policies in the area of trade and industrial policies illustrates the interplay of several factors in the determination of policy design and implementation. In some sense, there was an erosion of policy autono-my, given that the International Monetary Fund and donors could almost retain veto power on policy choices. Lack of clear ownership of eco-nomic policy meant that policymakers operated without conviction. It is therefore not surprising that the manufacturing subsector steadily declined, contributing less than 3 percent to the GDP by 2006.

It is in the services sector that growth has been rather impressive. Liberalisation of the telecoms sector provides an example of a relatively successful services reform. An estimated 450,000 jobs have been creat-ed to serve the mobile phone industry, including many more as informal sector vendors of prepaid recharge cards. Similarly, the development of Internet services has led to the opening of an estimated 5,000 cybercafés. Other areas for services growth include banking and finance, transport, especially air, and tourism.

It is evident that Nigeria has the potential to become a regional finance and transportation hub. The new Financial Sector Strategy, a complement to Vision 2020, was initiated by the Central Bank in 2007 and has the objective of making the country the financial centre of the continent by the year 2020. Nigerian banks are already extending their tentacles to neighbouring West African countries, while others have moved as far as Kenya, Rwanda, Uganda, and South Africa. In the aviation sector, Nigerian airlines are providing much of the air transport services for West Africa. Another potentially important area is expansion of services in the gas and petroleum sector. Ambitious targets have been set for local content in the oil and gas industry from a low of 5–25 percent to a minimum of 70 percent by the end of 2010.

National Economic Empowerment and Development Strategy

During 2004–2007, economic policy was anchored on the National Economic Empowerment and Development Strategy (NEEDS). A programme aimed at engineering a new prosperity, its pillars centred on value reorientation, fostering accountability and transparency, fighting corruption, reducing poverty, and creating wealth and jobs. NEEDS aimed to boost the productive sector of the economy, rebuild infrastructure, and position the private sector as the key driver of growth. In addition to rehabilitating infrastructure such as roads, harbours, ports, and power, NEEDS aimed to enhance the productivity of the real sector, in particular, agriculture and industry, as well as development of small and medium enterprises (SMEs) and socioeconomic empowerment of people and job creation. (See Figure 9.1.)

One of the laudable achievements recorded in the Nigerian economy was the successful bank recapitalisation in 2006. It was an exercise that saw the total overhaul of the banking system and pruned 100 existing banks to 25 strong banks. Confidence was restored with more public patronage and credit facilities. As a result of insider problems and the global financial meltdown, however, capital markets have been in the doldrums since the spring of 2008. The subsequent fall in values of shares generated toxic assets that affected the liquidity of commercial banks. Revelations of serious corporate problems, bordering on fraud, resulted in the Central Bank dismissing five of the chief executives of banks, in addition to pumping over 600 billion naira in bailout funds.

Figure 9.1   Sectoral Composition of the Nigerian GDP (US$), 2009

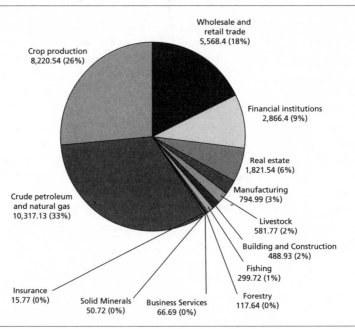

Source: Economic Associates Quarterly, Lagos, Nigeria, June 2009.

One of the most salutary developments in recent years has been the fact that Nigeria was successful in negotiating an exit from the Paris Club list of debtors in December 2005, when the United States and seven other nations signed a debt-reduction agreement with the government. As a consequence, debt-servicing obligations declined from 36 percent of GDP in 2004 to less than 4 percent in 2009.

In April 2009, the minister of commerce and industry announced a new trade and industrial policy for the country. The political context for the policy is the medium-term goal of achieving the government's Seven-Point Agenda, meeting the internationally agreed targets for the Millennium Development Goals for poverty alleviation and Vision 2020, which aims to put Nigeria among the twenty largest economies within the coming decade. The objective is to establish a thriving manufacturing sector anchored on low production costs, a highly skilled and motivated labour force, and high value-added, competitive products whilst fostering wealth creation, reducing poverty, and boosting employment. The policy document formally acknowledges that these objectives cannot be achieved without renewed commitment to macro-economic policy reforms that ensure improvements in overall economic performance, with all that this implies for budgeting, expenditure management, and fiscal policy.

The new policy also emphasises the need for the overhaul of the regulatory architecture underpinning trade and industrial activities, especially protection of foreign investments and intellectual property rights, relaxation of restrictive trade practices, enforcement of industrial and commercial standards, as well as consumer protection, and revision of weights and measures to align them with best international practices.

To achieve these measures would foster domestic commerce while enhancing exports promotion. In addition, the government is committed to building strong partnerships with international financial institutions and agencies that would provide trade-related development assistance. Government acknowledges the role of the private sector as the main driver for industrial and commercial prosperity. It also emphasises the role of public-private partnerships in building infrastructure for long-term sustainable development. Such partnerships are also seen as important vehicles in the building of industrial parks in such sectors as petrochemicals, textiles, fertilizers, biofuels, solid minerals, agro-processing, and engineering and machine tools.

Institutionally, the new policy accords a central role to the federal government in providing an enabling macroeconomic environment and incentives, promoting exports, strengthening R&D and the financial architecture for accessible credit, and developing human capital and skills. The Federal Ministry of Commerce is expected to take the driver's seat in coordinating and implementing the new policy. The ministry reports to the National Council on Commerce and Industry, the highest policymaking body on industrial matters, bringing together state governments and the various ministries, departments, and agencies under the president's leadership.

Nigeria's current industrial policy thrust is anchored on deregulation and privatisation of the economy, leaving government to play the role of facilitator, concentrating on the provision of incentives, policy, and infrastructure that are necessary to enhance the private sector's role as the engine of growth.

Vision 2020 and the Quest for Accelerated Transformation

The most recent initiative in macroeconomic policy is the Vision 2020 blueprint. At the core of this long-term plan is the critical role of manufacturing, structural transformation, and enhanced national competitiveness. Vision 2020 is a comprehensive perspective plan embracing targeted policy actions in the political system; macroeconomic management; and key sectors such as agriculture, health, education, manufacturing, and infrastructure. Manufacturing is expected to be the key driver. Given that manufacturing currently constitutes only 4.13 percent of GDP, the objective is to raise it to 23.4 percent over the long term and to achieve a capacity utilisation level of 85.5 percent by 2018. The modelling framework for Vision 2020 supports a structural shift of the macroeconomy from primary production to an increasingly high value-added secondary/tertiary production using an appropriate mix of technology, incentives, institutional architecture, and a national system of innovation, research and development, and human capital development. If Nigeria is to be among the twenty largest economies by 2020, it would require an annual growth rate of 15.95 percent and an annual investment growth rate in real terms of 30.5 percent. This is based on the assumption that the country currently occupying the twentieth position, the Netherlands, with a nominal GDP of US$844 billion, will be growing at an annual rate of between 1 and 2.2 percent during the period.

To achieve the Vision 2020 objective, the nation's human capital has been identified as its most important asset, critical to the attainment of the desired economic growth. In this light, one of the central themes of the Vision 2020 blueprint is to enhance national productivity and overall welfare (National Planning Commission 2009). It is well understood that if the country is to achieve its plan of being among the largest economies within the coming decade, its GDP would have to jump from the long-term average of 7.8 percent to a sustained high of 12.5 percent per annum from 2010 to 2020. This would lift its GDP from the current US$212.1 billion to approximately US$900 billion in 2020. In terms of strategy, efforts would be made to optimise existing growth drivers—agriculture, energy (oil and gas), and wholesale and retail trade—whilst speeding up by quantum leaps the role of such potentially strong drivers as manufacturing, information and communication technologies, finance, minerals and metals, building, construction and real estate, SMEs, and tourism.

Evolution of Bilateral and Multilateral Aid

During the 1960s, Nigeria emerged as a moderately prosperous country, largely dependent on revenues from commodity exports such as cocoa, groundnuts, cotton, rubber, and palm produce. Given the pro-Western stance of the Balewa administration, beyond maintaining a principle of good neighbourliness, the leadership had a rather lukewarm attitude towards pan-Africanism. The government was keener to maintain its traditional relationship with Britain and the Commonwealth than with the Eastern Bloc and other developing countries. Although authorities did reaffirm the nonaligned status of the country, there was a conscious effort to steer clear of more radical elements in the developing world. Beyond the token humanitarian assistance to its neighbours, Nigeria did not make any major commitment to aid giving.

The civil war, however, was a turning point. The Gowon administration realised that without the help of its neighbours and of the Soviet Union working together with Britain and the United States, winning the war and securing the ante-bellum peace would have been more difficult. Coincidentally, the ending of the war in January 1970 saw the expansion of the oil sector as the oil majors returned to the oil fields, resulting in unprecedented earnings from petroleum exports. These earnings provided the finance needed for postreconstruction as well as for the pursuit of a more ambitious foreign policy. In 1974, during an official visit to the Caribbean island nation of Grenada, General Yakubu Gowon discovered that the country was nearly paralysed by a national strike because public-sector workers had not been paid for months. There and then, Gowon was said to have announced the immediate underwriting of the entire bill for all outstanding salaries of the Grenada government. The exact amount that was spent was never revealed. When Gowon was criticised back home, he was said to have famously retorted that the country's problem was not money, but how to spend it.

After the lacklustre postwar regime of General Gowon was overthrown, the Murtala/Obasanjo administration appeared to have a more focused commitment to foreign policy. In 1976, a committee headed by Professor Adebayo Adedeji articulated the concept of Africa as "the centrepiece" of Nigerian foreign policy. This new focus was the basis of renewed actions in support of liberation movements in southern Africa, with Nigeria taking on a new role as de facto leader of the Frontline States in the United Nations.

During 1983–1985, foreign policy thinkers, led by scholar-diplomat Professor Ibrahim Gambari, developed the theory of "concentric circles" as the framework of national policy. It was felt that the idea of "Africa as centrepiece" was much too general to be of operational relevance. The notion of concentric circles gave priority first to national interest, then to the neighbouring ECOWAS, and then thirdly to Africa and the rest of the world (Ajulo 2007).

The administration of General Ibrahim Babangida took major steps to boost relations within the West African subregion through the vehicle of personal diplomacy. Bilateral agreements were strengthened during visits while grants were provided in several instances. For example, in July 1988, President Babangida visited the island nation of Cape Verde, where, among other things, he donated the sum of US$76,700 toward the building of a new polytechnic. He also gave an undisclosed number of scholarships to enable Cape Verdian students to pursue higher studies in several Nigerian universities. During a visit to Ouagadougou, Burkina Faso, Babangida donated funds for the construction of a primary school, in addition to providing 500 tonnes of bitumen for road construction and vehicles towards hosting the ECOWAS summit in the Burkinabe capital. During a subsequent state visit to Sierra Leone, Babangida undertook to build a medical school in Freetown and provided funds for a distinguished Nigerian medical scientist and educator, Professor Ige Grillo, to be seconded there as founding dean.

Diplomatic insiders estimate that Nigeria has spent over US$60 billion in financial assistance to various African and Caribbean countries. So-called rescue operations, consisting largely of grants, have been made to countries ranging from Benin Republic to Zimbabwe, Cape Verde, Guinea, Senegal, Niger, Togo, Liberia, and Mali (Fayomi and Adejola 2007, p. 481). Several others have benefitted from Nigerian goodwill and financial assistance, including Caribbean countries such as St. Vincent and the Grenadines, St. Kitts/Nevis, British Guyana, Suriname, Barbados, the Bahamas, and the Commonwealth of Dominica. Nigeria also gave the Caribbean Development Bank the sum of US$5 million to enable it to support Caribbean Commission countries with the financing of various development projects. In 1988, Nigeria gave a grant of US$1 million to Jamaica, following a hurricane that wreaked havoc on the Caribbean island country.

It seems evident that much of the initial preoccupation of the country's foreign policy was the political liberation of Africa. As such, the economic aspects of foreign policy were initially geared towards serving these political objectives. Greater emphasis was given to bilateral economic assistance during the Babangida years (Asobie 1991). In 1986, after bombing raids carried out by the racist South African government's Air Force on Zambia, Zimbabwe, and Botswana, some US$60 million was donated by the Nigerian government between 1986 and 1988. A special fund amounting to 100 million naira was launched in 1988 to assist the South West African People's Organization (SWAPO) to campaign for independence elections in Namibia (Ogwu and Olukoshi 1991, p. 86). During 1988–1990, several grants were provided to the neighbouring country of Equatorial Guinea, among them some 10 million naira by way of a trade loan; a grant of US$5 million; and the financing of the construction of a hospital, polytechnic, and agricultural development project. Some of the bilateral assistance to African countries has been in terms of scholarships given to African students to study in Nigerian institutions of higher education. Nigerian foreign aid to Angola in 1975 amounted to some 13.5 million naira (Ogwu and Olukoshi 1991, p. 167).

A strong element of such assistance has been by way of concessional oil resources, largely consisting of oil sales below world market prices (Aluko 1976). General Gowon, for example, extended concessional oil assistance to the Bahamas. In February 1975, the government articulated a clearer policy on concessional petroleum sales to African countries with two conditions: (1) The countries must have their own refineries for processing crude petroleum; and (2) they had to ensure that products from the crude oil supplies not be re-exported to third countries (Fayemi and Adejola 2007, p. 481).

Technical Aid Corps Scheme

Established in 1986 by decree, the Technical Aid Corps (TAC) emerged as a foreign policy tool to promote goodwill and foster social and economic development in partner countries. TAC is structured to provide human capital assistance in all fields of social and economic development. It also symbolises the enduring values and practical demonstration of the crucial role of South-South cooperation. The aims and objectives of the scheme include

- Sharing Nigeria's know-how and expertise with other members of the African, Caribbean and Pacific Group of States (ACP)
- Giving assistance on the basis of assessed and perceived needs of recipient countries
- Promoting cooperation and understanding between Nigeria and recipient countries
- Facilitating meaningful contact between youths of Nigeria and those of recipient countries
- Complementing other forms of assistance to ACP countries
- Ensuring a streamlined programme of assistance to other developing countries
- Acting as a channel through which South-South collaboration is enhanced

• Establishing a presence in countries which, for economic reasons, Nigeria has no resident diplomatic mission

According to available data, between 1987 and 2008, nearly 2,000 TAC volunteers were deployed to thirty-three countries in Africa, the Caribbean, and the Pacific. It is generally recognised that one of the main strengths of the scheme is the fact that it is a people-oriented and people-centred assistance programme that fills crucially important gaps in the human capital needs of its partner countries. Indeed, so popular and so successful has the scheme become that it has attracted the interest of the Commonwealth Secretariat, the United Nations Volunteer Service, and the Japanese Agency for International Cooperation, all of which have sought some partnership and cooperative relationship with TAC.

It is evident that TAC has brought obvious dividends to both the giver and receiver. Nigerians sent abroad have acquired new skills and experiences, which they have been able to bring back home. The country has benefitted from immense goodwill garnered from sending its experts to serve in other countries. Tangible benefits have been recorded by the activities of technical assistance personnel in recipient countries (Daura 2006). For example, in Kenya, the two medical volunteers who served in Shelter Afrique were later retained as directors in that United Nations agency and also were said to be instrumental in Shelter Afrique's investment in a housing development in Bayelsa State. In the east African country of Uganda, TAC volunteers were responsible for the design and implementation of the IT network of the Kampala Institute of Teacher Education. In the Caribbean nation of Dominica, Nigerian TAC volunteers successfully designed and launched a new healthcare delivery system while one of the volunteers was retained as pioneer director of the primary healthcare system. In Zambia, a volunteer was said to have designed and launched the first programme in dentistry at the Medical School of the University of Zambia. In Gambia, one of the Nigerian volunteers became the first vice-chancellor of the country's pioneer university. In Jamaica, another volunteer drew up the first of the country's national land survey. Several other success stories have been registered in countries as diverse as Fiji, Seychelles, and Sierra Leone.

Clearly, the TAC scheme has been a success. However, there are some challenges. In the first place, the amount that has been expended so far remains shrouded in mystery. There is no evidence of any detailed and critical evaluations, especially during its first and second decades, so as to internalise any lessons learned. There is also no evidence that volunteers have been subjected to any form of debriefing so the country can learn from their experiences and loop these into foreign policy actions. A major lacuna is the francophone countries. For obvious reasons of language, few Nigerian graduates have proficiency in French, and those few that do barely meet the needs of the Nigerian market. Given that most of Nigeria's neighbours are French-speaking, some effort should be made to encourage Nigerian volunteers to be proficient in French so they are able to serve in francophone countries.

Nigeria and the African Development Bank

For much of its independent existence, Nigeria has been a major contributor to multilateral institutions. Within the African context, the country has been a major contributor and/or dominant shareholder of such institutions as the African Development Bank Group, Shelter Afrique, Afrexim Bank, and the ECOWAS Fund for Compensation and Development, which was transformed into the ECOWAS Bank for Investment and Development. In most African regional institutions in which Nigeria has been involved, it has contributed as much as 40 percent to the operational costs of those institutions. There was a period when Nigeria virtually underwrote the entire operational budget of the Organization of African Unity (OAU)/African Union at a time of fiscal difficulties when most member countries were not forthcoming. Indeed, according to former OAU Secretary-General Salim Ahmed Salim, without Nigeria's help at crucial turning points, the secretariat in Addis Ababa would have ground to a halt (Salim 2009).

At the inception of the African Development Bank (AfDB) in 1964, with an initial share capital of UA250 million (US$470 million) by the twenty-five member countries, Nigeria was the third-largest shareholder, following Egypt and Algeria (One AfDB unit of account, UA, = US$1.25). Egypt had the largest initial subscription of US$30 million and a voting power of 10.1 percent, followed by Algeria with a contribution of US$24.50 million and a voting power of 8.60 percent. Nigeria came third with an initial subscription of UA24.10 and a voting a power of 8.49 percent. These initial subscriptions followed the allocation formula that was determined on the basis of population and gross national product at the time. In 1982, when AfDB President Boubacar Ndiaye opened up participation to nonregional member countries, the share capital increased from UA250 million to UA21.9 billion (equivalent to UA30.7 billion by 1998).

This expansion increased the share participation of nonregionals from 33.3 to 40 percent, with the proportion of the voting powers of the regional member countries reduced from 66.6 to 60 percent.

With Nigeria's growing influence in international economic relations, due to increased petroleum resources, the government was able to significantly increase its share ownership in AfDB. At year-end 2005, Nigeria's subscriptions stood at UA197.86 million, representing a voting power of 8.974 percent. By the end of 2005, the total voting power of the first twelve shareholders stood at a total of 55.861 percent, with nonregionals wielding greater votes than ever.

Nigeria Trust Fund

The Nigeria Trust Fund (NTF) is a special AfDB fund created in 1976 by agreement between the African Development Bank Group and the Nigerian government. Its objective is to assist the development efforts of the AfDB's low-income regional member countries whose economic and social conditions and prospects require concessional financing.

The NTF became operational in April 1976 following approval of the agreement establishing it by the AfDB board of governors. Its initial capital of US$80 million was replenished in 1981 with US$71 million. The NTF deploys its resources to provide financing for projects of national or regional importance with the aim of fostering economic and social development of the low-income regional member countries (RMCs) whose peculiar social and economic conditions require nonconventional terms of financing. It lends at a 4 percent interest rate with a twenty-five-year repayment period, including a five-year grace period. In 1996, the NTF had a total resource base of US$432 million. In April 2003, the AfDB Board of Governors considered and approved a number of proposals aimed at enhancing the effectiveness of the NTF. These included

- Adjusting the interest rate for NTF loans from 4 percent to a 2–4 percent range, to increase concessionality
- Allocating 10 percent of NTF annual net income as a contribution to the Highly Indebted Poor Countries (HIPC) Trust Fund
- Appropriating NTF corpus resources to finance activities under the Technical Cooperation operation of the bank
- Reaching an agreement with the Bank Group to support programmes benefitting its regional member countries
- Introducing more flexibility in the investment of NTF resources, pending their use in financing projects

Under the terms of the agreement establishing the NTF, fund operations were envisaged to come to an end thirty years after the agreement came into force. Although the bank and Nigerian authorities agreed to two one-year extensions of the agreement's original expiry date of April 25, 2006, no new loans or grants have been approved from the NTF window since that date. In November 2006, an evaluation of the fund's activities was commissioned, and the exercise was completed in July 2007. On the basis of the evaluation exercise, findings, and recommendations, and subsequent to meetings held between the bank and Nigerian authorities in November 2007, the agreement was extended for a period of ten years beginning from April 26, 2008.

As at December 31, 2008, cumulative disbursements from the NTF window amounted to UA213.15 million (African Development Bank 2009). The loans provided by the fund have benefitted many countries across the continent and have been awarded in highly concessional terms. As at year's end 2008, some fifty-nine loans were fully disbursed for a total of UA196.20 million, representing 92.05 percent of cumulative disbursements. The fund's net income fell from UA19.84 million in 2007 to UA5.99 million in 2008, mainly because of the fall in money market returns, debt write-offs, and provision for impairment on loans and related charges. However, NTF reserves increased from UA144.88 million in 2007 to UA158.19 million by the end of 2008.

Nigerian Technical Cooperation Fund

The Nigerian Technical Cooperation Fund (NTCF) was developed in April 2004 as a grant window to complement the resources of the NTF, consisting of some US$25 million drawn from the net income of the NTF. Its objectives are to pool the human capital of recipient countries from the African Diaspora to assist in the rebuilding of war-torn countries and provide technical assistance grants for the identification and preparation of bankable projects. The bulk of resources are used to finance procurement of consultancy services, of which 80 percent is set to come from Nigeria while the remaining 20 percent comes from other African regional member countries.

From all indications, NTF outcomes have been, at best, a mixed blessing. Although its resources have been welcomed in recipient countries, it is doubtful this has translated into goodwill or even leverage for Nigeria. From the lessons of experience, countries that contribute to the shareholdings of multilateral banks do so for reasons of altruism as well as national self-interest. Given that these institutions wield enormous influence in national development policies of recipient countries, donor countries often jealously guard their voting powers as a means of exerting policy influence on those institutions and, via those institutions, on regional member countries. According to a former career official, vice president for operations, and one-time presidential candidate, given the size of Nigeria as the largest shareholder in the AfDB Group, one would expect the country to play the following roles (Ogunjobi 2007):

- Assume a leadership role in policymaking and strategic direction of the AfDB Group
- Use the NTF and NTCF resources to further both economic interests and foreign policy objectives of Nigeria as well as Africa
- Maximise economic and other benefits from using technical and financial resources of the AfDB Group
- Wield effective influence and have full representation at the senior management level of the AfDB

In practice, the experience has been that Nigeria has never fully exercised influence commensurate with its status and voting power. Nigerian influence remains weak at the highest levels of management, while Nigerian staff have felt they have not been given their due when it comes to promotion within the professional ranks.

Issues and Challenges Facing Nigeria's Economic Assistance

From the foregoing, it is evident that Nigeria has been a major player in promoting South-South cooperation for development. The country has committed enormous resources for promoting economic development in the developing countries of Africa, the Caribbean, and the Pacific. In some cases, notably the TAC scheme, Nigeria has been a pacesetter and model for other relatively prosperous developing countries. Obviously, the capacity to provide assistance directly correlates with the level of development and availability of government revenues. As we have seen, the country remains a monocultural-dependent economy. A strong industrial base and a prosperous economy are prerequisite for achieving the leadership role that Nigeria intends to play on the continent.

It has been suggested that Nigeria and South Africa constitute the two regional hegemons on the continent (Adebajo 2006). South Africa maintains a growing aid programme that is rigorously linked to its trade and commercial interests on the continent, through the South African Development Bank. Nigeria recently created the African Finance Corporation, which has been embroiled in controversy. A government-appointed investigation panel in 2007 indicted a former governor of the Central Bank, allegedly for money laundering, gross abuse of power, and professional misjudgement. The report was not released officially for political reasons.

One major element of the political economy of Nigerian foreign policy is its structural incoherence. According to one of the nation's leading diplomats and international relations specialists, Ibrahim Gambari:

> The management of Nigeria's petroleum resources has been so inept and corrupt that the country's oil 'boom' has almost become its economic and social 'doom'. Throughout recent history, Nigeria's vast human resources have rarely been matched by entrepreneurship, unity, integrity, or vision on the part of the country's political leadership. . . . It is now widely recognised that in Nigeria there is a direct relationship between domestic politics and the making of foreign policy. The domestic system and the conduct of political business invariably affect the conduct of external relations. . . . Nigeria's foreign policy has never been directly related to the needs of the masses of its people. Rather, this policy has been formulated, articulated, and implemented in highly elitist circles, reflecting the needs and aspirations of national elite of political, business, bureaucratic, military and traditional ruling groups. Not very cohesive, Nigeria's national elite is deeply divided along ethnical, regional, religious and ideological lines. (2008, p. 79)

Nigerian international assistance efforts have never been rooted in a clearly articulated vision of the national interest. At the All-Nigeria Conference on Foreign Policy held at the National Institute for Policy and Strategic Studies in 1986, President Ibrahim Babangida urged participants to seek a clearer definition of the national interest, with priority to be accorded the issue of "national security" (Egwu 2007). That particular conference distilled the essential elements of Nigerian national interests as consisting of

- National independence
- National cohesion
- Territorial integrity

- Security of citizens in terms of food, shelter, health, and housing
- Promotion of the national values of discipline, self-reliance, and patriotism

Given Nigeria's external image problem, the country's unparalleled generosity on the continent has not always been appreciated. Many citizens across the world have been recipients of dubious Nigerian 419 e-mails and faxes requesting the transfer of incredibly large amounts of money. Until recently, Nigeria was on the small list of countries with weak money-laundering legislation and controls. On Christmas Day, December 25, 2009, a young Nigerian and scion of a prominent banking family attempted to blow up an aircraft on US soil. The Obama administration immediately replied by placing Nigeria on the list of terrorist countries. Recipients of the gifts proffered by Prometheus may not be ingrates. It is simply the case that Nigeria's political economy, its poor image, and lacklustre reputation defeat any aims that provision of largesse would serve to achieve.

In 1977, the noted Kenyan scholar, Professor Ali Mazrui, observed that with its vast resources and huge population, Nigeria was well on its way to being the "the first major black power in modern international politics," predicting that the country was poised to overtake Britain and France as a world power by the end of the century (Ajulo 2007, p. 42). It is a profound irony that the first decade of the twenty-first century finds Nigeria in a far worse state than Mazrui had prophesied. A combination of factors such as poor economic management, weak leadership, massive corruption and ethno-religious conflicts have destroyed Nigeria's prestige and weakened its influence on African and world affairs. It is clear that no amount of grants or financial assistance could change this perception of Nigeria as a chaotic and irresponsible behemoth. Indeed, former US ambassador to Nigeria, Princeton Lyman, told Nigerian leaders to exorcise themselves of the illusion of grandeur, in essence prophesying doom for the future of the country. While Lyman is entitled to his opinions, there is no denying that Nigeria faces a profound crisis of leadership. The Nigerian people may continue to believe in their manifest destiny in the world, but the future of the country and its very survival remain at stake.

It is crucial that Nigeria evolve a new generation of transformational leaders—statesmen who have a vision of the country's high destiny. Linked to this is the need to articulate a new vision of foreign policy for the twenty-first century. In the emerging global hierarchy of nations, competitiveness, economic growth, and industrial prowess are factors that will determine the extent of a country's power and influence. The Vision 2020 project needs to be closely aligned to a new definition of national purpose. There must also be a new strategy anchored on international economic diplomacy so that the country's assistance programmes directly support long-term trade and investment interests. Economic statecraft must serve as the handmaiden of national interest and the promotion of collective aspirations on the world stage. While there will always be a place for charity in the affairs of nations, generosity without an eye for the promotion of the national interest amounts to a pursuit of illusions.

Bibliography

Adebajo, A., 2006, "Prophets of Africa's Renaissance: Nigeria and South Africa as Regional Hegemons," Occasional Paper Series No. 3, Nigerian Institute of International Affairs, Victoria Island, Lagos, Nigeria.

African Development Bank Group, 2009, the *2008 Annual Report,* Tunis, Tunisia.

Ajulo, S.B., 2007, "Nigeria's Interests in West Africa, 1983–1999: Streaks of Continuity and Discontinuity," in B. Akinterinwa, ed., *Nigeria's National Interests in a Globalising World: Further Reflections on Constructive and Beneficial Concentricism*, Bolytag International Press, Ibadan, Nigeria, pp. 3–67.

Asobie, H.A., 1991, *Nigerian Journal of International Studies*, vol. 15, no. 1. p. 86.

Bauer, P., 1972, *Dissent on Development*, Harvard University Press, Cambridge, MA, US.

Bull, H., 1977, *The Anarchical Society: A Study of Order in World Society*, Columbia University Press, New York, US.

Central Bank of Nigeria, various years, *Statistical Bulletin*, Lagos, Nigeria.Centre for Global Development, 2006, *Building Africa's Development Bank: Six Recommendations for the AfDB and Its Shareholders*, Report of the AfDB Working Group, Centre for Global Development, Washington, DC, US.

CIA, 2009, *World Fact Book*, Washington, DC, US, p. 20.

Daura, M., 2006, "The Technical Aid Corps Scheme: Background and the Journey So Far," in M. Daura, ed., *Nigeria's Technical Aid Corps: Issues and Perspectives*, Dokun Publishing, Ibadan, Nigeria, pp. 3–16.

Egwu, D., 2007, "National Interests, Globalisation and the Challenge of Constructive and Beneficial Concentricism," in B. Akinterinwa, ed., *Nigeria's National Interests in a Globalising World: Further Reflections on Constructive and Beneficial Concentricism*, Bolytag International, Ibadan, Nigeria, pp. 677–700.

Fayomi, A.O., and Adejola, A.R., 2007, "Nigeria's Aid Policy in the Caribbean," in B. Akinterinwa, ed., *Nigeria's National Interests in a Globalising World: Further Reflections on Constructive and Beneficial Concentricism*, Bolytag International, Ibadan, Nigeria, pp. 470–492.

Gambari, I.A., 2008, "From Balewa to Obasanjo: The Theory and Practice of Nigeria's Foreign Policy," in A. Adebajo and A.R. Mustapha, eds., *Gulliver's Troubles: Nigeria's Foreign Policy after the Cold War*, University of Kwazulu Natal Press, Scottsville, South Africa, pp. 58–80.

Hayter, T., 1971, *Aid as Imperialism*. Penguin, Harmondshire, UK.

Hollis, M., and Smith, S., 1991, *Explaining and Understanding International Relations*, Clarendon Press, Oxford, UK.

Holsti, K.J., 1994, *International Politics: A Framework of Analysis*, Prentice-Hall, Englewood Cliffs, NJ, US.

Joseph, R., 1987, *Democracy and Prebendal Politics in Nigeria: The Rise and Fall of the Second Republic*, Cambridge University Press, Cambridge, UK.

Lewis, P., 2007, *Growing Apart: Oil, Politics, and Economic Change in Indonesia and Nigeria*, University of Michigan Press, Ann Arbor, MI, US.

National Bureau of Statistics, Nigeria, 2007, *Statistical Bulletin*, Abuja, Nigeria.

National Planning Commission, 2009, Report of the Vision 2020 National Technical Working Group on Manufacturing, Vision 2020 Secretariat, Abuja, Nigeria, July.

Okeahalam, C., and Murinde, V., 2008, *An Evaluation of the Financial Performance of the African Development Bank*, Birmingham Business School, University of Birmingham, Edgbaston Birmingham, UK.

Ogunjobi, B., 2007, "Nigeria and the African Development Bank," in B. Akinterinwa, ed., *Nigeria's National Interests in a Globalising World: Further Reflections on Constructive and Beneficial Concentricism*, Bolytag International Press, Ibadan, Nigeria, pp. 378–412.

Ogwu, J., and Olukoshi, A., eds., 1991, "Economic Diplomacy in the Contemporary World and the Nigerian Experience," *Nigerian Journal of International Studies*, vol. 15, nos. 1 and 2 (November).

Ogwu, J., and Olukoshi, A., eds., 2001, *The Economic Diplomacy of the Nigerian State*, Frankad Publishers/Nigerian Institute of International Affairs, Lagos, Nigeria.

Okigbo, P.N., 1989, *National Development Planning in Nigeria 1900–1992*, James Currey/Heinemmann/Fourth Dimension, London, Portsmouth, and Enugu.

National Bureau of Statistics. 2009, *Social and Economic Statistics*, Abuja, Nigeria.

Riddell, R., 1987, *Foreign Aid Reconsidered*, Johns Hopkins University Press, Baltimore, MD, US.

Smith, M., and Hollis, S., 1991, *Explaining and Understanding International Relations*, Clarendon Press, Oxford, UK.

World Bank, 2008, Nigeria Growth and Competitive Report, Washington, DC, US.

Yates, D. A., 1996, *The Rentier State in Africa: Oil Rent Dependency and Neocolonialism in the Republic of Gabon*, Africa World Press, Lawrenceville, NJ, US.

Yusif, M. M., 2008, "The TAC Scheme and the Pursuit of Nigeria's Foreign Policy Objectives: Problems and Prospects," Department of Political Science, Bayero University, Kano, presented at 11th Orientation Exercise of TAC, Ministry of Foreign Affairs Nigeria, Makurdi, Benue State, May 29.

10

Multilateral Water Organisations and Nigeria's National Interest: Lake Chad Basin Commission and Niger Basin Authority

Tijjani Muhammad Bande

A state's national interest informs and guides its relations with other states. These interests as well as their power determines how states interrelate in the international system. From this standpoint, foreign policy is the systematic attempt by states to defend and advance their national interests in their interaction with other states and external bodies. The United Nations, African Union (AU), and Economic Community of West African States (ECOWAS) have been important arenas for advancing Nigeria's interest. Less well known is the way in which other forums contribute, with implications for the defence of Nigeria's interest—for example, natural factors that bring states together irrespective of their differences. These include but are not restricted to shared oceans, rivers, and lakes. Management of transnational waters requires the involvement of all states that directly or indirectly share economic, social, or even politico-strategic stakes. The management of transnational waters can be a source of cooperation or conflict. Yet, international laws governing the utilisation of waters are often vague, if not contradictory. For most African states the attainment of peace and development through regional integration is a high priority.

Nigeria's national interest concerns its survival and development as a sovereign nation under sustained peace, security, and political stability. The 1999 Constitution specifies its foreign policy objectives as

- Promotion and protection of national interest
- Promotion of African integration and support for African unity

- Promotion of international cooperation for the consolidation of universal peace and mutual respect among all nations and elimination of discrimination in all its manifestations
- Respect for international law and treaty obligations as well as seeking the settlement of international disputes by negotiation, mediation, conciliation, arbitration, and adjudication
- Promotion of a just world economic order

The River Niger and Lake Chad not only provide access to Nigeria but to other countries in the West and Central African subregions, providing water for agricultural and domestic use, conservation, and hydroelectric power generation. Fishing is also a source of livelihood for millions of Nigerians living along the basins of the Niger and Lake Chad. Proximity offers an opportunity to constructively engage other states and advance the cause of socioeconomic integration in Africa.

This chapter examines two important transnational water management organisations in West Africa: The Lake Chad Basin Commission (LCBC) and the Niger Basin Authority (NBA), established to manage, regulate, and harmonise activities of states around the waters. Sources of data for the study were mainly secondary, supplemented by in-depth, semistructured interviews with one former chief executive of each of the authorities and the current head of Nigeria's Lake Chad Development Authority.

Transnational Waters: Cooperation and Conflict

Management of water at domestic and international levels has been a source of both conflict and cooperation. Westing argues that "competition for limited . . . freshwater leads to severe political tensions and even war" (1986, p. 231). Seragelding concludes that "the wars of the next century [twenty-first] will be about water" (1995, p. A–13). The battle over control of the Suez Canal was fierce among major powers from the late nineteenth century to the middle of the twentieth century. Today control of the Persian Gulf, the Mediterranean Sea, and the Red Sea is a major issue in international strategy (both commercial and military). Scholars who study transnational waters, such as Cooley (1984) and Remans (1985), point to the potential of water as a cause of violent conflict in the twenty-first century (Wolf 1998). The problem is compounded by insufficient consideration of water quality issues in decisions, a lack of specificity in rights allocations, disproportionate political power by special interests, and a general neglect of environmental concerns in water resource decisionmaking (Wolf 1998; Butts 1997). Mostert (2003) stresses that unilateral action often triggers water conflict—for example, upstream water diversion that threatens to harm other parties that share the resource.

Conflicts among communities over rights to ponds and other water points are not uncommon. Fortunately, few disputes have resulted in violent conflict. Table 10.1 provides the date, nature of conflicts, and the countries involved.

Table 10.1   Selected Cases of Water Conflicts

Date	Nature of Conflicts and Countries Involved
1948	The partition of India and Pakistan led to the division of the Indus Basin in an overlapping fashion. This dispute over irrigation exacerbated tensions in the Kashmir region and brought the two states to the brink of war. However, twelve years of World Bank–led negotiations resulted in the 1960 Indus Waters Agreement.
1951–1953	Israel and Syria exchanged sporadic fire over Israeli water development works in the Huleh basin, which lies in the demilitarised zone between the two states.
1958	In the middle of pending negotiations over Nile waters, Sudanese general elections, and an Egyptian vote on Sudan-Egypt unification, Egypt sent an unsuccessful military expedition into the territory during a dispute between the two states. When tensions eased, a Nile Waters Treaty was signed.
1963–1964	The 1964 boundaries left Somali nomads under Ethiopian rule and led to border skirmishes between Somalia and Ethiopia over the Ogaden Desert, which includes critical water resources (as well as oil resources). Hundreds of people were killed before a ceasefire was negotiated.
1965–1966	War ensued between Israel and Syria over an Arab plan to divert the Jordan River headwaters to preempt an Israeli national water barrier, an out-of-basin diversion plan from the Sea of Galilee. However, construction of the Syrian diversion was halted in July 1966.
1975	When the flow of water from the Euphrates filled upstream dams, Iraq complained that the diminished flow reaching its territory would no longer be tolerated and asked the Arab League to intervene. Syria presented a similar claim. After mutually hostile statements, Syria pulled out of an Arab League technical committee formed to mediate the conflict. In May 1975, Syria closed its airspace to Iraqi flights, and both countries reportedly deployed troops to their mutual border. Saudi Arabia's timely intervention and mediation prevented escalation of the conflict.
1989–1991	Two Senegalese peasants were killed over grazing rights along the Senegalese River, which forms a boundary between Mauritania and Senegal. This incident sparked serious ethnic and land reform tensions in the region. Civilians along the border towns of both states were killed before each country deployed its army to restore order. Sporadic violence, however, continued until diplomatic relations were restored in 1991.

Source: Wolf 1998, pp. 4–5.

Of the seven historical cases of armed conflict over water, three did not escalate into physical combat. Wolf maintains that "there has never been a single war fought over water" (1998, p. 5) in modern times. Perhaps some minimum level of humanity is involved here: How far would any state or community go if wilfully denied access to so vital a resource as water?

Although there is a considerable body of literature concerning transnational freshwater management, Mostert contends there is "little information on how these institutions were developed and how they function in practice" (2003, p. 1) and perhaps even no information regarding how states strategise the use of transnational waters to achieve national interests. To minimise this theoretical lacuna is to study transnational waters from the framework of what Mostert refers to as PC-CP (potential conflict to cooperation potential). The PC-CP project, a UNESCO and Green Cross International framework, examined and promoted the potential of transitional water resources becoming a catalyst for regional peace and development through the triple issues of dialogue, cooperation, and participative management. In understanding how transnational waters influence conflict and/or cooperation, three issues can be discerned:

1. Collective problems in which relevant states have similar interests, such as restoration of an international lake (for example, the various projects initiated for the resuscitation of Lake Chad, such as the Inter-basin Water Transfer project) and the joint development of a boundary river
2. Negative externality problems, which result in a situation whereby actual or proposed activities in a given country would have adverse effects on another, such as upstream water diversion or water pollution
3. Positive externality problems which occur when activities of a member state would be beneficial to another, such as constructing a dam to reduce flooding downstream

Scenarios (1) and (2) characterise the situation of Lake Chad and Niger River basins. Although a potential for conflict exists, cooperation has largely ensued. Given this, two questions are important: (1) How are the basins managed by their respective authorities within the challenges of limited available resources? (2) How does Nigeria advance its national interests through participation in both LCBC and NBA? These are considered in the following sections.

Lake Chad Basin Commission

Lake Chad is the fourth largest in Africa after lakes Victoria, Tanganyinka, and Nyassa. It shares boundaries with Chad, Nigeria, and Niger, but its hydrographic basin extends to Algeria, Libya, Sudan, and Cameroon (see Figure 10.1). According to Kahumba (2007), the Lake Chad catchment area is approximately 2,370 square kilometres, and seven states share its basin: Chad, Cameroon, Central African Republic, Niger, Nigeria, Libya, and Sudan.

Establishment and Mandate

The LCBC was established on May 22, 1964, by the Fort Lamy (N'Djamena) Convention and Statutes by the governments of Cameroon, Chad, Niger Republic, and Nigeria. In 1994, the Central African Republic was admitted as the fifth signatory. Sudan was admitted in July 2000, increasing the LCBC jurisdiction from 966,955 to 1,035,000 square kilometres (LCBA 2008). Libya was formally admitted in January 2010. The convention recognises the sovereign right of each member state over basin water resources within its own territory but forbids unilateral exploitation of lake water where such use detracts from the interests of other states (see Table 10.2). The convention also recognises the right of member states to plan projects within the conventional basin in consultation with the LCBC (Hodge 2006; LaRoche 2008).

The LCBC mandate encompasses trans-boundary water and land, economic integration, peace, and security matters. However, the actual convention limits such mandate to economic objectives. LaRoche argued that the LCBC convention and statutes focused mainly on the water sector to the detriment of other water-related resources. Nevertheless, Article 9 of the convention states that

> The Member States undertake to refrain from adopting, without referring to the Commission beforehand, any measures likely to exert a marked influence either upon the extent of water losses, or upon the form of the annual hydro graph and limnograph and certain other characteristics of the Lake, upon the conditions of their exploitation by other bordering states, upon the sanitary condition of the water resources or upon the biological characteristics of the fauna and the flora of the Basin. (LaRoche 2003, p. 23)

Figure 10.1:   Map of Lake Chad Basin

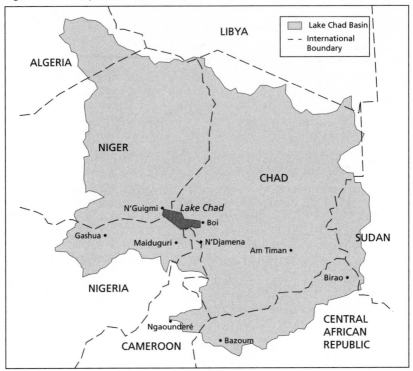

Source: Kombe 2009, p. 10.

This article addresses the negative externality problems that could potentially affect friendly relations among member states. The common vision of the LCBC member states is for a "basin where land, water and all natural resources are to be conserved, sustainably exploited, managed in an integrated manner and shared equitably in order not only to eradicate poverty and improve living standards of the people in the Lake Chad basin, but also to ensure peace, security, cooperation and sound economic development of the region" (Adamu 2005, p. 33).

The key mission of the commission, as stated in Article IX of its statutes, is to "collect, evaluate and disseminate information on projects prepared by Member States and to recommend plans for common projects and joint research programmes in the Lake Chad Basin"; ensure the most efficient utilisation of the basin's waters; examine complaints and promote the settlement of disputes and the resolution of differences; and "supervise the implementation of the provisions of the present Statute and the Convention to which it is annexed" (LCBC 2008).

Table 10.2   Distribution of the Lake Chad Basin in Member Countries of the LCBC

Country	Basin Surface Area (km^2)	Portion of Basin (%)	Country Surface Area (km^2)	Portion of Country in Basin (%)
Chad	1,109,201	46.3	1,284,000	86.4
Niger	671,868	28.0	1,267,000	53.0
Central African Republic	217,340	9.1	622,980	34.9
Nigeria	180,364	7.5	923,770	19.5
Algeria	89,694	3.7	2,381,740	3.8
Sudan	81,360	3.4	2,505,810	3.2
Cameroon	46,049	1.9	475,440	9.7
Libya	1,548	0.1	1,759,540	0.1
Total	2,397,423	100	11,220,280	—

Source: LCBC 2008, p. 2.

The commission has also developed what is popularly referred to as Lake Chad Vision 2025, which states in part that

> The Lake Chad Region would like to see by the year 2025 the Lake Chad—common heritage—and other wetlands maintained at sustainable levels to ensure the economic security of the freshwater ecosystem resources, sustained biodiversity and aquatic resources of the basin, the use of which should be equitable to serve the needs of the population of the basin thereby reducing the poverty level. (LaRoche 2008, p. 23)

Many maintain, however, that more integration of the convention with the vision is needed. On one hand, the convention hardly addresses the need for the basin to be managed in accord with an ecosystem approach. On the other hand, Vision 2025, which was based on the framework of Africa Water Vision for 2025 with inputs from development partners, incorporates the ecosystem approach and stresses an integrated water resources management approach. The ecosystem approach recognises that water, land, and living resources must be managed as part of an integrated system rather than on a sector-by-sector basis. This is a daunting task, given often conflicting directions among relevant ministries, even within member states (e.g., water resources, agriculture, transportation, and health).

Nevertheless, little reference is made to groundwater. Adenle (2004) argues that the only reference to groundwater is in Chapter I, Article 4 of the convention, which states that the "development of the said basin and in particular the utilisation of surface and ground waters shall be given its widest connotation." Adamu (2010), who was LCBC executive secretary between 2000 and 2009, further laments the neglect of groundwater by the LCBC and member countries, particularly with the depletion of surface water resources (Interview, January 12, 2010, Kaduna, Nigeria). Ngatcha et al. (2007) conducted a study to determine groundwater recharge in Lake Chad in order to evaluate its sustainable yield.

Results show that important recharge zones are located in topographically higher areas (Mandara Mountains and Guera and Batha massifs) and where sand dunes are exposed. Indirect recharge to groundwater is by seepage through the beds of Lake Chad, Rivers Logone-Chari, local ponds, and nonpermanent rivers (Komadugu-Yobe, Yedseram, Mayos). More needs to be known about the interactions between groundwater and surface water.

Lake Chad can be a source of improving the livelihood of member states' citizens, as well as an arena for the creation and re-creation of cultures. Little wonder that the Council of Ministers of member states has consistently requested the LCBC to be more effective and efficient in discharging its responsibilities. For example, at the end of its meeting in Niamey, Niger, in 2003, the council agreed that "an experienced consulting firm should be awarded the contract for an organizational, accounting and financial audit of LCBC" (LaRoche 2008, p. 24).

Structure and Operations

The commission is structured as follows:

- The Summit of the Heads of State, which meets biannually, is the highest decisionmaking body.
- The Council of Ministers meets annually to approve the commission's budget.
- The Secretariat, which conducts the day-to-day business of the commission, is headed by an executive secretary and is headquartered in N'Djamena, Chad. The executive secretary post is now permanently retained by Nigeria.
- Committees are established on an ad hoc basis to conduct other technical activities of the commission.

According to Iliya (2010), current head of Nigeria's Chad Basin Development Authority in Maiduguri, from January 2010, the LCBC funding burden is shared as illustrated in Table 10.3.

Table 10.3   LCBC Fund-Sharing Formula Among Member States (2010)

Country	Former Sharing Formula (1964–2009)	Current Sharing Formula (from 2010)
Nigeria	52%	40%
Cameroon	26%	20%
Libya	Not yet a member	18%
Chad	1%	11%
Niger	7%	7%
Central African Republic	4%	4%
Total	100	100

Sources: Iliya 2010; LCBC 2008, p. 5.

Even though Table 10.3 shows that Nigeria accounts for 40 percent of statutory funding, until January 2010 the contribution of Nigeria was approximately 52 percent. It should be noted also that because Sudan has not yet ratified the convention it is not yet assigned a quota in the LCBC fund-sharing formula. Other sources of funding for the commission include international development partners, such as the United Nations, World Bank, UN Educational, Scientific and Cultural Organization, UN Environmental Programme (UNEP), UN Development Programme (UNDP), UN Habitat, African Development Bank, UN Economic Commission for Africa, German Ministry for Economic Cooperation and Development/German Agency for Technical Cooperation, Arab Bank for Economic Development in Africa, ECOWAS, Economic and Monetary Community of Central African States, Global International Waters Assessment, Food and Agricultural Organisation (FAO), World Metrological Organisation, Islamic Development Bank, Réseau International des Organismes de Bassin, Global Water Brigades, World Wildlife Fund, International Union for Conservation of Nature, Commission on Climate Change and Development, Global Environment Fund (GEF), European Union (EU), and African Union (Adamu 2005).

Development partners have also been funding projects on the Lake Chad Basin. For instance, in 1989, UNEP and the UN Sudano-Sahelian Office jointly provided assistance for the Transboundary Diagnostic Analysis of Lake Chad in order to identify environmental problems in the region. Upon completion of the exercise, seven critical problems were identified (Adamu 2008) and policy actions are being taken to address them (Interview with Adamu 2010). In addition, the LCBC/GEF project on Reversal of Land and Water Degradation Trends in the Lake Chad Basin

Ecosystem was funded by the GEF through the World Bank. Similarly, the Hydro-Chad Project, which costs US$855,000, was supported by the BADEA (Arab Bank for Economic Development in Africa) with a sum of US$250,000. The aim of the project was to provide quick access to ready, accurate, and reliable hydro-meteorological data of the Lake Chad Basin for integrated water resource management and socioeconomic development of the region. The Mega Chad Project, which aimed at promoting the use of renewable energy resources and conservation of economic floral species in the dry lands of Mega Chad, was funded by Belgium through UNEP, implemented by the University of Maiduguri, and coordinated by the commission. The Integrated Pest Management Project, a pilot project on integrated pest management (IPM) for sustainable subsistence farming in the Lake Chad Basin, was funded by African Development Bank (AfDB) with a sum of 1.5 billion CFA franc. The objective of the project was to test and validate modern IPM techniques over a period of two years, with a view to reducing by at least 50 percent crop losses caused by pests, weeds, and crop diseases affecting millet and sorghum in twenty selected villages of Lake Chad Basin (Adamu 2005, 2010).

Nigeria has been a consistent supporter of the commission's activities, providing leeway to work within LCBC to advance its interests. Blench (1997) states that of the major basins, the most effluent parts of the lake, Komadugu-Yobe, and Ngadda and Yedseram river systems are within Nigeria. Water control within Nigeria is divided into (1) structures intended to draw water from Lake Chad and (2) those on the Ngadda and Yedseram river systems, which reduce the flow of the lake. Within Nigeria, the two most significant projects drawing water from the lake are the Baga Polder and the South Chad irrigation projects. The Baga Polder was constructed in the 1970s to irrigate a pilot scheme of 500 hectares. Conversely, the main structures reducing water flows into the lake are the Alau Dam southeast of Maiduguri on the Ngadda River and the Lower Yedseram. Live storage volume of the dam is approximately 106 million cubic metres. The dam was also to supply the urban water needs of Maiduguri, but has not done so. Its drainage area is 4,105 square kilometres and includes part of the Sambisa swamp, which detains inflows from the Ngadda River. Similarly, the Jere Bowl in the swampland northeast of Maiduguri is fed by the Ngadda River, which supports an integrated farming, fishing, and pastoral economy (Blench 1997; Iliya 2010).

Main Achievements

The LCBC has recorded significant achievements, including the successful demarcation of international boundaries between Chad, Niger,

Nigeria, and Cameroon at various times between 1988 and 1992 (Adamu 2010). Similarly, the LCBC has successfully prepared a master plan for the basin in collaboration with experts from member states and supported by FAO, UNDP, and UNSO. It was adopted by the LCBC Summit of the Heads of State and Government, and an international campaign was launched to save the lake in 1994.

From the master plan, a strategic action plan was developed, which identified thirty-six projects as priority to ensure continued existence of the basin's natural resources, including water transfer from the Oubagui River to Lake Chad. It is instructive that Nigeria contributed approximately US$5 million out of the required US$6.7 million for feasibility studies of this important work. Another crucial achievement of the LCBC is the preparation of the Vision 2025 document, which identifies causes of the current environmental degradation as global climate change, unsustainable decisions, lack of good policy and political will among member states, poor coordination mechanism, poverty, and the region's fragile economic situation.

Similarly, the challenges to integrated management of the Lake Chad Basin's resources were identified and include conservation to preserve water resources, restoration of vegetation, and protection of aquatic ecosystems; restoration of the lake level, including wetlands; prevention of desert encroachment; data collection; and regional cooperation (LCBC 2008). Strengthening subregional cooperation and institutional reforms were among the strategies suggested to redress problems. Hodge (2006) observes that, in 1964, Lake Chad measured 25,000 square kilometres, but, due to persistent water diversion and drought, it has shrunk to a mere 5 percent of its original size. The problem of Lake Chad's gradual disappearance has caused a progressive serious water shortage which affects all other development projects along the basin.

To address this problem, the LCBC submitted a memorandum to the meeting of its convention's Permanent Technical Committee on Water Resources, in Niamey, Niger, September 11–14, 2001, on "Draft agreement on the equitable utilisation, development, conservation, management and protection of the international waters of the Conventional Lake Chad Basin." The memorandum identifies critical gaps in the convention statutes. For instance, it argues that the convention does not have any legal instrument to ensure that a member state concludes an agreement with the other members before it proceeds on the water project. Similarly, the convention fails to offer water allocation rules. The LCBC Memorandum of 2001 noted that the water resources management problem within the basin gave rise to two bilateral agreements of water utilisation: one between Chad and Cameroon (Mondou Agreement) and the other between Nigeria and Niger (brokered by the Nigeria-Niger Joint Commission, NNJC). However, these bilateral agreements have the potential to jeopardise activities of the LCBC.

Problems and Challenges

The major problem facing the LCBC is funding. Statutory annual dues are not remitted in time, if at all (see Table 10.4). Adamu (2008), for instance, lamented that despite the various decisions of the Summit of the Heads of State, resolutions of commissioners, and vigorous followup by the executive secretary to ensure member states pay their contributions on time, the financial condition of LCBC remains precarious. He noted that, as at March 2008, no country had paid its 2007 contribution, except Nigeria and Chad, which paid only part of their contribution arrears within the period, totaling about 814,438,195 CFCA. Outstanding arrears from member states amounted to 3,396,141,585 CFCA.

Lack of timely payment of contributions has contributed to LCBC becoming heavily reliant on development partners (see Table 10.4). Other problems of the LCBC include weak coordination of projects; weak economic situation of member states; rigid legal frameworks; effects of global climate change in lake and wetlands shrinkage, drought, and desertification; and inefficient integrated water resource management at national and regional levels.

In addition, an operational issue arises from "overall fragmentation of scientific effort, responsibility, and weakening of capacities at all levels. As a consequence, the organisation's ability to function on a day-to-day basis is retarded" (Hodge 2006, p. 10). An important aspect of water resource and environmental management is data gathering and information sharing. Systems of data collection and exchange, including information regarding availability of water resources, water users, hydro-systems, and land management, are essential to any water cooperative system. Only Article IX(b) of the convention addresses this, though not the collection of information for the purposes of monitoring resources with a view to proper management. This is an important lacuna that must be addressed. Information sharing and monitoring by the LCBC can douse tension and suspicion and increase trust among member states.

Niger Basin Authority

The NBA, otherwise known in French as Autorité du Bassin du Niger, is a nine-member (Benin, Burkina Faso, Cameroon, Chad, Cote d'Ivoire, Guinea, Mali, Niger, and Nigeria) intergovernmental organisation estab-

Table 10.4   **Breakdown of Outstanding Arrears of LCBC Member States**

Country	Outstanding Arrears	Since (year)
Nigeria (52%)	1,242,723,942 CFCA	2006
Cameroon (26%)	948,723,814 CFCA	2004
Chad (11%)	537,898,840 CFCA	2003
Niger (7%)	392,733,866 CFCA	2002
Central African Republic (4%)	274,061,123 CFCA	2000

Source: Adamu 2008, p. 7.

lished to manage and harmonise development of River Niger basins for the benefit of its members. River Niger, from which the NBA derives its name, encompasses a basin area of 2.2 million square kilometres and is one of the world's longest rivers—almost 4,200 kilometres (see Figure 10.2). The basin lies variously in the humid, subhumid, arid, and subarid climatic regions of West Africa where rainfall varies between 100 and 2,300 millimeters per annum.

The River Niger system sustains remarkable biological communities, featuring thirty-six families and nearly two hundred and fifty species of freshwater fish, of which twenty are found nowhere else in the world. Eleven of the eighteen families of freshwater fish endemic to Africa are represented in the river as well as hippopotami and crocodiles. The Niger's only delta, which is in Nigeria, contains West Africa's largest mangrove forest. The Niger River Basin hosts a population of approximately 100 million people, 80 percent of whom are in Nigeria. In fact, 65 percent of Nigeria's population is estimated to live in the basin. Of the nine countries that share the river and its basin (see Figure 10.2), Mali, Niger, and Nigeria have the largest share of 30.3, 28.3, and 23.8 percent, respectively. The Fouta Jalon Mountains in Guinea, which lie at an altitude of approximately 800 meters, provide the main source of water for the river. Its main tributary is the River Benue located in Nigeria (Ayibotele 2010).

Establishment and Mandate

The Niger River Commission (NRC) was established in 1963, and its main functions were principally consultative and sought to ensure that a national project of any country sharing the river and its basin did not negatively affect the territory of another member state (Niasse 2008). The NRC was refounded on November 21, 1980, as the NBA, through a convention agreed to by the nine-member states in Faranah, Guinea. The NBA has a mandate that geographically covers an area of 2,200,000

Figure 10.2   Map of West Africa Showing River Niger and Its Basin

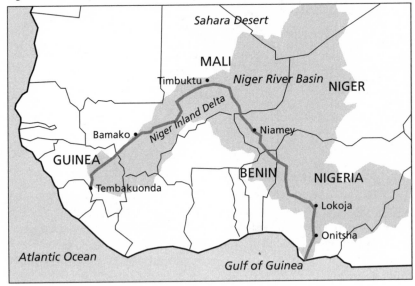

Source: Niasse 2005, p. 4.

square kilometres (Adenle 2004). Chapter II, Articles 3 and 4, of the 1980 NBA Convention specify that the NBA aims in particular to promote cooperation among member states and to ensure an integrated development of the Niger Basin in all fields by developing all its necessary resources including water. Similarly, Article 4.1 states that the NBA shall be responsible for six issues, one of which deals with surface and groundwater resources. It states that the NBA shall be concerned with the "initiating and monitoring of an orderly and rational regional policy for the utilisation of the surface and underground waters in the basin." Article 4.1a states that the NBA shall be responsible for the "harmonisation and coordination of national development policies in order to ensure an equitable policy as regards sharing of the water resources among member states." To achieve the six objectives listed under Article 4 of the convention, the agreement states under Article 4.2a–g that it shall undertake seven activities: (1) statistics and planning, (2) infrastructure, (3) water control and utilisation, (4) environment control and preservation, (5) navigation control and regulation, (6) land and agro-pastoral development, and (7) financing projects.

In addition, Article 4c, in particular, is concerned with water control and utilisation. Perhaps because of its importance in facilitating cooperation and/or conflict among member states, the item is further subdivided into six activities: (1) regulation of the flow and drainage of the main waterway; (2) flood control; (3) construction and maintenance of dikes; (4) prevention and control of drought and desertification; (5) prevention of soil erosion and sedimentation; and (6) setting up of structures and works for development, including salt water and drainage control. However, Article 4.2d identifies three activities that deal with the environment: (1) protection of the environment comprising the establishment of norms and measures applicable to the states in alternative uses of waters in the basin, (2) prevention and reduction of water pollution, and (3) preservation of human health and genetic resources (fauna and flora). According to the convention, the member countries "pledge not to undertake any work on the portion of the River, its tributaries and sub-tributaries under their territorial jurisdiction which pollute the waters or modify the biological features of the fauna and the flora." This clause is particularly important to Nigeria, to ensure that one of its important rivers and a tributary to the Niger—Benue—would not be negatively affected (Adenle 2004; Ayibotele 2010).

Structure and Operations

According to M.B. Tuga (2009), executive secretary of the NBA from 2000 to 2009, the NBA has a four-tier organisational structure: (1) Summit of Heads of State and Government, (2) Council of Ministers, (3) Technical Committee of Experts, and (4) an Executive Secretariat. The secretariat is headed by an executive secretary responsible for day-to-day administration of the NBA—implementing policies, programmes, and projects (Interview with M.B. Tuga, December 31, 2009, Birnin-Kebbi, Nigeria). The secretariat consists of five sections or departments: (1) Administration and Finance, (2) Water Resources, (3) Navigation, Transportation, and Telecommunication; (4) Agriculture and Livestock; and (5) Documentation and Information. The Summit of Heads of State is the authority's highest decisionmaking body and meets bi-annually to give policy direction. The Council of Ministers comprises all ministers of water resources of member countries and meets once every year to approve the budget for the commission. The Committee of Experts includes directors of water resources of member countries, who are responsible for preparing agenda items and documents for Council of Ministers' meetings.

The post of the executive secretary, whose status is equivalent to an ambassador and a minister at national level, is a political one. The secretariat, located in Niamey, Niger Republic, has two divisions: (1) Technical and (2) Administration and Finance. The NBA Convention provides representation from member states in the staffing of the organisation. Nevertheless, posts are usually advertised, and candidates from member states compete for positions. Equal representation from member states must be ensured in appointing secretariat staff. The post of executive secretary is advertised once a vacancy exists, and nominations are made by Heads of State of member countries. Currently, according to Tuga (2009), the secretariat has fifty-three staff, twenty-three of which are "foreign" (from member states), while the remaining staff are "local" (from Niger). In addition, focal structures in each country are headed by a coordinator, who as a director ensures the implementation of policies. Project management teams exist at regional and national levels, and regional coordinators oversee more than 100 staff. Meetings are rotated among member countries.

Sources of funding for the NBA are both internal and external. Internal sources include mandatory contributions from member states, which are shared as illustrated in Table 10.5.

The financial contribution of a member state is largely determined by the portion of the river it occupies. Nigeria, for example, has the largest portion—approximately 70 million of the 106 million square kilometres of the river.

External sources of funding for the NBA are international organisations and development partners, which contribute approximately 90 percent of the authority's budget. According to Tuga (2009), a Committee

Table 10.5   Funding Formula for NBA

Member State	Prior to 1995[a]	Current Contribution[b]
Nigeria	14.95%	30%
Mali	12.76%	20%
Niger	12.50%	18%
Guinea	11.18%	10%
Benin	10.73%	5%
Cameroon	10.12%	7%
Cote d'Ivoire	9.78%	5%
Burkina Faso	9.16%	4%
Chad	8.81%	1%
Total		100

Sources: Ayibotele 2010, p. 8.; Tuga 2009.
Notes: a. Percentage contribution before 1995 review. b. Current percentage contribution from member states.

of Development Partners led by the World Bank harmonise their activities and minimise conflict among them. Development partners include the World Bank, UNDP, United States Agency for International Development, FAO, Canadian International Development Agency, AfDB, Germany, France, Japan, and Korea. For example, within the last seven years the World Bank has provided US$500 million for water resources, of which US$300 million was for rehabilitation of the Kainji Dam alone. Furthermore, a joint project by the World Bank and UNDP was awarded in 2003 and expected to be completed in 2009, to define the transboundary framework for sustainable development of all member states of the Niger River Basin. At a cost of US$30.27 million, the project aims at strengthening the capacity of member states for understanding the basin's land and water resources (IW:LEARN 2010).

In 2007, the World Bank provided a credit of US$500 million to fund development of the Niger Basin. Its aims were to increase water resource productivity, boost hydropower generation, and foster economic growth in all nine member countries over the next twelve years. The renovation of Kainji and Jebba hydropower plants in Nigeria are part of this project. The World Bank also aims to strengthen the capacity of the NBA for efficient coordination and harmonisation of development programmes and policies in the region. Funding was awarded in two phases. The initial US$185 million went to Nigeria, Guinea, Benin, Mali, and Niger, while the second US$315 million was slated for Burkina Faso, Cameroon, Chad, and Cote d'Ivoire (VOA 2007). Development partners, however, express scepticism over the successful implementation of projects they help finance. A case in point was the insistence by partners in 2007 that Muhammad Tuga's tenure, which had ended, be extended by another two years in order to ensure the successful completion of projects. The Summit of the Heads of State and Government agreed (Tuga 2009).

Problems and Challenges

A careful analysis of the provisions of the NBA Convention calls attention to the need for further review. In some provisions, the NBA appears to be too ambitious. For instance, Rangeley et al. (1994) observe that the size of the NBA membership has posed a serious challenge to how such lofty objectives could be achieved. Niasse (2005) argues that it is often difficult to ensure efficient joint management of a river that is more than 4,000 kilometres long, with a basin covering 2.2 million square kilometres shared by nine countries with various economic capabilities and different sociopolitical and cultural attributes. Indeed, as a result of this problem, there have been calls for the division of the basin into two smaller and more manageable river basin organisations.

The NBA has been in serious financial difficulty since the 1990s, and often payment of salaries has been a problem (Tuga 2009; Rangeley et al. 1994). One problem internal to the convention is harmonisation and coordination by member states of their water resource development policies. The institutional, technical, and financial capacities needed for such a task are not readily available. At the level of the secretariat, internal rivalries among staff affects the implementation of NBA policies and programmes. The problem is more daunting as the NBA is a multilateral organisation, comprising nationals from the nine member countries. In addition, there are conflicts of interest among countries, usually addressed at the Council of Ministers meetings (Tuga 2009). Other problems facing the NBA include the recruitment of inexpert staff, as member states nominate personnel to key positions who tend to have allegiance to their home states rather than to the organisation, perhaps regardless of technical competence. Trained and qualified staff are often not placed in positions relevant to their training and expertise. Between 1980 and 1986, serious mismanagement of NBA finances resulted in the executive secretary being relieved of his post. Staff salaries could not be paid and credit bills accrued. Indeed, by 1994, at the 16th Session of the Council of Ministers held in Bamako, Mali, the NBA financial situation worsened to the extent that member states were asked to pay the salaries of their nationals working at the secretariat. However, the NBA was reinvigorated with the intervention of the Nigerian government under General Sani Abacha in 1996 to pay all outstanding salary arrears of staff.

Within the institutional framework of the NBA, cooperation with member states and intergovernmental organisations and domestic basin development organisations is weakly defined and can lead to serious problems. For example, the NBA could not rely on the Liptako Gourma Authority and the NNJC to obtain the necessary data and information in the preparation of its Master Plan for Development. Nonetheless, the NBA's major problem is a lack of political will from member states (Ayobotele 2010, p. 7).

Major Achievements

Despite these problems, the NBA has recorded important achievements. The fact that none of the member states has gone to war against another is a tremendous accomplishment. Furthermore, a revised convention was formulated and signed by member states in 1987 to address the shortcomings of the original version. Member states are also to refrain from carrying out any works likely to pollute the waters or adversely affect the characteristics of the fauna and flora on any section of the river, its tributaries, and subtributaries within their territorial jurisdictions.

At the 2001 Summit, the following decisions were reached: (1) to prepare a new vision for the NBA; (2) to improve policy direction and supervision; (3) to improve the institutional framework of the authority; and (4) to mobilize member states, subregional organizations, and the international community to support the NBA in its effort at rational and equitable management of the Niger Basin resources (Niasse 2008 and 2005; Ayibotele 2010). Despite new provisions, the new convention did not define the legal status of projects, let alone the mode of financing of common works by member countries.

There is also a remarkable improvement in the payment of contributions by member states. In fact, by September 2001, Benin, Cameroon, and Nigeria have all paid their current contributions, while Mali, Niger, and Guinea had paid their arrears and part of their current dues. According to Tuga (2009), member states are now more forthcoming in meeting their financial obligations to the NBA.

Nevertheless, it can be argued that most of the achievements of the NBA, apart from maintaining cooperation in the face of disagreement among member countries, are limited to conducting basic studies, developing operational tools necessary to conduct its activities, and the issues of environmental protection, such as the control of silting and water hyacinth. To minimise bureaucratic bottlenecks and improve administration and good governance, the heads of state of member countries adopted a declaration, known as the Paris Declaration, which defines the general principles of good governance for the river basin. Niasse (2005) argues that, through this declaration, the NBA member states initiated a consultation process aimed at adopting a shared vision of the river and its development. This exercise has ultimately produced an ambitious long-term development programme—the NBA Master Plan.

There are signs of potential trouble, however. Niasse (2005) identifies five bilateral agreements between member states. These are

1. A January 1999 agreement between Nigeria and Benin relating to the development of a hydroelectric power station in Dyodyonga on Mekrou River
2. A 1990 agreement between Nigeria and Niger on the equitable sharing, conservation, and development of their resources in the subbasins of Maggia, Lamido, Gada-Goulbi, Tagwai-El Fadama, and Kamadugu-Yobe, which is part of LCBC jurisdiction

3. A July 1988 agreement between Niger and Mali concerning cooperation in the use of water resources of the Niger River;
4. A hydrological management project of the Upper Niger between
   Guinea and Mali, which aims to improve hydrological knowledge
   in order to enhance the ecology management policies of the
   Upper Niger Basin
5. A Nigeria-Cameroon Protocol Agreement of January 2000
   aimed at coordinating the release of water from dams and consulting each other with respect to water projects from conception to implementation

While these agreements demonstrate the relevance of the sub-
sidiary principle, they may still lead to difficulties. Take, for example,
the NNJC. Niasse (2005) argues that Nigeria has invested heavily in
irrigation schemes and hydropower projects in the downstream part of
the River Niger (Kainji and Jebba dams, 1.6 million hectares of irrigat-
ed land, river transport installations, and urban water supply). Nigeria's
fear is that construction of dams upstream, such as the Kandadji Dam
project in Niger and Taoussa Dam project in Mali, would lead to
reduced inflow to its Nigerian dams. Several Nigerian authorities have
expressed their concern on dam construction upstream as well as their
opposition to any dam project on the Niger River that would involve a
reduction of more than 10 percent volume of inflow received annually
in Nigeria. Considering that climate variability over recent years has
resulted in a drop of 20 to 50 percent in average annual flows into the
River Niger (as in most major rivers in West Africa) and taking into
consideration the fact that climate change could lead to further reduc-
tions in river discharges, it is possible that climate variability will result
in the withdrawal of more water from the River Niger than downstream
countries such as Nigeria would consider acceptable. Downstream
countries could blame upstream dams and irrigation schemes for what
might be due to climate variations. What this calls for is a more determined effort to listen to the legitimate interests of all members and to
devise more rational ways of addressing issues.

Nigeria's Role in LCBC and NBA

Nigeria played a pivotal role in the establishment of both the LCBC and
NBA and points to their importance in furthering its national interest, as
well as efforts to support African integration. Despite the numerous
domestic and international challenges that Nigeria has encountered in its

fifty years of independence, the country has made an enormous contribution in the sustenance of the two regional water commissions. Nigeria is the most economically powerful state among all member states of the LCBC and NBA and has used its economic power to ensure steady funding of both organisations, which explains how the country has continued to provide leadership to the two organisations. Not only does Nigeria pay the highest statutory contribution to both bodies, it also has been consistent in remitting its contribution. In fact, in the 1990s when the NBA was in serious financial difficulty, it was Nigeria that came to its rescue, by building a befitting accommodation for the executive secretary and paying all outstanding arrears of staff salaries.

In the case of the LCBC, the position of the executive secretary is permanently reserved for Nigeria. In the NBA, though the position is not formally reserved for Nigeria, since its establishment, the country has continuously provided its executive secretary. In sum, the fact that the LCBC and NBA have continued to exist and provide relevant developmental activities along the two major West African basins demonstrates Nigeria's commitment to African development and integration, which are key elements underpinning its interests.

Nigeria has consistently used its position within ECOWAS and Africa with development partners to garner significant support for the two water authorities. For example, Nigeria has been instrumental in securing AfDB grants for the NBA and used its leeway to obtain financial support from international donors such as UNESCO, UNDP, UN Habitat, and the EU. It is worth noting that international development partners are the second most important financiers of LCBC and NBA activities. For example, it was the leadership role of Nigeria that led to GEF, through the World Bank, to fund the Reversal of Land and Water Degradation Trends in the Lake Chad Basin Ecosystem Project. In the case of the NBA, Nigeria's leadership role helped in securing financial assistance from the World Bank. Recently, the bank has provided approximately US$500 million for water resource development and another US$300 million for rehabilitation of the Kainji Dam. Nigeria has also provided US$5 million for research to the LCBC.

Conclusion

The role of transnational waters in facilitating the achievement of Nigeria's national interest is well demonstrated through the importance of the Niger River and Lake Chad basins. They serve not only as a catalyst for economic development and sources of livelihood for Nigerians and other nationals living near the basins but are essential for hydropower generation. LCBC and NBA are instruments for forging regional integration through dialogue and cooperation. The spillover effects of success—or failure—of the management of these transnational waters directly impact the lives of Nigerian citizens. However, the nature and pattern of the management of these two important regional water systems offers reason for both hope and despair. Their formation is indicative of the member countries' resolve to cooperate and develop the basin and waters for their mutual benefit. However, the nonchalance, as evidenced by late payment of statutory contributions, raises serious questions regarding the ability to improve the capacity of the organisations to achieve their aims and objectives, and contributes to overdependence on development partners for funding.

Notwithstanding their poor economic conditions, member countries should improve their overall support to the LCBC and NBA. Any conflict between Nigeria and an upstream country over the two waters could jeopardise their national interests. Nigeria must provide serious leadership to the two organisations. After fifty years of independence, the challenges of regional integration remain formidable. The LCBC and NBA provide a veritable mechanism of strengthening regional integration and cooperation for the benefit of Nigeria and its neighbours. The security of Nigeria depends very much on the security along its borders. Both its security and foreign policy objectives can be realised through these water authorities. This is only possible if the nation continues to provide leadership and financial support to the multilateral water organisations as it works to improve its own impressive record of supporting them. This is in the interest of the required attainment of peace and development in Africa, key elements in Nigeria's understanding of its national interest.

Bibliography

Adamu, M.S., 2005, "Managing Water Resources of the Lake Chad Basin," presented at the International Commission on Irrigation and Drainage Conference, Beijing, China, September 10–18.

Adamu, M.S., 2008, Annual Report of the Lake Chad Basin Commission, presented to the 54th Ordinary Session of the Council of Ministers, Preparatory to the 12th Summit of Heads of States of the Lake Chad Basin Commission (LCBC), Abuja, Nigeria, March 26.

Adenle, D., 2004, "Groundwater Resources and Environmental Management in Niger River Basin Authority and Lake Chad Basin Commission Agreements," presented at the International Conference organised by Network of

International Commissions, Transboundary Basin Organisations, and African Network of Basin Organisations, at Dakar, Senegal, November 3–6.

Ayibotele, N.B., 2010, "Transboundary Organisation in the Niger River Basin," www.gwptoolbox.org/images/stories/cases/en/cs%2046%20transbound-ary.pdf, accessed January 15, 2010.

Blench, R., 1997, "The History and Future of Water Management of the Lake Chad Basin in Nigeria," in H. Jungraithmayr, D. Barreteau, and U. Seibert, eds., *L'Homme et l'eau dans le Bassin du Lac Tchad*, ORSTOM, Paris.

Butts, K., 1997, "The Strategic Importance of Water," *Parameters*, Spring, pp. 65–83.

Cooley, J., 1984, "The War Over Water," *Foreign Policy*, vol. 54 (Spring), pp. 3–26.

Hodge, S., 2006, "Knowledge Innovation Systems and Technology Diffusion Strategies for Ecosystems Management in Africa—Case Study: Lake Chad Basin Commission," *Africa Policy Journal*, vol. 2 (Fall).

IW:LEARN (International Waters Learning Exchange and Resource Network), 2010, "Reversing Land and Water Degradation Trends in the Niger River Basin," www.iwlearn.net/iw-projects/Fsp_112799468181, accessed January 21, 2010.

Kahumba, R., 2007, "Sharing Water for Regional Integration," presented at International Conference on Small Hydropower—Hydro, Sri Lanka, October 22–24.

Kombe, M.D., 2009, "The Project for Water Transfer from Oubagui to Lake Chad," in *Adaptive Water Management in the Lake Chad Basin: Addressing Current Challenges and Adapting to Future Needs*, World Water Week, Stockholm, Sweden, August 16–22, International Water Institute, Stockholm.

LaRoche, D.A., 2008, "Institutional Assessment of the Lake Chad Basin Commission—LCBC," Final Report, unpublished manuscript, June 11.

LCBA (Lake Chad Basin Commission), 2008, "The Lake Chad Basin: A Bet in Danger for the Future," Roundtable to Save Lake Chad Background Paper, presented at a High-Level Conference on Water for Agriculture and Energy in Africa: The Challenges of Climate Change, Sirte, Libyan Arab Jamahiriya, December 15–17.

Mostert, E., 2003, "Conflict and Cooperation in International Freshwater Management: A Global Review," *International Journal of River Basin Management*, vol. 1, no. 3, pp. 1–12.

Ngatcha, B.N., Mudry, J., and Leduc, C., 2008, "The State of Understanding on Groundwater Recharge for the Sustainable Management of Transboundary Aquifer in the Lake Chad Basin," presented at IV International Workshop on Transboundary Water Management, Thessaloniki, Greece, October 15–18.

Ngatcha, B.N., Jacques, M., and Jean, S. R., 2007, "Groundwater Recharge from Rainfall in the Southern Border of Lake Chad in Cameroon," *World Applied Sciences Journal*, vol. 2, no. 2, pp. 125–133.

Niasse, M., 2005, "Climate-Induced Water Conflict Risks in West Africa: Recognising and Coping with Increasing Climate Impacts on Shared Watercourses," presented at International Workshop on Human Security and Climate Change, organised by Centre for the Study of Civil War,

International Peace Research Institute, Oslo, Norway, and Centre for International Environmental and Climate Research at the University of Oslo for the Global Environmental Change and Human Security Programme (GECHS), held at Holme Fjord Hotel, Asker, Norway, June 21–23.

Niasse, M. 2008, *Transboundary River Basins*, ECOWAS Executive Secretariat, Abuja, Nigeria.

Rangeley, R., Thiam, B.C., Andersen, R.A., and Lyle, C., 1994, "International River Basin Organizations in Sub-Saharan Africa," World Bank Technical Paper No. 250, World Bank, Washington, DC, US.

Remans, W., 1985, "Water and War," *Humantäres Völkerrecht*, vol. 8, no. 1.

Seragelding, I., 1995, "Water Resources Management: New Policies for a Sustainable Future," *New York Times*, August 10.

VOA (Voice of America), 2007, "World Bank Sending $500 Million Funding for Niger Basin Development," www1.voanews.com/english/a-13-2007 -07-04-voa35-66780562.html, (accessed January 22, 2010).

Westing, A.H., ed., 1986, *Global Resources and International Conflict: Environmental Factors in Strategic Policy and Action*, Oxford University Press, New York, US.

Wolf, A.R., 1998, "Conflict and Cooperation Along International Waterways," *Water Policy*, vol. 1, no. 2.

11

Conclusion: Defining the Achievements and Challenges of Nigeria's Foreign Policy

Attahiru M. Jega

Nigeria's foreign policy has engendered fifty years of largely positive relations with the country's immediate neighbours, despite remarkable differences in size, resources, and language, as well as diverse colonial traditions and experiences. The country's leading role in peacekeeping, democratisation, and regional integration in the West African subregion and the prominent role it played in the struggle against apartheid and in support of liberation movements in southern Africa are proud achievements. Mutually beneficial bilateral and multilateral relations with non-African countries in the international arena have also been fostered.

Nigeria has deployed significant resources in pursuit of its foreign policy even in periods of declining fortunes. For example, the country provided £15 million pounds sterling to peacekeeping operations in the Belgian Congo in the 1960s; underwrote US$80 million of Organization of African Unity (OAU) peacekeeping operations in Chad in 1982; and was estimated to have spent US$10–$14 billion on peacekeeping in Liberia and Sierra Leone (Dike 2010). It contributed US$20 million to the South West African People's Organization (SWAPO) in the 1989 elections in Namibia (Kuna 2006)—huge investments that in material terms may not have yielded commensurate dividends. Mailafia (Chapter 9) also asserts that Nigeria has not only used its petrodollars to "oil" its friends' distressed economies, it has sometimes "oiled" their leaders as well.

Whether in the United Nations, the Commonwealth, the Non-Aligned Movement (NAM), or through other bilateral or multilateral avenues, Nigeria has enjoyed constructive engagements and made significant contributions in the global arena. From a relatively unknown neo-colony that took its first tentative steps in October 1960, symbolically marked by Prime Minister Tafawa Balewa's address to the UN

General Assembly, Nigeria is now, in the first decade of the new millennium, a well-known, important player in international politics. Its peace-keeping and peacebuilding roles in West Africa have made it a leader to be reckoned with by the dominant powers and international organisations interested in the subregion. Similarly, its leadership in the struggle against apartheid through the UN and the Frontline States has been widely acclaimed. Whatever indices are used to define actors contributing to peace, democratisation, and development in the contemporary era, Nigeria would earn a deserved mention. Indeed, a recent joint statement on Nigeria by the United States, France, UK, and the European Union stated:

> Nigeria is one of the most important countries in sub-Saharan Africa, a member of the UN Security Council, a global oil producer, a leader in ECOWAS, a major peacekeeping contributing country, and a stabilizing force in West Africa. . . . Nigeria's stability and democracy carry great significance beyond its immediate borders. (*Guardian* 2010, p. 3)

Yet, given its size, resource endowment, and vast potential, contemporary Nigeria's role on the global stage leaves much to be desired—barely respected or merely tolerated in some cases and accused of hegemony in the subregion by others. As Mustapha has rightly observed, "Despite its many strong points, there is still a feeling that Nigeria's diplomacy is punching below its rightful weight" (2008, p. 369). Notwithstanding a relatively good record in international relations, as amply illustrated by the contributors to this book, formidable, if not profound, challenges have constrained the formulation and execution of Nigeria's foreign policy. Significant achievements are commendable and noteworthy, especially at the subregional and continental levels, but there are numerous and substantial missed and wasted opportunities. Looking back at fifty years of Nigeria's foreign policy, one sees much to be proud of. However, positive initiatives are too often offset by avoidable contradictions and inconsistencies pervasive in the conduct of Nigerian foreign policy. These contradictions may have beclouded, if not eroded, gains that have accrued from global engagements and interactions.

In this concluding chapter, notable achievements are reviewed, key challenges are identified, and future prospects are discussed. Finally, general recommendations are offered. In all, the achievements are many, the challenges have been enormous, and future prospects are bright if foreign policy objectives are repositioned, domestic socioeconomic and political foundations strengthened, and the machinery for its execution reformed and reinvigourated.

Notable Achievements

In its global preoccupation with peace and security, democracy, and development, Nigeria has, in spite of constraints and limitations, made constructive contributions and recorded notable achievements.

Peacekeeping, peacebuilding, peace enforcement, and peace-support operations constitute a major area of achievement in Nigeria's involvement in global affairs. Beginning with participation in the UN Mission in the Congo (1960–1964) to its foray in Chad (1979–1982); through its contributions to UN missions in Lebanon (1978–1981) and Bosnia-Herzegovina (1992–1995); its involvement with African Union (AU) missions in Darfur, Sudan (since 2004); and its leadership in the Economic Community of West African States (ECOWAS) through the Economic Community of West African States Monitoring Group operations in Liberia (1990–1998) and Sierra Leone (1996–2000), as well as its interventions in Guinea-Bissau (1998–2000) and Cote d'Ivoire (since 2000), Nigeria has helped to contain conflicts, minimise suffering, restore order, reconstruct war-torn societies, and pave the way for transitions to civil rule and democratisation. Thousands of military, police, and increasingly civilian personnel have been involved in these missions and operations (with over 1,000 recorded casualties in Liberia and Sierra Leone alone, according to Dike [2010]), which essentially focused on ending disputes and bringing stability to war-ravaged countries and regions.

Nigeria's role in support of the liberation struggles in southern Africa is widely acknowledged. The assistance it provided to liberation movements in South Africa, Angola, Mozambique, and Namibia was tremendous and contributed to the attainment of those countries' independence. Nigeria's membership in the Frontline States, its leadership in the UN Special Committee against Apartheid, and consistent activism in the UN General Assembly, the Commonwealth, and NAM mobilized international support for the isolation of the racist regime in South Africa and paved the way for its eventual demise and replacement with majority rule under a democratic dispensation.

The promotion of subregional and continental unity, peaceful coexistence, and economic integration is another arena in which Nigeria has made significant contributions. Its role in the Monrovia Group was decisive in the creation of the OAU in 1963, just as its leadership and commitment was instrumental in the creation and nurturing of ECOWAS in 1975. Similarly, Nigeria was one of four African countries whose leaders piloted the creation of the AU in 2002 as well as the New Partnership for Africa's Development (NEPAD) in 2001. Indeed,

Nigeria's role in subregional and continental political and economic associations and organizations has strengthened solidarity, enhanced good neighbourliness, facilitated unity, and expanded opportunities for collective human security, progress, and development.

Through bilateral and multilateral relations, Nigeria has demonstrated the capacity for being its "brother's keeper," contributing in various ways to economic development in many African nations. For example, through its active participation in the Lake Chad Basin Commission (eight member countries) and the Niger Basin Authority (nine member countries) (see Chapter 10), Nigeria has worked towards harnessing and managing common water resources for the agricultural and socioeconomic development of member states and expanded the scope of subregional economic integration. Using the Technical Aid Corps managed by the Ministry of Foreign Affairs, Nigeria has also since the 1980s contributed skilled personnel, including doctors, nurses, engineers, and teachers, to many African and Caribbean countries despite the fact that a shortage of these categories of human capital exists in the country itself. Similarly, through its participation in the African Development Bank, Nigeria has spread its petrodollars and extended financial assistance facilities to needy African countries in order to finance development programmes and projects. Through bilateral agreements, it has provided crude oil at subsidized rates to many African countries, including Ghana and Kenya.

In international organizations such as the UN and its specialised agencies; the Commonwealth; the African, Caribbean and Pacific Group of States; and NAM, Nigeria has not only been an active member but has led many commendable initiatives, contributing ideas and technocrats for the attainment of global objectives of security, peaceful existence, human rights, and economic development. Nigerians have held key positions in the UN (for example, Ibrahim Gambari, chair, UN Special Committee against Apartheid and, subsequently, undersecretary and secretary general's special envoy; and General Martin Agwai, commander of peacekeeping operations in Darfur). Further, in the Economic Commission for Africa, Adebayo Adedeji has served as secretary-general; in the Commonwealth, Emeka Anyouku was named secretary-general; in OPEC, Rilwan Lukman served as secretary-general; and, at the World Bank, Ngozi Okonjo-Iweala is managing director and Oby Ezekwesili is executive director. In the OAU, the AU, NEPAD, and ECOWAS, Nigeria's contributions to global diplomacy are truly substantial, wide-ranging, and remarkably consequential.

At another level, as Mohammed's contribution in Chapter 8 illustrated, through its membership in OPEC, Nigeria has forged strong relations with oil-producing countries, particularly in the Middle East and the Arab world. Nigeria has taken initiatives to increase national participation in the strategic oil sector and stabilise production, and has sought to work with OPEC on pricing and distribution of oil globally while guaranteeing a stable source of income for financing domestic socioeconomic development. Successes and achievements may not have been substantial in comparison to those in other areas, but Nigeria's participation in OPEC highlights the fascinating contradictory dynamics and pressures that characterise and condition the conduct of foreign policy.

In many fundamental respects, there are sufficient achievements to celebrate after fifty years of Nigeria's independence. But it is important to pay greater attention to the challenges that have prevented the maximisation of the country's vast potential and the impact of those challenges on the continued scope of Nigeria's power and influence in the global arena. Coming to terms with these challenges will set the requisite stage for greater success in years to come.

Major Challenges

Many factors have accounted for the lack of attainment of Nigeria's appropriate position of power and influence in global political and economic relations. Some of these are associated with the influence of domestic processes on foreign policy, but intertwined are historical and structural influences, as well as external factors. A determined effort must be made to address the negative impact of these challenges as Nigeria contemplates the next fifty years of greater involvement in the global world.

One of the main challenges arises from the nature and character of Nigeria's colonial history and the associated legacies of colonialism. As a postcolonial society, inherently embedded socioeconomic contradictions in the Nigerian political economy find expression in decisionmaking and policy execution, particularly in shaping and influencing foreign policy. For example, the manner in which the country was cobbled together by British colonialists has engendered a relative lack of a collective sense of nationhood, which constrains all policies, especially foreign policy. First, the infusion of mutual fears and suspicions as a framework for relationships among Nigeria's multiethnic and religious groups has ensured that little coherently defined national ethos exists (Mustapha 2008, p. 370). A natural corollary of this has been confusion and ambiguity, which characterises the definition of Nigerian national interest and the lack of commitment of the elite to its pursuit.

Second is the nature of Nigeria's federal system and its impact on foreign policy. Ordinarily, as Wheare has observed, "federalism and foreign policy go ill together" (1963, p. 183). In the Nigerian context, the intensely and somewhat peculiarly adversarial regional system engendered by colonialism has tended to undermine a united front in the conduct of foreign policy. Third, institutions and processes are not deeply entrenched and work epileptically, if at all—such that informal channels tend to substitute formal ones. Consequently, half-hearted or clandestine decisions result in serious repercussions for the entire system. Nigeria's foray into Chad in the late 1970s and its decision to join the Organisation of Islamic Countries in the mid-1980s illustrate this. In a general context, most foreign policy successes tend to be happenstance rather than the outcome of strategic analysis and due process.

Fourth, there are ample illustrations of decisionmakers' behaviour significantly influencing foreign policy decisionmaking. From the Balewa to Yar'Adua–Jonathan governments, whether under civilian or military dispensations, the leader's disposition significantly affected the outcome of foreign policy decisions. Leaders who have held onto the foreign policy portfolio have been characterized as egotistic. Pronounced policies are zealously executed by loyal ministers of foreign affairs, with hardly any review or input from professionals in the ministry. Less-inclined leaders have presided over more inert foreign policy formulations.

Fifth, and perhaps most significantly, is the impact of the socioeconomic and political context at the domestic level on foreign policy. In this regard, perpetual crises in the Nigerian political economy associated with poor governance, stunted economic growth, poverty and inequality, insecurity, and violent ethno-religious and communal conflicts have combined to undermine the credible and effective pursuit of foreign policy objectives. A sustainable foreign policy is necessarily connected to a stable political and economic domestic setting. Conversely, an unstable socioeconomic and political context places enormous domestic pressures and constraints on foreign policy.

At conceptual and methodological levels, Nigeria has been constrained by problems of focus, strategy, and lack of structures to conceptualise or implement a well-defined foreign policy. There is little if any strategic planning or projection of outcomes. What is the framework and where are the agendas? What are the defined interests in the short, medium, and long term? What mandate are diplomats given? Seasoned diplomats are often embarrassed or concerned by the lack of answers to these questions. Nigeria has been muddling through its foreign policy, albeit with sometimes surprising outcomes.

This has not always been the case. In 1961, an all-Nigeria conference on foreign policy held in Lagos, Nigeria, helped define a postindependence agenda. In the late 1970s, a special review panel headed by Adebayo Adedeji attempted to define Nigeria's foreign policy objectives more coherently. With only minor modifications, this has remained the constitutionally enshrined basis for Nigeria's foreign policy. Subsequent efforts to redefine and refocus the conceptual and methodological policy framework have met with little success. For example, the resolutions of the 1986 Kuru national conference on foreign policy did not receive official approval. In 2001, a panel under General Joe Garba, Nigeria's foreign minister during the Murtala-Obasanjo regime, drafted a National Defence Policy in a bid to give greater coherence to certain key aspects of Nigeria's foreign policy. Despite these efforts, glaring examples of a lack of coordination between key government agencies driving foreign and defense policies, the Ministry of Defence and Ministry of Foreign Affairs, persist. With regard to peacekeeping operations, it seems that no operational framework or forum for activities coordination functions properly.

Another important illustration of the lack of focus and coordination in foreign policy is the evident disconnect between diplomatic and political activity and the economic dividend of foreign policy. For example, when peace returned to Sierra Leone, countries moved in to reap the dividends of a US$10 billion reconstruction programme, while Nigeria literally packed its bags and left. The Nigerian government has not aided private-sector initiatives in countries where Nigeria has intervened.

The absence of coherence in foreign policy is compounded by a lack of strategic planning in the pursuit of identified objectives. Given this, opportunities are rarely seized and often missed. Threats are either not perceived or underestimated. Anticipated responses are haphazard. As Rourke has aptly stated, "[T]he course of world politics is the story of the motivations and calculations of the actors and how they put those into action" (2008, p. 65). Lack of a clear and implementable strategic plan obstructs and frustrates how motivations and calculations are actualised. Illustrations abound. For example, even in peacekeeping missions where successes have been highly celebrated, there have been bitter lessons learnt as a result of lack of planning and adequate preparation. Ambassador Kingibe has observed that Nigeria was often pushed into "hot potatoes" by others, as exemplified by the country's mission in Chad in the late 1970s and early 1980s: "The real world is a heartless one, when you are mid-river they leave you on your own" (2009).

While the machinery of foreign policy is absolutely vital to the attainment of defined objectives and goals, it has for too long been neglected. Foreign policy staff lack motivation, many are not well-trained, and the lack of specialisation in the Ministry of Foreign Affairs is glaring. For example, the ministry lacks professional negotiators, and desk officers are ill-equipped to participate in negotiations in specialised disciplines. Indeed, the ministry has been criticised for not adapting to the changing international climate. Research capacity is lacking; qualified personnel are given virtually no training; and embassies are understaffed, ill-equipped, and underutilised. The Foreign Service Academy has long been underfunded and requires refocusing and reorganising. Recent reforms address allowances rather than the need to enhance professionalism through curriculum review, rigorous training, retraining, and capacity building. Intellectual resources available in the official foreign policy think tank, the Nigerian Institute of International Affairs, are insufficiently tapped.

Future Prospects

Nigeria will continue to be a key player in the international system given its size, resources, and acknowledged role in Africa, as well as the increasing unwillingness of dominant powers such as the United States and UK to commit resources and personnel to the continent's hot spots of conflict. However, in the final analysis, the extent to which Nigeria expands the scope of its role in the globalised world will be related to the extent to which its polity and economy become sustainable within the framework of democratic governance. Progress in democratisation and economic development are inextricably linked to increased international leadership roles and responsibilities, requiring a conducive domestic environment for foreign policy decisionmaking and implementation. This is the major challenge to be tackled, as Mustapha aptly suggests, "of re-engineering of the constitutional, political and economic system, with twin objectives of reducing areas of contention and promoting public welfare" (2008, p. 371).

The dynamic global environment is rapidly changing, and concerns for sovereignty, survival, and economic development remain primary preoccupations of nation-states. In the globalised world, what Albright has termed "forward-looking initiatives on diplomacy and development" are required (2008, p. 134).

Specific Recommendations

First and foremost, a thorough reassessment and reevaluation of Nigeria's foreign policy, similar to that undertaken in the 1970s under Adedeji, is long overdue in order to reposition Nigeria to attain greater heights in its global undertakings in the new millennium. Such a review must provide a clearer definition and articulation of national interests as well as a reprioritisation of attainable foreign policy objectives.

More specifically, the following recommendations are noteworthy. First, Nigeria should remain actively involved in efforts to strengthen subregional and continental economic integration. Subregions in Asia and South America are reaping the benefits of regional and continental economic integration; there is no reason why African countries should be left behind in these endeavours. Important ECOWAS protocols for free movement of people and goods should be signed and aggressively implemented. Second, Nigeria must increasingly utilise international organisations as forums for economic relations. In particular, platforms that strengthen South-South cooperation and contribute to stronger strategic partnership with emerging economies, such as Brazil, Russia, India, and China, should be forged. Third, with regard to Nigeria's involvement with peacekeeping, it is important that a clear policy framework be established. This would go a long way in determining rational modes of intervention as well as improving relations and coordination among agencies involved with peace support operations, such as police headquarters and the ministries of Defence and Foreign Affairs.

The Ministry of Foreign Affairs must be strengthened, reformed, and reinvigourated to enable it to meet standard requirements for driving foreign policy in the coming decades. Competence, expertise, and specialisation should be ensured, and training and retraining of professional staff must be provided on a regular basis. Staff recruitment into the ministry must be rigourous, competitive, and merit based. Existing staff should be reoriented and better motivated. Indeed, choice of ministry leadership must draw from the most brilliant and respected Nigerian diplomats whose qualities and experience command respect and garner influence in the international system. The country has witnessed embarrassing occasions, such as during the tenure of Tom Ikimi as minister of foreign affairs under General Sani Abacha, over the matter of Nigeria's expulsion from the Commonwealth following the hanging of Ken Saro Wiwa, when the amateurism, arrogance, and abrasiveness of the country's foreign policy drivers compelled drastic measure to be meted out. Such situations might be avoided through the meritorious appointment of competent and experienced diplomats.

Other countries make strenuous effort to ensure that the rights of their citizens are adequately protected and that they are considered innocent until proven guilty no matter the severity of the allegation. The manner in which Nigerian citizens are increasingly maltreated abroad for alleged crimes, without their rights being protected by Nigerian embassies, has raised concerns about the clarity and lack of focus of *citizens' diplomacy* in Nigeria's foreign policy. Citizens' diplomacy should be reassessed in line with the global trend.

In the final analysis, attention must be paid to enduring reforms in the Nigerian polity and economy in order to bring about democratic governance and sustainable development as a foundation for Nigeria to play its role on the global political stage. The country's transition from military to civil democratic rule has been fragile, but the thin roots it has sprouted must be nurtured in order to set a firm foundation for economic growth and development and a concomitant virile foreign policy. It is significant to note that legacies of prolonged military rule have significantly impacted the formulation and conduct of foreign policy. The magnitude of the challenge is in many fundamental respects attributable to these legacies. Therefore, as Nigeria consolidates the gains of civil democratic rule, with increased transparency, respect for due process, and stronger institutions, there is continued hope for the future prospects of Nigeria's foreign policy.

References

Albright, M., 2008, *Memo to the President Elect*, HarperCollins Publishers, New York, US.

Dike, P., 2010, "Nigeria and the Quest for an Enduring Security Mechanism in Africa," presented by Nigeria's Chief of Defence Staff, at the Royal United Services Institute, London, March 26; published in *The Guardian*, April 4.

Guardian, 2010, Report on a Joint Statement signed by Hillary R. Clinton, US Secretary of State; David Miliband, British Foreign Secretary; Catherine Ashton, French Foreign Minister and the EU High Representative, January 30.

Kingibe, B., 2009, Contribution to Methodology workshop organized by the Yar'Adua Centre on Nigeria's Foreign Policy, Abuja, Nigeria, October 15.

Kuna, M., 2006, "The Role of Nigeria in Peace Building, Conflict Resolution and Peacekeeping in Africa since 1960," in S. Adamu and A. Siddique, eds., *Nigeria and the United Nations*, Abdullahi Smith Centre for Research and Training, Zaria, Nigeria, pp. 58–74.

Mustapha, A. R., 2008, "Challenges for Nigeria's Foreign Policy in the Post–Cold War Era," in A. Adebajo and A. R., Mustapha, eds., *Gulliver's Troubles: Nigeria's Foreign Policy after the Cold War*, University of Kwazulu Natal Press, Scottsville, South Africa, pp. 369–382.

Rourke, J.T., 2008, *International Politics on the World Stage*, 12th ed., Mc Graw-Hill, New York, US.

Wheare, K.C., 1963, *Federal Government*, 4th ed., Oxford University Press, London.

Acronyms

ACP: African, Caribbean and Pacific Group of States
AEC: African Economic Community
AfDB: African Development Bank
AFL: Armed Forces of Liberia
AFRICOM: US African Command
ASF: African Standby Force
AU: African Union
BP: British Petroleum
CCC: Congo Conciliation Committee
CFAF: Communauté Financière Africaine Franc
DBSA: South African Development Bank
EBID: ECOWAS Bank for Investment and Development
ECA: Economic Commission for Africa
ECOMOG: Economic Community of West African States
    Monitoring Group
ECOWAS: Economic Community of West African States
ESF: ECOWAS Standby Force
ETLS: ECOWAS Trade Liberalization Scheme
EU: European Union
FNLA: National Front for the Liberation of Angola
FPU: Formed Police Unit
GDP: Gross Domestic Product
GEF: Global Environment Fund
IMF: International Monetary Fund
IPM: Integrated Pest Management
LCBC: Lake Chad Basin Commission
MDGs: Millennium Development Goals

MFA: Ministry of Foreign Affairs
MOU: memorandum of understanding
MPLA: Popular Movement for the Liberation of Angola
NAM: Non-Aligned Movement
NBA: Niger Basin Authority
NCCI: National Council on Commerce and Industry
NEEDS: National Economic Empowerment and Development Strategy
NEPAD: New Partnership for African Development
NIGCON: Nigerian Contingent
NPF: Nigeria Police Force
NPFL: National Patriotic Front of Liberia
NTCF: Nigerian Technical Cooperation Fund
NTF: Nigeria Trust Fund
OAU: Organization of African Unity
ODA: official development assistance
ONUC: UN Operation in the Congo
OPEC: Organization of Petroleum Exporting Countries
PSO: peace support operation
R&D: research and development
RECs: Regional Economic Communities
RUF: Revolutionary United Force
SAP: Structural Adjustment Programme
SMC: Standing Mediation Committee
SMEs: Small and Medium Enterprises
SWAPO: Southwest African People's Organization
TAC: Technical Aid Corps
UDAO: Union Douarniere Entre Des Etats De L'Afrique Occidentale
UDEAO: Union Douarniere Des Etats De L'Afrique De L'Ouest
UEMOA: Union Economique et Monetaire Ouest Africaine
ULIMO-J: United Liberation Movement of Liberia — Johnson
ULIMO-K: United Liberation Movement of Liberia — Koroma
UN: United Nations
UNAMID: African Union/United Nations Hybrid Operation in Darfur
UNDP: United Nations Development Programme
UNDPKO: UN Department of Peacekeeping Operations
UNEP: United Nations Environment Programme
UNESCO: United Nations Educational, Scientific and
    Cultural Organization
UNIFIL: UN Interim Force in Lebanon
UNMIL: UN Mission in Liberia
UNITA: Union for the Total Independence of Angola

UNMIBH: UN Mission in Bosnia and Herzegovina
UNMIK: UN Mission in Kosovo
UNMIS: UN Mission in Sudan
UNMIT: UN Mission in East Timor
UNMSIL: UN Mission in Sierra Leone
UNO: United Nations Organization
UNOCI: UN Mission in Cote D'Ivoire
UNSO: United Nations Sudano-Sahelian Office
USA: United States of America
USAID: United States Agency for International Development
VOA: Voice of America
WAHO: West African Health Organization
WAMA: West African Monetary Agency
WAMZ: West African Monetary Zone
WAPP: West African Power Pool
WMO: World Meteorological Organization
WRCU: Water Resources Coordinating Unit
WWF: World Wide Fund for Nature
ZANU-PF: Zimbabwe African National Union – Patriotic Front

The Contributors

Tijjani Muhammad Bande (BSc, Ahmadu Bello University; M.A., Boston University; Ph.D., University of Toronto) is director-general of the National Institute for Policy and Strategic Studies and professor of political theory at Usman Danfodiyo University, Sokoto, Nigeria. He served as director-general of the African Training and Research Centre in Administration for Development, Tangier, Morocco (January 2000 to February 2004), and was vice-chancellor of Usman Danfodiyo University (February 2004 to February 2009). Professor Bande was awarded Nigeria's national honour of the Officer of the Order of the Federal Republic in 2005.

Hamid Bobboyi, BA, PhD (Northwestern University, Evanston, Illinois, US), was a senior research fellow and former director of Arewa House, Ahmadu Bello University, Kaduna, Nigeria. He has published several papers and books on the history and politics of Nigeria and has served as visiting scholar to several universities in Europe, United States, Asia, and the Middle East. He is currently the director, Centre for Regional Integration and Development, Abuja, Nigeria.

Okechukwu Ibeanu is a professor of political science and former dean of Social Sciences at the University of Nigeria, Nsukka. He is presently the director of the Institute for Development Studies at the same university. Professor Ibeanu was recently a visiting professor in Conflict, Security and Development at King's College, London. He is also the special rapporteur of the United Nations Human Rights Council on the adverse effects of toxic wastes on human rights. Professor Ibeanu has published extensively on politics, environment, and conflict in Nigeria, including *Direct Capture: The 2007 Nigerian Elections and the Subversion of Popular Sovereignty* (2009); *Between the Theory and Practice of Democracy in Nigeria* (2008); *Women, Children and Internal Conflict in Nigeria* (2007); *Elections and the Future of Democracy in Nigeria* (2007); and *Oiling Violence: The Proliferation of Small Arms and Light Weapons in the Niger Delta* (2006).

Attahiru M. Jega is a professor of political science and former vice-chancellor, Bayero University, Kano, Nigeria. He obtained his BSc in political science from Ahmadu Bello University, Zaria, Nigeria, and his master's degree and PhD from Northwestern University, Evanston, Illinois, US. He was a former director of the Centre for Democratic Research and Training, Bayero University (2000–2004), and former president of the Academic Staff Union of Universities (1988–1994). In 2010 he was appointed chairman of the Independent National Electoral Commission. Jega has published widely on Nigerian politics, especially on the themes of identity transformation, transition to democracy and democratisation, governance, and elections. He was awarded the national honor, Officer of the Federal Republic, in 2005.

Obadiah Mailafia is founder and director of the Centre for Policy and Economic Research, a macro-economics and public policy think tank based in Abuja, Nigeria. He is also a member of the National Economic Management Team, the council of advisers to the president on the economy. An economist and former banker, he has interests in monetary policy, development economics, public finance, and international affairs. Dr. Mailafia began his career as a fellow of the National Institute for Policy and Strategic Studies, Kuru, Nigeria, subsequently becoming an associate professor and head of Department of Regents Business School, London. He later joined the Planning and Budgeting Department of the African Development Bank, serving in Côte d'Ivoire and Tunisia. He is a former deputy governor of the Central Bank and one-time adviser to the president on economic and policy matters. Dr. Mailafia holds a BSc in social sciences (economics, politics, and sociology) honours degree from Ahmadu Bello University in Nigeria, the *diplôme* in international economics from the École National d'Administration (ENA-IIAP), and a PhD from Oriel College, University of Oxford, England.

Abubakar Siddique Mohammed read political science at Ahmadu Bello University, Zaria, Nigeria. At the University of Grenoble, France, he obtained the *diplome d'etude approfondi* in energy economics and policy, and at the Ecole Des Hautes Etudes en Sciences Sociales, Paris, he obtained a PhD in socio-economy of development. Dr. Mohammed teaches in the Department of Political Science, Ahmadu Bello University, Zaria, Nigeria, and is current director, Centre for Democratic Development Research and Training, Zaria. Dr. Mohammed has published numerous articles and monographs and edited two books. He is currently engaged in a major study on facts and impressions of contemporary Nigerian history, politics, and society.

Okello Oculi is executive director, Africa Vision 525 Initiative. His publications include *Discourses on African Affairs* (2000); *Song for the Sun in Us* (2000); *A Political Economy of Malnutrition: Nigeria, Kenya and Jamaica* (1986); and several other literary works. He co-edited *Brain Gain: Discourses on Governance* (2008). A correspondent columnist for the Nairobi-based newspaper, *Daily Nation*, Oculi's written conference papers include "The Great Lakes Region and African Strategic Issues" (2009); "Challenges of Sovereignty for a United States of Africa" (2009); and "Challenges in Integration through Regional Parliaments: ECOWAS and the European Parliament" (2010). Oculi was educated at Makerere University, Uganda; Stanford University, California, US; Essex University, England; and University of Wisconsin, US.

Andrew Okolie obtained his PhD in sociology from the University of Toronto and has taught at universities in Nigeria, Canada, and the United States. He was teaching at the University of Toronto when he was appointed a senior special assistant (policy and program monitoring speech writing) in Nigeria's presidency. On leaving government in 2006, he worked as the deputy director and head of Secretariat Administration of the Atiku Abubakar Presidential Campaign Organization, Abuja, Nigeria. He was a visiting professor at Teachers College, Columbia University, New York (2007–2008), and is currently the director general, Atiku Centre, a research and advocacy NGO, based in Abuja, Nigeria.

Eghosa E. Osaghae is professor of comparative politics and vice chancellor of Igbinedion University, Okada, Nigeria. Before taking up appointment at Okada, he was leader of the Ford Foundation–funded Programme on Ethnic and Federal Studies and director of the Centre for Peace and Conflict Studies at the University of Ibadan, Nigeria. He has held academic appointments and fellowships in Liberia, South Africa,

Sweden, Austria, India, Northern Ireland, England, and the United States. He is a recipient of the Best Paper Award at the Eighth Annual Conference of the International Association for Conflict Management in Helsignor, Denmark (1996); the Best Article Award for 2004 of the African Politics Conference Group, a coordinate group of the American Political Science Association, African Studies Association, and International Studies Association (2004); and the 2004 Lawrence Dunbar Reddick Memorial Scholarship Award for the best article on Africa published in the *Journal of Third World Studies*. Osaghae is chair of the Governing Board of the Community Relations and Conflict Resolution Centre in Ibadan. His publications include *Researching Conflict in Africa: Insights and Experiences* (United Nations University Press, 2005), *Crippled Giant: Nigeria Since Independence* (C. Hurst, 1998), *Between State and Civil Society in Africa* (CODESRIA, 1994).,and several articles in leading international journals.

Julie G. Sanda is a principal research fellow at the African Centre for Strategic Research and Studies, National Defence College, Nigeria. A political scientist, she is head of the Department of Conflict, Peacekeeping and Humanitarian Studies and member of the College Steering Group. Sanda served on the Committee of the Chief of Army Staff that developed a peace support operations doctrine for the Nigerian Army. She is also editor of the *Africa Peace Review Journal* and has contributed to several books on Nigeria's foreign policy, conflict management, peace, and security. A graduate of the University of Jos (1983), and Ahmadu Bello University, Zaria, Nigeria (1987), where she is also a doctoral candidate at present, she was a Fulbright Junior Scholar at the Eliot School of International Affairs, George Washington University, Washington, D.C. (1990–1991). Sanda was also at the Institute de Fédéralisme, Université de Fribourg under a Swiss federal government scholarship (1996–1997). In this regard she has been course administrator for the United Nations Senior Mission Leaders' Courses conducted for the Economic Community of West African States (2007 and 2010) and the African Union (2008).

Index

nities of River Niger system, 217; calls for basin division into more manageable river basin organizations, 222; and cooperation among member states and to ensure integrated development of the basin, 218; coordination of national development policies to ensure an equitable policy, 218–219; decisions reached for new vision and improvements, 223; and establishment of LCBC and NBA, 224–225; establishment and mandate of, 217–219; internal and external sources of funding for, 220–221; major achievements of, 222–223; and Nigeria's investment in irrigation schemes and hydropower projects, 224; nine-member intergovernmental organization to manage and harmonise development of River Niger basins, 216–217; population of 200 million people in, 17; problems and challenges of, 221–222; secretariat and executive secretary of, 219; serious financial difficulty of, 222; structure and operations of, 219–221; World Bank provision of credit to fund development of, 221

Niger, regional mediation groups in, 61

Nigeria: achievements and challenges in, 229–238; absence of coherent foreign policy in, 235; and aid deployed in pursuit of national ambitions, 179; arguments for special contribution as permanent member, 42; and attainment of permanent seats for Africa in UN Security Council, 41; attempt to assist needy members of the Commonwealth while receiving assistance from others, 46; bank recapitalization in 2006, 187; benefits from Commonwealth scholarship scheme and Rhodes Scholar programme, 47; and bourgeoning economy predicated on rise in oil revenues, 129; call for collectivist strategic position of two African countries as permanent members, 41; call for redirection of, 30; as chronically unstable and conflict-ridden, 6; chal-

lenges arising from nature and character of colonial history and legacies of, 233; conservative and pragmatic perspective on, 17–18; constructive engagements and significant contributions in global arena, 229; contribution to consolidation of peace and security in the subregion, 138; contribution to global efforts at knowledge production for use by PSO industry, 91; and contribution of skilled personnel to African and Caribbean countries, 232; cordial relations with OPEC member countries of Middle East, 172; and creation of OAU and AU, 231; debates concerning socioeconomic issues affecting Africans' health, 41; debt-reduction agreement with government, 188; decision to involve itself in the Congo, 92; and defining of postindependence agenda, 234–235; and democratization for sustainable peacebuilding, 8; determination to be key player in stabilizing efforts in the subregion, 102; and diplomatic actions opposing the European-settler government in Zimbabwe, 40; diplomatic manoeuvres complementing military intervention in, 69; economic policy anchored on National Economic Empowerment and Development Strategy (NEEDS), 187; emergency summit to extend urgent assistance to Angola, 28; engagement with subregional body predicated on faith in regional unity and integration, 134; engagement with ECOWAS and issue of democracy and good governance, 138; enhancement of global stability through peacekeeping and peacemaking, 9; era of petrodollar economy in, 129; and evolution of bilateral and multilateral aid, 190–193; failure to maximize gains of PSO in area of logistics, 91; and federal government role enabling microeconomic environment and incentives, 189; federal system and its impact on foreign policy, 233–234; formidable challenges

Statement of Petroleum Policy in Member Countries of 1968, 156; embargo on oil supply to US, 159; formation of, 154–155; framework for oil-rich endowed nations to provide assistance to less-endowed counterparts, 178; and frantic demand's impact on spot market trading in limited stocks, 161–162; Iranian revolution contribution to market destabilization, 161; and members with control of 90 percent of global exports of oil, 155; and Middle East holdings of major global crude oil-production, 151; OAPEC demand for substantial increase in crude oil prices, 159; and Petroleum Decree No. 51 vesting the entire ownership and control of all petroleum, 156–157; principal of creating, 155; and relationship between transnational oil companies and their host governments, 155

Parliament, restructuring of, 133
Peace support operations (PSO): articulating a shared, comprehensive, and strategic vision for, 94; and establishment of dedicated coordination unit within MFA, 95; as growth area in nation's defence and police sectors, 91; imperative of, 94–95; as overarching policy within policy and embedded with national foreign policy, 94
Peacekeeping: involvement of military in, 92; as metaphor for Nigeria's numerous failings at home, 118; practice of reward better troops on foreign assignments, 116–117; and principle dictating that army should not send itself to war, 93; serving as income augmentation for the military as an institution, 116; tangible and intangible gains derived from, 89
Peacekeeping and Nigeria's national interest: informed attempt at identifying, 117; peacekeeping role in relations with countries in the region, 117

Preventive diplomacy, and country investment to prevent crises, 121

Revolutionary United Front (RUF): confrontation of ECOMOG, 68; founders of, 104; invasion of Sierra Leone from its Liberian base, 68
Rwandan genocide, and UN mission mandate's failure to stop, 83

Shagari, Shehu: government of, 30; and North-South Dialogue, 43; and realist phase, 20
Sierra Leone: changing political fortunes in, 106; excesses of exclusionary one-party rule, 67–68; history of, 67; initial objectives to end the civil war via interventions, 54–55; and military coups overthrowing new democratic government, 110; organized elections in, 68; peacebuilding and democratization processes in, 70; propellants of peacekeeping interventions in, 57; UN imposed arms embargo on, 69; youth-based radical opposition movement to terminate the twenty-three-year rule, 68; war and control of diamond mining, 104
South Africa: growing aid programme linked to its trade and commercial interests, 199; involvement in promotion of democracy, 53–54; objective of ending apartheid, 25; open support for UNITA and FNLA, 27; military superiority to capabilities of Frontline States, 25; roles in "stabilising" southern African region, 59
Strasser, Valentine: recruitment of street kids and criminals into the army, 104
Structural Adjustment Programme (SAP), poor implementation of, 183

Taylor, Charles: as major factor in Sierra Leone's civil war, 66; and National Patriotic Front of Liberia (NPFL) invasion, 65
Technical Aid Corps (TAC): aims and objectives of, 193–194; challenges and success in, 194–195; emergence as foreign policy tool to promote

About the Editors

Attahiru M. Jega is professor of political science and former vice chancellor, Bayero University, Kano. He obtained a bachelor's degree in political science from Ahmadu Bello University, Zaria, and his master's and PhD from Northwestern University, Evanston, Illinois. Professor Jega is former director of the Centre for Democratic Research and Training and former president of the Academic Staff Union of Universities. He is widely published on Nigerian politics. Professor Jega was recently appointed chairman of the Independent National Electoral Commission, the body established to oversee Nigeria's electoral process.

Jacqueline W. Farris is the director general of the Shehu Musa Yar'Adua Foundation and a member of its board of trustees. She received a bachelor's degree in political science and urban development from Michigan State University and served in a number of capacities with Ambassador Andrew Young during his tenure in the U.S. House of Representatives, the U.S. Mission to the United Nations, and Atlanta city government. Mrs. Farris co-edited *Shehu Musa Yar'Adua: A Life of Service,* the official biography of Shehu Yar'Adua.